StatView®

Using StatView

Copyright

Technology License Notices

ISBN: 1-58025-162-5

Origin

StatView began with Jim Gagnon and Daniel S. Feldman, Jr. Subsequent versions of StatView owe credit also to developers Joe Caldarola, Alex Benedict, Ania Dilmaghani, William F. Finzer, Keith A. Haycock, and Jay Roth. StatView has enjoyed its celebrated place in the international marketplace thanks to the ongoing efforts of Hulinks (Japanese StatView), ALSYD (French StatView), Cherwell (German StatView), and many others in the United States and worldwide.

In 1997, John Sall, Senior Vice President and Cofounder of SAS Institute Inc., led SAS Institute's acquisition of StatView and undertook its development.

Credits

Recent development of StatView was completed by Eric Wasserman, Ph.D., and Charles Soper. Clifford Baron led recent product design and development efforts. Colleen Jenkins, Director of the Statistical Instruments Division, guided StatView's entry into the Statistical Instruments offerings of SAS Institute, with sales, marketing, and technical support from Bob McCall, Chuck Boiler, Bonnie Rigo, Nick Zagone, and Mendy Clayton. Annie L. Dudley led the testing efforts of Nicole Hill Jones and Brenda Sun; early testing was done by Sid Butts and Bruce Gilbert. Ann Lehman, Ph.D., Kristin Rinne, Terri March, and Lynn Scott made production possible.

The manuals were written by Erin Vang. Authorship credit for significant portions of the *StatView Reference* is due to Nicholas P. Jewell, Ph.D. (Division of Biostatistics and Department of Statistics, University of California-Berkeley, logistic regression and survival analysis), Clifford Baron (QC analysis and survival analysis). Additional contributions were made by Daniel S. Feldman, Jr., Samantha Sager, Pete Schorer, and Phil Spector, Ph.D. (Department of Statistics, University of California-Berkeley). Erin Vang also coordinated localization and revised the help systems originally created by Clifford Baron.

Statistical consulting was provided by Phil Spector, Ph.D., Alan Hopkins, Ph.D., and Nicholas P. Jewell, Ph.D.

Acknowledgements

We are grateful of StatView users around the world for their continued support, and particularly for their comments, criticisms, suggestions, and praise. A special note of recognition is due the users who have volunteered their time to beta test StatView.

It is through the efforts of all the people named above and many more whom we could not list that we are able to accomplish our mission: to enable *anyone*—not just an expert—to perform data analysis and present results. We do so by creating, marketing, and supporting statistical and data analysis software that is easy to use and is therefore accessible to those who practice, teach, or are learning data analysis.

Finally, we thank the Technical Support and Professional Services Divisions of SAS Institute, whose contributions enable us to move forward and truly deliver on that mission.

Overview

The StatView manual comes in two volumes, *Using StatView* and *StatView Reference*. This volume, *Using StatView*, shows how to work with StatView.

1. The first chapter, "Tutorial," steps you through every phase of a data analysis product with StatView, from collecting and entering data, to analyzing data, to presenting your results. If you read nothing else, read the tutorial.

Subsequent chapters expand on the concepts introduced in the tutorial.

2. "Datasets" discusses the structure of StatView datasets—how to arrange your data for StatView, how to enter and edit data in the dataset window, how to work with StatView's data attributes, and how to use category and compact variables.

3. "Importing and exporting" shows how to get datasets into StatView from other programs, through Microsoft Excel files and plain text (ASCII) files.

4. "Managing data" shows StatView's special tools for generating and transforming variables, sorting data, and studying subsets of your data.

5. "Analyses" shows how to build and modify analyses—statistical tables and graphs—and how to work with tables and graphs in the view window.

6. "Templates" shows how to recycle a complete set of analyses by applying it as a template to other datasets—a quick set of steps that can save you countless hours.

7. "Customizing results" shows how to redesign the appearance of StatView's tables and graphs to suit your needs and preferences.

8. "Drawing and layout" shows how you can assemble analysis results into a full-color presentation, complete with annotations and enhancements you draw yourself.

9. "Tips and shortcuts" shows how to use various online help facilities and how to set preferences to suit your way of working. Then, it demonstrates example documents and templates, answers common questions, and gives troubleshooting suggestions.

The second volume, *StatView Reference*, presents a reference chapter for each analysis, reviewing statistical ideas, then detailing data requirements, dialog box options, results, and related templates. Finally, each chapter demonstrates the analysis with a step-by-step exercise. The last chapter in *StatView Reference* is "Formulas," a comprehensive reference for the mathematical expression language used throughout StatView. Finally, *StatView Reference* is where you'll find algorithms and formulas, a glossary of statistical terms, and references.

StatView's keyboard and mouse shortcuts are summarized on the *StatView Shortcuts* quick reference card.

Examples

If you try examples shown in the manual, your results might look a little different from ours. Some differences you might see:

1. In a dataset, variable attribute settings (type, format, number of decimal places, etc.) can cause values to look different.

2. We often resize or scroll windows to focus the readers attention on a specific item, and we often change display attributes such as plotting symbols, line types, and colors to accommodate black-and-white printing.

3. Illustrations show both Windows and Macintosh versions of StatView. Interface elements such as title bars, window sizing controls, scroll bars, combo boxes or pop-up menus vary slightly between platforms. If important interface elements differ, we show both Windows and Macintosh illustrations side by side; Windows first, then Macintosh.

4. International system configurations can cause numeric, currency, and date/time formatting to differ. We use a variety of formats in our examples.

5. Be aware that StatView performs numeric calculations in the fullest precision of the machine you are using; therefore, results can differ slightly among platforms.

6. Previous StatView versions represented missing values by bullets (•), and illustrations in these manuals continue to use bullets for maximum visibility. However, StatView currently represents missing values in the dataset and elsewhere in the program with periods (.)

Keyboard and mouse chords

Often in StatView, special keyboard and mouse **chords** let you perform special functions. A chord is any combination of simultaneous keystrokes and/or mouse actions.

For example, if you hold the Shift key while mouse-clicking several variables in the variable browser (and then release the key and the mouse button), you can select multiple adjacent variables at once. We write "Shift-click" to describe this action. Or, you can Copy the current selection into the clipboard by holding the Control key (Windows) or the Command key (Macintosh) and typing the letter "c," then releasing both keys. We write "Type Control-C" (Windows) or "Type Command-C" (Macintosh) to describe this action. Another example: you can select several *nonadjacent* variables in the variable browser by holding the Control key (Windows) or the Command key (Macintosh) and clicking the variable names. We write "Control-click" (Windows) or "Command-click" (Macintosh). When Windows and Macintosh chords differ, we describe each separately; Windows first, then Macintosh. StatView's keyboard and mouse shortcuts are summarized on the *StatView Shortcuts* quick reference card.

Some chords require holding several keys as well as clicking with the mouse. For example, you can Control-Shift-Alt-double-click (Windows) or Command-Shift-Option-double-click (Macintosh) a variable name in the browser to clone an analysis with the Split By button.

(Windows only) You can perform special functions by using the second mouse button. If you are right handed, the first mouse button is the left button, and the second mouse button is the right button. We describe clicking with the second button as "Right-click."

Contents

1 Tutorial 1

2 Datasets 49

3 Importing and exporting 99

4 Managing data 107

5 Analyses 131

6 Templates 161

7 Customizing results 179

8 Drawing and layout 203

9 Tips and shortcuts 221

Index 257

Tutorial

Data analysis the StatView way

Data analysis is hard enough without software getting in your way. That's why StatView is designed to be easy to use. We're not saying your research will be easy. If research were easy we'd have a cure for the common cold by now. We're just saying that you should be able to concentrate on your research instead of your software.

So we designed StatView to be simple, consistent, flexible, and powerful. We think that if you spend just an hour with this tutorial, you'll learn everything you *need* to know to get around in StatView. And you'll also know where to look in StatView for the trickier techniques you *want* to know.

We designed StatView to do everything you need to do, starting with data spreadsheets and going all the way through your project to full-color presentations. And we made it dynamic, so that any changes you make to your data along the way automatically trickle through all your analyses. So you can change any graph or any table any time, directly, in place, without having to redo anything. So you can fix that one tiny error you made weeks ago—quickly, the morning of your presentation.

All of StatView's advanced analyses work the same way as the simple ones, so once you know how to build one analysis, you can build any analysis. (If you need a quick review of some of the statistical techniques, we'll give you a hand with that, too.)

Why should I bother with a tutorial?

This tutorial is meant to get you started using StatView by stepping through typical activities in each phase of a data analysis project:

1. Manage data (collect data, enter or import data into StatView, find and fix errors, sort groups, get a feel for the numbers)

2. Analyze data (explore the data, look for patterns, test your hypotheses, turn raw data into information)

3. Present information (put together persuasive graphs, annotate results with your comments, call attention to the discoveries that lead to your conclusions)

It is also meant to give you a taste of chocolate.

What?!

No, seriously! By the time you finish this tutorial, you will be craving a candy bar. What's more, you'll know which candy bars are the most nutritionally sound.

Usually you concentrate on your data, not StatView. But now we want you to concentrate on how StatView works, so we're going to use a simple, fun dataset—something you won't have to think about too much.

Don't take it too seriously: we're not trying to get a grant, cure cancer, or influence public opinion. That's what *you* do. We just try to help by providing simple, powerful software.

Manage data

In any data analysis project, the first thing you have to do is collect data. We'll introduce the sample dataset you'll be using in this tutorial.

Then you need to get it into StatView. Some common ways to do this:

1. Enter the data by hand into StatView's data window
2. Import the data from a text file or another application, such as Excel
3. Open a StatView dataset that somebody else created

We'll step you through each possibility.

Our sample data

Background

Since 1994, the United States Food and Drug Administration (FDA) has required uniform, easy-to-read nutrition labeling for nearly all foods. The purpose of the new label is to reduce confusion and help consumers choose more healthful diets. Unlike prior labeling laws, the reform requires that even such items as candy bars carry full nutrition labels, and also requires that nutritional facts per realistic serving must be reported, including total calories, total fat, saturated fat, cholesterol, sodium, total carbohydrate, dietary fiber, sugars, protein, vitamins A and C, calcium, and iron.

The United States Department of Agriculture (USDA) and the Department of Health and Human Service (HHS) have teamed up to produce the Food Guide Pyramid, which recommends eating a variety of foods, an appropriate number of calories, and a modest amount of fat—specifically, 30% or fewer of your total number of calories per day should be calories from fat, and only a third of those should be calories from saturated fat. Fat is the densest source of calories, at 9 calories per gram. (Alcohol is a close second at 7 calories per gram.)

For adults consuming 2000 calories per day (which is about right for moderately active women and somewhat sedentary men), that works out to no more than 65 grams of fat, no more than 20 grams of which are saturated fat.

Chocolate

We want to know how many candy bars can fit into this daily diet. The first thing we need to do is gather nutritional data. We went clipboard in hand to a few stores near our Berkeley, California offices and stood in the candy aisle copying down nutritional facts about every candy bar we could find.

We also included some non-bar candies like M&Ms and Reese's Pieces, because they're very similar to many candy bars. Once we'd made that decision, it seemed only fair to include other non-chocolate candies, such as Skittles and Super Hot Tamales. Was this a good decision, theoretically? Maybe, maybe not. We'll have to study that in our analysis. Fortunately, StatView has all sorts of tools for excluding "weird" cases from analyses, so if it's a mistake, we won't suffer too much.

Then we came back to the office (miraculously, without a single candy bar!) and sat down to enter the data.

Enter data by hand

Here's a small part of the dataset:

Brand	Name	Serving/ pkg	Oz/pkg	Calories	Total fat g	Saturated fat g
M&M/Mars	Snickers Peanut Butter	1	2	310	20	7
Hershey	Cookies 'n' Mint	1	1.55	230	12	6
Hershey	Cadbury Dairy Milk	3.5	5	220	12	8
M&M/Mars	Snickers	3	3.7	170	8	3
Charms	Sugar Daddy	1	1.7	200	2.5	2.5

StatView's data organization

These data are already organized the way StatView wants: each **case** or **observation** (each specific candy bar) is in a horizontal **row**, and various characteristics or **variables** appear in vertical **columns**. Each value occupies a **cell** in the table.

This row-and-column design is important. It means that any value in any column belongs to one row (one case, one observation, one candy bar) and only one row. The very organization of the numbers tells you something. For example, the 170 in the Calories column is not just any measurement of calories on any subject. It corresponds exactly to the Name in the same row: Snickers. It corresponds exactly to the measurement of total fat in the same row: 8 grams.

StatView holds its data in a dataset, a spreadsheet format in which columns represent variables (such as gender, weight, height) and rows represent cases (such as patients in a medical study or plots in a field study).

Start StatView

- Double-click the StatView icon

StatView

The first thing you see (after a splash screen) is a welcome message in a Hints window:

Keep an eye on the Hints window as you begin to work with StatView. As its welcome says, it gives helpful information about what you're doing, how to handle errors, and what to do next. You can close the window if you prefer. To reopen it at any time, select Hints from the View menu (Windows) or Window menu (Macintosh).

Start a new dataset

- From the File menu, select New
- You see an empty, untitled dataset. You can resize or move the window if you want. Take a moment to look at the parts of the window.

First notice the top row of **variable names**. Right now we have only one name, "Input Column." Let's change that to be our first variable name, Brand:

- Click the "Input Column" cell to select it
- Type a new name: Brand
- Press Enter or Return

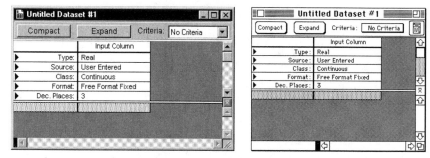

Now you have another empty "Input Column."

- Click the next column and type Name
- Press Tab to move to the next column, and type Serving/pkg
- Name the rest of the columns: Oz/pkg, Calories, Total fat g, Saturated fat g

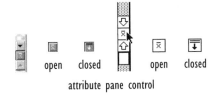

Next, notice the **attribute pane**. The top five rows of the dataset tell you the type, source, class, format, and decimal places for each variable. You can change each of these attributes directly: just click and hold the cell you want to change, then select the correct setting from the pop-up menu. You can show or hide as many of the rows as you desire by double-clicking or clicking and dragging the attribute pane control on the vertical scroll bar. Notice that the control changes appearance when the attribute pane is closed.

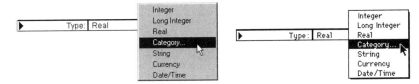

attribute pane control

The first attribute, **type**, indicates whether the data are integers, real numbers, categories (group memberships), string, currency, or date/time. Since our first variable, Brand, contains group or **category** data, we need to change the **type** to category:

- Scroll back to the first column
- Click and hold the mouse button on the Real cell in the attribute pane
- Select the correct type: Category
- Release the mouse button

The category data type is a timesaving feature in StatView. When a variable records group memberships, the same values are used repeatedly for many cases. For example, many different candy bars are manufactured by the major brands, Hershey, Nestle, and M&M/Mars. (Each candy bar is a case belonging to one of the brand groups.) Creating a category definition makes it faster to enter the data, prevents data entry errors, and saves RAM and disk space.

Here's how it works: first we create a **category definition** containing the group or level names we plan to use. Then we use this category definition to enter the data.

- Click New to create a new category definition

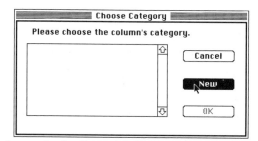

- Type the first Brand name in the Group label box: M&M/Mars
- Click Add
- Type the next name (Hershey) and click Add
- Type the last name (Charms) and click Add
- Click Done

StatView automatically sets Format and Decimal Places to "missing," since those attributes don't make sense for category variables. We'll discuss missing values some more later; "not applicable" is the idea here.

	Brand
Type:	Category
Source:	User Entered
Class:	Nominal
Format:	●
Dec. Places:	●

The second attribute, **source**, answers the question, "Where did these data come from?" Most data are user entered raw values, but others are computed from static or dynamic formulas (such as the sum of several variables), and others are generated by analyses (such as residuals from a regression).

The third attribute, **class**, tells how the data are to function: as **continuous** measurements (such as calories, fat in grams, etc.), as **nominal** data (such as our brand groups), or as **informative** (such as name labels or identification numbers). Since we've set type to category, Stat-View automatically sets class to nominal.

Having set all the attributes for Brand, we are ready to enter data. Now we can see the power of categories:

- Click the first empty (gray) cell in the Brand column to select it
- Type the first letter of the first value (M&M/Mars): m

StatView supplies the rest of the name. (If you had several groups beginning with M, you would need to type a few more letters.) All you need to do is accept the value:

- Press Enter or Return to move to the next cell

You can also enter category values by typing its number: 1 for the first group, 2 for the second group, etc., in the order that you defined them. This alone saves you time. Now think of how much time you'll save not having to correct your typing mistakes—especially on a hard-to-type name like M&M/Mars!

Let's try using both shortcuts to finish entering brand names:

- Type h and press Enter or Return
- Type 2 and press Enter or Return
- Type 1 and press Enter or Return
- Type c and press Enter or Return

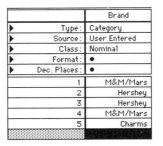

Now we're ready for the Name variable. First, we need to change its type from real to string, because the candy bar names are text, not numbers.

- From the Type pop-up menu, select String
  (In the Name column, click and hold Real, select String from the pop-up menu, and release the mouse button)

Again, we don't need to do anything with source, format, or decimal places. We do need to change Name's class from nominal to informative: (Name is not a grouping variable, because each value is unique. Rather, the names identify each case.)

- From the Class pop-up menu, select Informative

Now we can enter values:

- Click the empty cell in the first row for Name
- Type the first name: Snickers Peanut Butter
- Press Enter or Return to store the value and move to the next cell
- Enter the rest of the names the same way: Cookies 'n' Mint, Cadbury Dairy Milk, Snickers, Sugar Daddy

	Brand	Name
▶ Type:	Category	String
▶ Source:	User Entered	User Entered
▶ Class:	Nominal	Informative
▶ Format:	●	●
▶ Dec. Places:	●	●
1	M&M/Mars	Snickers Pean...
2	Hershey	Cookies 'n' Mint
3	Hershey	Cadbury Dairy...
4	M&M/Mars	Snickers
5	Charms	Sugar Daddy

The rest of the variables are all numeric, so we don't need to change their attributes. Notice that the cells all contain **missing values** (periods . for numeric variables, blank cells for character variables) right now, indicating that no values have yet been specified. Let's just enter the values:

- Click in the first cell for Serving/pkg and type the first value: 1
- Press Enter or Return to store the value and move to the next cell
- Enter the rest of the values the same way: 1, 3.5, 3, 1

Notice that StatView reformats the numbers to have three decimal places, which matches the current attribute setting for decimal places. (This setting only affects the way numbers are *displayed*; StatView stores values exactly as you specify them and carries the fullest precision supported by the hardware platform through calculations and analyses.)

- Enter the values for Oz/pkg: 2, 1.55, 5, 3.7, 1.7
- Enter the values for Calories: 310, 230, 220, 170, 200
- Enter the values for Total fat g: 20, 12, 12, 8, 2.5
- Enter the values for Saturated fat g: 7, 6, 8, 3, 2.5

Now take a moment to check your work. If any values are wrong, just click the cell, type a new value, and press Enter or Return.

Serving/pkg	Oz/pkg	Calories	Total fat g	Saturated fat g
Real	Real	Real	Real	Real
User Entered	User Entered	User Entered	User Entered	User Entered
Continuous	Continuous	Continuous	Continuous	Continuous
Free Format Fi...	Free Format Fi...	Free Format Fi...	Free Format Fi...	Free Format Fi...
3	3	3	3	3
1.000	2.000	310.000	20.000	7.000
1.000	1.550	230.000	12.000	6.000
3.500	5.000	220.000	12.000	8.000
3.000	3.700	170.000	8.000	3.000
1.000	1.700	200.000	2.500	2.500

An easy way to check for data entry mistakes is to view all rows of the attribute pane, and look at the summary statistics:

- Click and drag the attribute pane control ($\overline{x}$) downward to expose the twelve rows of **summary statistics** for each variable

	Name	Serving/pkg	Oz/pkg	Calories	Total fat g	Satu
Type:	String	Real	Real	Real	Real	Real
Source:	User Entered	User Entered	User Entered	User Entered	User Entered	User
Class:	Informative	Continuous	Continuous	Continuous	Continuous	Conti
Format:	●	Free Format Fi...	Free Format Fi...	Free Format Fi...	Free Format Fi...	Free
Dec. Places:	●	3	3	3	3	3
Mean:	●	1.900	2.790	226.000	10.900	5.300
Std. Deviation:	●	1.245	1.505	52.249	6.407	2.439
Std. Error:	●	.557	.673	23.367	2.865	1.09
Variance:	●	1.550	2.266	2730.000	41.050	5.950
Coeff. of Variation:	●	.655	.539	.231	.588	.460
Minimum:	●	1.000	1.550	170.000	2.500	2.500
Maximum:	●	3.500	5.000	310.000	20.000	8.000
Range:	●	2.500	3.450	140.000	17.500	5.500
Count:	●	5	5	5	5	5
Missing Cells:	●	0	0	0	0	0
Sum:	●	9.500	13.950	1130.000	54.500	26.50
Sum of Squares:	●	24.250	47.982	266300.000	758.250	164.
1	Snickers Pean...	1.000	2.000	310.000	20.000	
2	Cookies 'n' Mint	1.000	1.000	230.000	12.000	

If any of those statistics seem wrong, look for an error in the column. With large datasets, this trick can be a big time-saver. (Results can differ slightly among different platforms due to differences in numerics handling. For example, on some systems, the Sum of Squares for Oz/pkg is 47.982; on others, it is 47.983.)

We'll examine this summary pane later in the tutorial. For now, let's close the summary pane.

• Double-click the pane control to hide the summary statistics

Now let's make a few aesthetic adjustments. First, notice that all the Calories values are whole numbers. We can save memory by storing this variable with type integer.

• From the Type pop-up menu, select Integer

Also notice that the other variables have only one significant decimal place. It will be easier to view these numbers with just one decimal place.

• Control-click (Windows) or Command-click (Macintosh) the four variable names to select all four columns

Serving/pkg	Oz/pkg	Calories	Total fat g	Saturated fat g
Real	Real	Integer	Real	Real
User Entered	User Entered	User Entered	User Entered	User Entered
Continuous	Continuous	Continuous	Continuous	Continuous
Free Format Fi...	Free Format Fi...	●	Free Format Fi...	Free Format Fi...
3	3	●	3	3
1.000	2.000	310	20.000	7.000
1.000	1.550	230	12.000	6.000
3.500	5.000	220	12.000	8.000
3.000	3.700	170	8.000	3.000
1.000	1.700	200	2.500	2.500

• From the Decimal Places pop-up menu in any one of the columns, select 1
  (Click and hold the "3" cell in one of the columns, select 1, and release the mouse button)

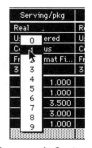

Let's also make the Name column wide enough for its values:

- Click any value in an unselected column to deselect the four columns
- Click and hold the border between Name and Serving/pkg
- Drag the border to the right and release the mouse button

Name	Se/ving/
String	Real
User Entered	User Enter
Informative	Continuous
▼	Free Form
●	1
Snickers Pean...	
Cookies 'n' Mint	
Cadbury Dairy...	

Name
String
User Entered
Informative
●
▼
Snickers Peanut Butter
Cookies 'n' Mint
Cadbury Dairy Milk
Snickers
Sugar Daddy

Let's close the attribute pane and save the dataset

- Double-click the pane control to close the attribute pane

	Brand	Name	Serving/pkg	Oz/pkg	Cal
1	M&M/Mars	Snickers Peanut Butter	1.0	2.0	
2	Hershey	Cookies 'n' Mint	1.0	1.5	
3	Hershey	Cadbury Dairy Milk	3.5	5.0	
4	M&M/Mars	Snickers	3.0	3.7	
5	Charms	Sugar Daddy	1.0	1.7	

- From the File menu, select Save
- Specify a filename Candy Bars First 5
- Click Save

Let's close this dataset.

- From the File menu, select Close Candy Bars First 5

Next, we learn how to import data.

Import data

Often you have data already entered in another application. StatView can read Excel files directly, and it can read plain text (ASCII) files exported by other applications.

Read an Excel file

Check the Update Doc installed in the StatView folder for the latest information on versions of Excel files that StatView can read.

- From the File menu, select Open
- For Files of type (Windows) or Show (Macintosh), select Excel
- Select the file Candy Bars.xls from the Sample Data folder
- Click Open

While StatView is importing the dataset, the cursor changes to a yin-yang, and a message window shows its progress:

StatView reads the entire Excel worksheet into a single StatView dataset. StatView reads only the values in each cell—it does not import functions, macros, or links. This is the complete Candy Bars dataset. Take a moment to scroll right and left to see all the variables, then scroll up and down to view all 75 rows.

		Brand	Name	Serving/pkg	Oz/pkg	Calories	Total fat g	Saturated fat g	Ch
	Type:	String	String	Real	Real	Integer	Real	Real	Inte
	Source:	User En...	User En...	User Entered	User Ent...	User Ente...	User Entered	User Entered	User
	Class:	Nominal	Nominal	Continuous	Continuous	Continuous	Continuous	Continuous	Con
	Format:	•	•	Free Format Fi...	Free For...	•	Free Format...	Free Format Fixed	•
	Dec. Places:	•	•	3	3	•	3	3	•
1		M&M/...	Snicker...	1.000	2.000	310	20.000	7.000	
2		Hershey	Cookies...	1.000	1.550	230	12.000	6.000	
3		Hershey	Cadbur...	3.500	5.000	220	12.000	8.000	
4		M&M/...	Snickers	3.000	3.700	170	8.000	3.000	
5		Charms	Sugar ...	1.000	1.700	200	2.500	2.500	
6		M&M/...	Twix P...	1.000	1.710	260	16.000	5.000	
7		Hershey	Twizzler	1.000	2.200	190	1.500	0.000	
8		Tobler	Toblero...	1.000	1.230	190	11.000	7.000	
9		Nestle	Crunch	1.000	1.550	230	12.000	7.000	
10		Hershey	Almond...	2.000	3.220	230	13.000	8.000	
11		Sherwood	Elana M...	1.000	1.600	200	10.000	6.000	
12		Hershey	Krackel	1.000	2.600	390	21.000	13.000	
13		M&M/...	M&Ms ...	1.000	1.740	250	13.000	5.000	
14		Bit-O-H...	Bit-O-...	1.000	1.700	200	4.000	2.500	
15		Nestle	100 Gr...	1.000	1.500	200	8.000	5.000	
16		Hershey	Skor	1.000	1.400	220	13.000	9.000	
17		Hershey	Twix C...	1.000	2.000	280	14.000	5.000	
18		M&M/...	Milky ...	1.000	1.570	160	5.000	3.500	
19		M&M/...	Mars	1.000	1.760	240	13.000	4.000	
20		Pearson	Peanut ...	1.000	2.500	340	16.000	3.000	
21		Nestle	Raisinet	1.000	1.580	200	8.000	4.000	

Candy Bars.xls (imported)

Compact Expand Criteria: No Criteria

StatView converts Excel data types and formats to the nearest StatView equivalents. (For details on how this works, see the chapter "Importing and exporting," p. 99.) We only need to change a few of the variable attributes.

- Change Brand from type string to category
  (Click and hold the Real cell in the Brand column, select Category, and release the mouse button)

(StatView automatically figures out how to define the category by scanning the values present in the column. You may examine the definition, if you want, by selecting Edit categories from the Manage menu.)

- Change Name from class nominal to informative

If you were going to use this dataset for a real analysis, you might also want to make some aesthetic adjustments. (You aren't going to use this dataset, so you may prefer to close the file and skip ahead to the next section, "Open a dataset," p. 13.)

- Control-click (Windows) or Command-click (Macintosh) the names Serving/pkg, Oz/pkg, Total fat g, and Saturated fat g to select all four columns
- From the Decimal Places pop-up menu, select 1
- Click and drag over the variable names for Brand and Name to select both columns
- Click and drag the border between their names to widen both columns
- Shift-click or click and drag over all the numeric variables' names to select those columns
- Click and drag the border between any two variable names to make all the columns narrower at once
- Double-click the $\boxed{\bar{x}}$ pane control to close the attribute pane
- From the File menu, select Save
- Change the filename if you want, then click Save
- Close the file

Read a text file

In this exercise, we will import a plain text (ASCII) file. Most applications have an option to save in a plain text format. StatView can read files delimited by tabs, spaces, commas, returns, or any character you specify.

- From the File menu, select Open
- Choose the Text file format
- Select Candy Bars.txt from the Sample Data folder
- Click Open
- Click Import
  (Our sample file is tab delimited, so we don't need to change any settings)

```
╔══════════ Import ══════════╗
  Please specify how this text file looks.
  Items may be separated with tabs and:
  ☐ spaces ☐ commas ☐ returns ☐ [    ]
     Number of variables:      [ 0 ]
  ☐ Convert small integers to Categories
  ☒ Import non-numeric data as type string
  ☐ Make variables with errors have type string
        ( Cancel )  ( Import )
```

StatView reads the values in each column of the text file and does its best to guess the appropriate attributes.

	Brand	Name	Serving/pkg	Oz/
▶ Type:	String	String	Real	Real
▶ Source:	User En...	User En...	User Entered	User
▶ Class:	Nominal	Nominal	Continuous	Conti
▶ Format:	●	●	Free Format Fi...	Free
▶ Dec. Places:	●	●	1	3
1	M&M/...	Snicker...	1.0	
2	Hershey	Cookies...	1.0	

Notice that StatView made the same guesses for this file as it did for it's Excel equivalent. You would need to make the same adjustments to its attributes. (You may experiment with it if you like.)

• Close the dataset

Open a dataset

Often you will begin your StatView data analysis sessions by simply opening a StatView dataset—perhaps one you saved the day before, perhaps one you received from a colleague. Since all display attributes are saved along with the values, you just open the file and begin your analysis.

• From the File menu, select Open
• Select Candy Bars Data from the Sample Data folder
• Click Open

A complete dataset with attributes all set and ready to go appears:

Candy Bars Data

| Compact | Expand | Criteria: | No Criteria |

	Brand	Name	Serving/pkg	Oz/pkg	Calories	Total fat g
1	M&M/Mars	Snickers Peanut Butter	1	2	310	20
2	Hershey	Cookies 'n' Mint	1	1.55	230	12
3	Hershey	Cadbury Dairy Milk	3.5	5	220	12
4	M&M/Mars	Snickers	3	3.7	170	8
5	Charms	Sugar Daddy	1	1.7	200	2.5
6	M&M/Mars	Twix Peanut Butter	1	1.71	260	16
7	Hershey	Twizzler	1	2.2	190	1.5
8	Tobler	Toblerone	1	1.23	190	11
9	Nestle	Crunch	1	1.55	230	12
10	Hershey	Almond Joy	2	3.22	230	13
11	Sherwood	Elana Mint	1	1.6	200	10
12	Hershey	Krackel	1	2.6	390	21
13	M&M/Mars	M&Ms Peanut	1	1.74	250	13
14	Bit-O-Honey	Bit-O-Honey	1	1.7	200	4
15	Nestle	100 Grand	1	1.5	200	8
16	Hershey	Skor	1	1.4	220	13
17	Hershey	Twix Caramel	1	2	280	14
18	M&M/Mars	Milky Way Lite	1	1.57	160	5
19	M&M/Mars	Mars	1	1.76	240	13
20	Pearson	Peanut Nut Roll	1	2.5	340	16
21	Nestle	Raisinet	1	1.58	200	8
22	Sherwood	Elana Mocca	1	1.6	230	13

Analyze data

Sort data

One of the most important (and overlooked!) data analysis tools is sorting. It would be easier to get a feeling for these candy bars if they were grouped by brand. Let's also alphabetize them within each brand.

- From the Manage menu, select Sort
- Select Brand and click Make Key
- Double-click Name

The up arrows (⇧) next to each sort key indicate ascending sort (least to greatest numerical sorting, alphabetical text sorting). If you preferred descending sort, you could click the arrow to change it to a down arrow (⇩).

```
┌══════════════════════ Sort ══════════════════════┐
│                                                   │
│            Select the keys for this sort:         │
│                                                   │
│      Uariables:                    Sort Keys:     │
│     ┌───────────────┐▲           ┌─────────────┐▲ │
│     │ Serving/pkg   │░           │ ⇧ Brand     │░ │
│     │ Oz/pkg        │░           │ ⇧ Name      │░ │
│     │ Calories      │░  ┌─────────┐             │  │
│     │ Total fat g   │░  │Make Key │             │  │
│     │ Saturated fat g│░ └─────────┘             │  │
│     │ Cholesterol g │░  ┌──────────┐            │  │
│     │ Sodium mg     │░  │Remoue Key│            │  │
│     │ Carbohydrate g│▼  └──────────┘            │▼ │
│     └───────────────┘              └─────────────┘ │
│                                                   │
│                           ┌────────┐  ┌────────┐  │
│                           │ Cancel │  │   OK   │  │
│                           └────────┘  └────────┘  │
└───────────────────────────────────────────────────┘
```

- Click OK

Quiz

(Quizzes are optional. If you're in a hurry, skip ahead to the next section.) Now scroll through the dataset and get a feel for the data. See if you can answer some questions just by looking at the data.

Which candy bar manufacturers make the most candy bars? Notice that Hershey, Nestle, and M&M/Mars appear in big clumps. This wasn't obvious before we sorted.

Which candy bars have been popular enough to spawn sequels? Snickers, Reese's Peanut Butter Cups, Milky Way and others have several varieties. Before sorting the names, we couldn't see these easily.

Examine summary statistics

In most data analysis packages, if you want basic descriptive statistics (means, standard deviations, and so forth), you need to type some commands. If your data change, you need to start over. In StatView, all you have to do is open a pane in the dataset window. If your data change, the statistics update automatically.

- Click and drag the attribute pane control ($\boxed{\overline{x}}$) downward to expose the twelve rows of **summary statistics** for each variable

- Scroll to the right so you can see the numeric variables

	Serving/pkg	Oz/pkg	Calories	Total fat g	Saturated fat g	Chole
Type:	Real	Real	Integer	Real	Real	Integ
Source:	User Entered	User En…	User En…	User Ent…	User Entered	User
Class:	Continuous	Continu…	Continu…	Continuous	Continuous	Cont
Format:	Free Format	Free Fo…	●	Free For…	Free Format	●
Dec. Places:	1	2	●	1	1	●
Mean:	1.3	2.19	243.027	11.9	6.2	5.28
Std. Deviation:	.9	1.15	61.996	5.7	3.4	5.42
Std. Error:	.1	.13	7.159	.7	.4	.626
Variance:	.8	1.33	3843.5…	32.8	11.6	29.4
Coeff. of Variation:	.7	.53	.255	.5	.6	1.02
Minimum:	1	1.2	125	0	0	0
Maximum:	4.5	6	450	29	15	20
Range:	3.5	4.8	325.000	29	15	20.0
Count:	75	75	75	75	75	75
Missing Cells:	0	0	0	0	0	0
Sum:	99	164.21	18227…	890.5	462.5	396.
Sum of Squares:	187.5	458.11	4714069	13000.8	3711.2	4268

Edit data

These summary statistics can help you spot and fix data entry errors quickly. For example, let's change the top Oz/pkg value from 1.25 to 125—dropping a decimal point is a common data entry error.

- Click the cell to select it
- Type 125
- Press Enter or Return

	Serving/pkg	Oz/pkg
Type:	Real	Real
Source:	User Entered	User En…
Class:	Continuous	Continu…
Format:	Free Format	Free Fo…
Dec. Places:	1	2
Mean:	1.3	3.84
Std. Deviation:	.9	14.23
Std. Error:	.1	1.64
Variance:	.8	202.38
Coeff. of Variation:	.7	3.71
Minimum:	1	1.2
Maximum:	4.5	125
Range:	3.5	123.8
Count:	75	75
Missing Cells:	0	0
Sum:	99	287.96
Sum of Squares:	187.5	16081…
1	1	125
2	1	1

Notice that the summary statistics change right away—probably faster than you can see. Now notice that the Maximum is 125. That would be a big candy bar!

Also notice that the Mean candy bar is 3.84 oz., but the standard deviation is 14. We know that, if candy bar sizes are normally distributed, most candy bars should fall within two standard deviations of the mean. That would mean some candy bars have negative weight. Even if sizes aren't normally distributed, these statistics would *not* seem likely!

Either discovery would tell us to look for an error.

- Click the 125 cell
- Change it back to 1.25
- Press Enter or Return

	Serving/pkg	Oz/pkg
► Type:	Real	Real
► Source:	User Entered	User En...
► Class:	Continuous	Continu...
► Format:	Free Format	Free Fo...
► Dec. Places:	1	2
Mean:	1.3	2.19
Std. Deviation:	.9	1.15
Std. Error:	.1	.13
Variance:	.8	1.33

These statistics make more sense.

Quiz

Try to answer these questions by examining your summary statistics pane. You may need to scroll through the dataset to answer some questions. You also might want to resize the data window to be taller and wider.

What's the smallest number of calories per serving you can find in a candy bar? Look at Minimum for Calories. The least value is 125.

How much does the per-serving total fat vary from candy bar to candy bar? What's the average? See Range (or Minimum and Maximum) for Total fat g. The candy bars range from 0g to 29g per serving. They average just below the halfway mark at 11.9g, and most should fall within two standard deviations (10.4g) above or below that, if they're normally distributed. That's a pretty big spread.

If you were watching your fat intake, which candy bars would be good choices? The Minimum for Total fat g is 0g. Scroll through and look for the case(s) with 0 values to see that Super Hot Tamales are your choice. Other choices with small numbers are Big Hunk, York Peppermint Patty, Skittles, Sugar Daddy, Tiger Sport, and Twizzler.

How many candy bars are in the dataset? Look at the Count for Calories. The count is 75, which means we have 75 nonmissing cases. Since Missing Cells is 0, we also know that our dataset has 75 rows.

Did any manufacturers refuse to tell us about saturated fat? Look at Missing Cells for Saturated fat g. Since it's 0, we know that the manufacturers complied with rules and printed this information for all the candy bars.

When you're done, close the entire attribute pane.

- Double-click the pane control (▱) to shrink the pane
- Double-click it again to close it completely

Compute formulas

Before we move on to analysis, let's generate a formula. The guidelines say we can have up to 2000 calories a day. How many candy bars would that be, if we didn't eat anything else?

- From the Manage menu, select Formula
- Use the calculator pad or your keyboard to enter "2000 / "
- Double-click Calories from the list of variables in the upper left corner
- Click Compute

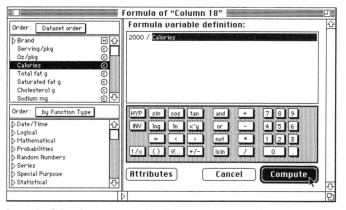

Now at the right end of the dataset, you should see a new variable with a boring name.

- Click that boring name (Column 18)
- Type a better name: Bars per day
- Press Enter or Return

Now you have a brand new variable whose values tell you how many of each candy bar you could eat. There's only one problem—you can't see the Name column anymore.

Not to worry! You can split the dataset window horizontally.

- Drag the horizontal split-pane handle to the right
  (It's the black bar to the left of the horizontal scroll bar)
- Scroll Brand and Name into view on the left side
- Scroll the right side to the end, so you can see Bars per day

Candy Bars Data

| Compact | Expand | Criteria: | No Criteria |

	Brand	Name	Bars per day	Input C
1	Adams & Brooks	Cup O Gold	12.500	
2	Annabelle	Abba-Zabba	8.000	
3	Annabelle	Big Hunk	8.696	
4	Annabelle	Look!	10.526	
5	Annabelle	U-No (Blue)	8.000	
6	Annabelle	U-No (Green)	8.000	
7	Bit-O-Honey	Bit-O-Honey	10.000	
8	Brown & Haley	Almond Roca	7.407	
9	Charms	Sugar Daddy	10.000	
10	Hershey	5th Avenue	7.143	
11	Hershey	Almond Joy	8.696	
12	Hershey	Bar None	8.000	
13	Hershey	Cadbury Caramello	10.526	
14	Hershey	Cadbury Dairy Milk	9.091	
15	Hershey	Cadbury Fruit & Nut	9.524	
16	Hershey	Cadbury Roast Almond	9.091	
17	Hershey	Cookies 'n' Mint	8.696	

(We also made the whole window small for this illustration. You can pick a size you like.)

It's easy to see you could have 12 Cup O Golds, or 8 Almond Joys, or 4 Mr. Goodbars, or 11 Peppermint Patties…

Oops! We forgot that these data are per *serving*, not per *bar*, and some of the candy bars are so big they have several servings per package! We need to fix that formula.

- Open the attribute pane
  Double-click the attribute pane control

- From the Source pop-up menu for Bars per day, select Dynamic formula
  Click and hold that cell, then release the mouse button

Now we just edit the formula in the dialog box to have another division term:

- Click just after the existing formula

- Click / in the keypad area of the formula dialog box, or type a / (slash)

- Double-click Servings/pkg from the list of variables

- Click Compute

Formula of "Bars per day"

Order: Dataset order

▷ Brand
Serving/pkg
Oz/pkg
Calories
Total fat g
Saturated fat g
Cholesterol g
Sodium mg

Order: by Function Type

▷ Date/Time
▷ Logical
▷ Mathematical
▷ Probabilities
▷ Random Numbers
▷ Series
▷ Special Purpose
▷ Statistical

Formula variable definition:

2000 / Calories / "Serving/pkg"

HYP	sin	cos	tan		and	+	7	8	9
INV	log	ln	x^y		or	–	4	5	6
	=	<	>		not	*	1	2	3
1/x	( )	if...	+/–		IsIn	/		0	.

| Attributes | | Cancel | | Compute |

The sad truth is we can only have 4 Almond Joys—that one had 2 servings per package. Accurate data analysis disappoints coconut and almond lovers everywhere.

Quiz

If you're in a hurry, you can skip past these quizzes. If you have the time, though, they'll give you some practice and help you learn more about the functionality you've learned.

You're supposed to limit total fat intake to 65 grams per day. How many candy bars could you eat if you were only worried about total fat? Create a new variable called "Total fat rule" with this formula:

> 65 / "Total fat g" / "Serving/pkg"

Now you are reduced to 8 Cup O Golds, or 2 Almond Joys, or 2 Mr. Goodbars. But, now you could have 16 York Peppermint Patties.

Only 20 grams of that total fat should be saturated fat. How many candy bars could you eat if you were only worried about saturated fat? Create a new variable called "Sat fat rule" with this formula:

> 20 / "Saturated fat g" / "Serving/pkg"

Yikes! More bad news! You're down to 4 Cup O Golds, 1 Almond Joy, or 1 Mr. Goodbar. And York Peppermint Patties are back down to 8.

Most people should try to get 25 grams of fiber per day. How many candy bars would that take? What's the best choice for fiber? Create a new variable called "Fiber rule" with this formula:

> 25 / "Dietary fiber g" / "Serving/pkg"

Clearly, candy bars are not a good source of fiber. Most would take more than 20 packages, and some don't have any fiber at all (see the missing values). If you open the summary statistics pane, you see that 4.2 is the Minimum—scrolling down, you find that's the Almond Joy.

Is there any candy bar that would give you enough fiber without putting you over the calorie and fat limits? This is a complex one, and we'll need to rely on StatView's logical functions to do it efficiently. Create another formula variable called "Composite" with this formula:

> if "Fiber rule" <= "Bars per day" AND
>   "Fiber rule" <= "Sat fat rule" AND
>   "Fiber rule" <= "Total fat rule"
> then 1
> else 0

Click the "if…" button in the keypad area of the formula dialog box. (Or type "if," or use the function browser in the lower left corner of the formula dialog box. We'll show you that in the "Managing data" chapter under "Function browser," p. 111.) Don't worry about formatting the formula exactly like you see here; we just broke the lines like this to make it easier to read.

Now scroll through the results, and see whether any candy bars have a "1," meaning they meet all the requirements. Tiger Sport is the only one: 12.5 Tiger Sports give you all the fiber you need, but you could have 16 before you broke the calorie rule, according to Bars per day.

	Brand		RDI	Bars per...	Total fat...	Sat fat r...	Fiber rule	Composite
72	Tootsie	Charleston Che	2	8.696	9.286	3.333	25.000	0.000
73	Tootsie	Jr Mints	4	10.526	16.250	8.000	●	●
74	Weider	Tiger Milk	15	12.500	10.833	20.000	●	●
75	Weider	Tiger Sport	15	16.000	32.500	40.000	12.500	1.000

Build an analysis

We've already analyzed these data quite a bit, without ever having left the dataset window. Now it's time to see some real analysis power.

- From the Analyze menu, select New View

Now you see StatView's **view window**. This is where you'll build statistical analysis tables, draw graphs, and put together presentations. Think of the view window as your paper.

Along the left side of view window is the **analysis browser**, which is a scrolling list of the statistical and graphical analyses you can create in StatView. To create an analysis, just select the analysis from the analysis browser, then click the Create Analysis button. (Some analyses, like Frequency Distribution, have little triangles in front of their names. Click any triangle to reveal a more specific set of choices.)

For example, we can get Descriptive Statistics about the candy bars:

- Click Descriptive Statistics
- Click Create Analysis

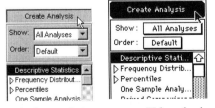

A dialog box asks which descriptive statistics we want. Take a look at "More choices" if you want to see all the descriptives StatView can do. For now, we will just compute the basic set of statistics.

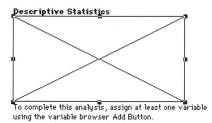

- Choose Basic
- Click OK

Now you should see an empty **analysis object**, with black selection handles indicating that the object is selected:

Descriptive Statistics

To complete this analysis, assign at least one variable using the variable browser Add Button.

The note on the empty object says what to do next. We use the **variable browser** to add variables to the empty analysis:

- Make sure the object is still selected (has black handles); if not, click it to select it
- In the Variable Browser, Shift-click to select Calories, Total fat g, and Saturated fat g
- Click Add

(Notice that each of these variables is marked with a ⓒ icon in the variable browser, indicating that the variables are continuous. Similarly, Brand has an Ⓝ icon for nominal, and Name has an ⬥ icon for informative. We made these class settings in the attribute pane of the dataset window, and now the browser reminds us. StatView also uses these settings to help you assign appropriate variables to each analysis.)

Ta-dah! You've completed your first analysis in StatView. Black handles indicate the object is still selected.

Descriptive Statistics

	Mean	Std. Dev.	Std. Error	Count	Minimum	Maximum	# Missing
Calories	243.027	61.996	7.159	75	125.000	450.000	0
Total fat g	11.873	5.728	.661	75	0.000	29.000	0
Saturated fat g	6.167	3.407	.393	75	0.000	15.000	0

While the analysis is selected (has black handles), notice that the variable browser marks which variables are used: each variable has an X marker. The X marker means the variable is an X (or independent) variable in the selected analysis. We'll see other markers later.

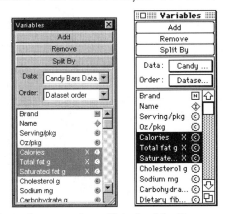

Here's the fun part. Analysis objects are incredibly flexible. You can:

1. add variables

2. split the analysis by a nominal (grouping) variable

3. remove variables

4. replace variables with different variables

5. change the way statistics are displayed

6. choose different statistics

7. etc., etc., etc.!

We'll try some of these things as we continue our quest for the ideal candy bar.

Remove variables

Let's just look at calories for now.

- Make sure the analysis is still selected (has black handles); if not, click it
- In the variable browser, select Total fat g and Saturated fat g
- Click the Remove button

Our analysis is updated, in place, to show just calories. Also, the variable browser updates so that only Calories has an X marker.

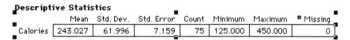

Descriptive Statistics

	Mean	Std. Dev.	Std. Error	Count	Minimum	Maximum	# Missing
Calories	243.027	61.996	7.159	75	125.000	450.000	0

Notice the analysis is really short and wide. It might look better if we flipped it sideways.

Edit a display

- Make sure the analysis is still selected
- Click the Edit Display button at the top of the view window

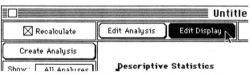

- Check Transpose rows and columns (click the checkbox so it has a check mark)
- Click OK

As easy as that, we've transposed the whole table:

Just as easily, we could have changed the table's number formats, borders, and row height.

Edit analysis parameters

You may not be surprised about how easy it is to transpose a table's display. Would you believe it is just as simple to change the parameters of an analysis?

• Make sure the analysis is still selected

• Click the Edit Analysis button at the top of the view window

Now we see the same dialog box of **analysis parameters** as when we first created the analysis. Almost all of StatView's graphs and analyses have a set of options for specifying exactly how to complete the analysis, and you can always change your mind by clicking Edit Analysis and making new choices.

• Click More choices

This expanded version of the analysis parameters dialog box lets us choose exactly which statistics we want. (Scroll down to see all the possibilities.) Since we know our dataset has no missing values, let's save space by turning off the Number missing option.

• Uncheck Number missing
(Click the box to remove the check mark.)

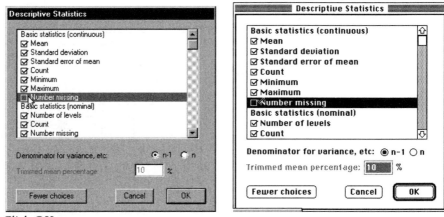

• Click OK

Descriptive Statistics	
	Calories
Mean	243.027
Std. Dev.	61.996
■ Std. Error	7.159
Count	75
Minimum	125.000
Maximum	450.000

Split by groups

How does per-serving calorie content of candy bars vary among the different brands? We can split this analysis by Brand group to find out:

• Make sure the analysis is still selected (if not, click the object to select it)
• In the variable browser, select Brand
• Click the Split By button

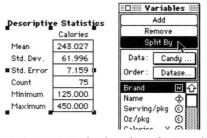

Now we have a table of descriptive statistics broken down by Brand groups. Unfortunately, it's so wide it runs off the window. Let's untranspose it.

• Make sure the analysis is still selected
• Click the Edit Display button at the top of the view window
• *Un*check Transpose rows and columns (click the checkbox to *remove* the check mark)
• Click OK

Descriptive Statistics
Split By : Brand

	Mean	Std. Dev.	Std. Error	Count	Minimum	Maximum
Calories, Total	243.027	61.996	7.159	75	125.000	450.000
Calories, Adams & Brooks	160.000	•	•	1	160.000	160.000
Calories, Annabelle	234.000	26.077	11.662	5	190.000	250.000
Calories, Bit-O-Honey	200.000	•	•	1	200.000	200.000
Calories, Brown & Haley	270.000	•	•	1	270.000	270.000
Calories, Charms	200.000	•	•	1	200.000	200.000
Calories, Hershey	267.931	80.462	14.941	29	170.000	450.000
Calories, Just Born	220.000	•	•	1	220.000	220.000
Calories, Leaf	226.667	15.275	8.819	3	210.000	240.000
Calories, M&M/Mars	236.250	37.394	9.349	16	160.000	310.000
Calories, Myerson	230.000	•	•	1	230.000	230.000
Calories, Nabisco	230.000	•	•	1	230.000	230.000
Calories, Nestle	231.667	39.200	16.003	6	200.000	280.000
Calories, Pearson	340.000	•	•	1	340.000	340.000
Calories, Sherwood	215.000	21.213	15.000	2	200.000	230.000
Calories, Standard	262.000	•	•	1	262.000	262.000
Calories, Tobler	190.000	•	•	1	190.000	190.000
Calories, Tootsie	210.000	28.284	20.000	2	190.000	230.000
Calories, Weider	142.500	24.749	17.500	2	125.000	160.000

This table shows descriptive statistics for the candy bars made under each brand name—for example, 160 is the mean calories per serving for the bars made by Adams & Brooks (of which there is only 1, according to the Count statistic), whereas all the different M&M/Mars bars average out to 236 calories per serving. The top row of the table shows statistics for the total, or for candy bars from all brands combined.

Clone an analysis with different variables

We're still interested in fat, so let's **clone** this table into a new one using the Total fat g variable:

- Make sure the analysis is still selected
- In the variable browser, select Total fat g
- Control-Shift-click (Windows) or Command-Shift-click (Macintosh) the Add button

Descriptive Statistics
Split By : Brand

	Mean	Std. Dev.	Std. Error	Count	Minimum	Maximum
Total fat g, Total	11.873	5.728	.661	75	0.000	29.000
Total fat g, Adams & Brooks	8.000	•	•	1	8.000	8.000
Total fat g, Annabelle	9.600	6.841	3.059	5	3.000	17.000
Total fat g, Bit-O-Honey	4.000	•	•	1	4.000	4.000
Total fat g, Brown & Haley	19.000	•	•	1	19.000	19.000
Total fat g, Charms	2.500	•	•	1	2.500	2.500
Total fat g, Hershey	14.603	6.140	1.140	29	1.500	29.000
Total fat g, Just Born	0.000	•	•	1	0.000	0.000
Total fat g, Leaf	11.667	1.528	.882	3	10.000	13.000
Total fat g, M&M/Mars	11.219	4.301	1.075	16	2.500	20.000
Total fat g, Myerson	10.000	•	•	1	10.000	10.000
Total fat g, Nabisco	14.000	•	•	1	14.000	14.000
Total fat g, Nestle	10.333	1.862	.760	6	8.000	12.000
Total fat g, Pearson	16.000	•	•	1	16.000	16.000
Total fat g, Sherwood	11.500	2.121	1.500	2	10.000	13.000
Total fat g, Standard	16.000	•	•	1	16.000	16.000
Total fat g, Tobler	11.000	•	•	1	11.000	11.000
Total fat g, Tootsie	5.500	2.121	1.500	2	4.000	7.000
Total fat g, Weider	4.000	2.828	2.000	2	2.000	6.000

Cloning an object makes a new copy of the object using the new variables, leaving the original object unchanged. (We could have added Total fat g to the original table instead, but two separate tables are easier to read.)

Notice that Split By Brand is still in effect. Let's clone this analysis for Saturated fat g, also:

- Make sure the analysis is still selected
- In the variable browser, select Saturated fat g
- Control-Shift-click (Windows) or Command-Shift-click (Macintosh) the Add button

Descriptive Statistics
Split By : Brand

	Mean	Std. Dev.	Std. Error	Count	Minimum	Maximum
Saturated fat g, Total	6.167	3.407	.393	75	0.000	15.000
Saturated fat g, Adams & B...	4.500	•	•	1	4.500	4.500
Saturated fat g, Annabelle	6.100	4.696	2.100	5	.500	11.000
Saturated fat g, Bit-O-Honey	2.500	•	•	1	2.500	2.500
Saturated fat g, Brown & H...	11.000	•	•	1	11.000	11.000
Saturated fat g, Charms	2.500	•	•	1	2.500	2.500
Saturated fat g, Hershey	8.103	3.434	.638	29	0.000	15.000
Saturated fat g, Just Born	0.000	•	•	1	0.000	0.000
Saturated fat g, Leaf	5.667	3.215	1.856	3	2.000	8.000
Saturated fat g, M&M/Mars	5.000	2.338	.585	16	.500	10.000
Saturated fat g, Myerson	5.000	•	•	1	5.000	5.000
Saturated fat g, Nabisco	1.500	•	•	1	1.500	1.500
Saturated fat g, Nestle	5.833	1.169	.477	6	4.000	7.000
Saturated fat g, Pearson	3.000	•	•	1	3.000	3.000
Saturated fat g, Sherwood	6.500	.707	.500	2	6.000	7.000
Saturated fat g, Standard	5.000	•	•	1	5.000	5.000
Saturated fat g, Tobler	7.000	•	•	1	7.000	7.000
Saturated fat g, Tootsie	4.250	2.475	1.750	2	2.500	6.000
Saturated fat g, Weider	.750	.354	.250	2	.500	1.000

Dotted red lines in the view window indicate page breaks.

Use Criteria to examine a subset

The numbers in the Count columns of these tables reveal that only Hershey, Nestle, and M&M/Mars have six or more different candy bars. (Annabelle has five, so you might want to include that brand as well; it's your choice.) Perhaps we should narrow our study to these three major brands. StatView makes it easy to do that.

- Bring the dataset window to the front by clicking it or by selecting Candy Bars from the Window menu

- From the Criteria pop-up menu, select New

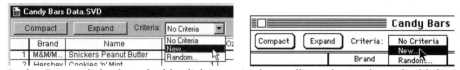

- In the Criteria dialog box, double-click items in the scrolling selection list to build the criteria definition:

Brand ElementOf {Hershey, "M&M/Mars", Nestle}

(Start by double-clicking Brand. Now you have a new set of choices: double-click ElementOf. Your choices change again: click Hershey, then M&M/Mars, and finally Nestle. Notice how StatView guides you through each step, so you don't have to learn any special rules.)

- In the Criteria name box, type a name for the criterion: Big Three

- Click Apply

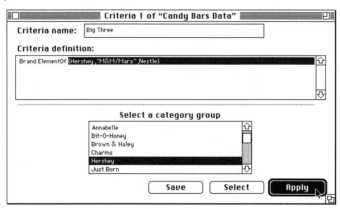

Look at the dataset window. Notice how the row numbers for candy bars made by other manufacturers are dimmed, indicating that the cases are not included in analyses. Also, the Criteria pop-up menu shows the criterion in effect.

```
┌────────────────────────────────────────┐
│ ▣░░░░░░░░░░░ Candy Bars Data ░░░░░░░░░░ │
│ ┌─────────┐ ┌────────┐  Criteria: ┌─────────┐ │
│ │ Compact │ │ Expand │            │Big Three│ │
│ └─────────┘ └────────┘            └─────────┘ │
```

	Brand	Name	Sat fat
1	Adams & Brooks	Cup O Gold	4.
2	Annabelle	Abba-Zabba	5.
3	Annabelle	Big Hunk	40.
4	Annabelle	Look!	5.
5	Annabelle	U-No (Blue)	1.
6	Annabelle	U-No (Green)	1.
7	Bit-O-Honey	Bit-O-Honey	8.
8	Brown & Haley	Almond Roca	1.
9	Charms	Sugar Daddy	8.
10	Hershey	5th Avenue	4.
11	Hershey	Almond Joy	1.
12	Hershey	Bar None	2.
13	Hershey	Cadbury Caramello	

Now, look at the view window—click the window or select Untitled View #1 from the Window menu. Notice how all your analyses have already updated themselves to show just the results for the big three brands.

And, so that you don't forget that you're looking at just a subset of your data, each object's title now includes "Inclusion criteria" information.

Descriptive Statistics
Split By : Brand
Inclusion criteria: Big Three from Candy Bars Data

	Mean	Std. Dev.	Std. Error	Count	Minimum	Maximum
Calories, Total	253.725	66.872	9.364	51	160.000	450.000
Calories, Hershey	267.931	80.462	14.941	29	170.000	450.000
Calories, M&M/Mars	236.250	37.394	9.349	16	160.000	310.000
Calories, Nestle	231.667	39.200	16.003	6	200.000	280.000

Descriptive Statistics
Split By : Brand
Inclusion criteria: Big Three from Candy Bars Data

	Mean	Std. Dev.	Std. Error	Count	Minimum	Maximum
Total fat g, Total	13.039	5.511	.772	51	1.500	29.000
Total fat g, Hershey	14.603	6.140	1.140	29	1.500	29.000
Total fat g, M&M/Mars	11.219	4.301	1.075	16	2.500	20.000
Total fat g, Nestle	10.333	1.862	.760	6	8.000	12.000

Descriptive Statistics
Split By : Brand
Inclusion criteria: Big Three from Candy Bars Data

	Mean	Std. Dev.	Std. Error	Count	Minimum	Maximum
Saturated fat g, Total	6.863	3.242	.454	51	0.000	15.000
Saturated fat g, Hershey	8.103	3.434	.638	29	0.000	15.000
Saturated fat g, M&M/Mars	5.000	2.338	.585	16	.500	10.000
Saturated fat g, Nestle	5.833	1.169	.477	6	4.000	7.000

Adopt variable assignments for a new analysis

If a picture is worth a thousand words, a graph must be worth a thousand statistics. Let's look at a box plot of these variables.

We can do this a number of ways. We could create a box plot analysis and add variables to it, just as we did to create our first descriptive statistics table. Or, we could select a table and then **adopt** its variable assignments for a new analysis:

• Select the first table by clicking it

• From the analysis browser, select Box Plot

• Click Create Analysis

StatView creates a box plot analysis object, and then automatically adds the Calories variable. StatView also assigns Brand as a Split By variable again, so that this box plot is the graphical equivalent of the statistics table.

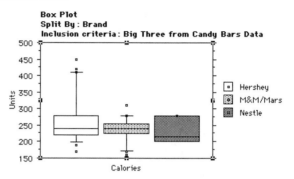

Quiz

Which brand offers the widest variety of calories per serving in its candy bars? Examine the box plots. The box-and-whisker for Hershey is more than twice as wide as the other boxes.

Which brand has the highest-calorie-per-serving candy bar? Again in the box plot, notice that Hershey's highest point is well above the maxima for the other two brands.

Which brand has the lowest-calorie-per-serving candy bar? M&M/Mars takes the honors here: its lowest point is right at the bottom of the graph.

Is the fat variation similar to the calorie variation? Do a box plot of Total fat g: select the Total fat g descriptive statistics table, select Box Plot from the analysis browser, and click Create Analysis. The only surprise is that Hershey has the lowest fat-content candy bar, while M&M/Mars has the lowest calorie-count candy bar.

Is the saturated fat variation similar? Similarly, do a box plot of Saturated fat g by starting with the statistics for Saturated fat g. Again, the results are similar. Hershey also has the lowest *saturated* fat content. Since saturated fat is part of the total fat, it is not surprising that these two go closely together. However, the plots show somewhat different distributions, which means that the proportions of *unsaturated* fat content (something nutrition labels don't report) do vary.

Are the other brands (besides Hershey, M&M/Mars, and Nestle) much different? Temporarily turn off the Big Three criterion: in the dataset window, select No Criteria from the Criteria pop-up menu. When you're ready to continue, select the Big Three criterion again.

Create an analysis with several parts

Sideways triangles (▷) sit in front of many items in the analysis browser. These triangles indicate that more detailed choices are available. Clicking the triangle tips it downward (▽) and reveals a list of possible results. Some even have subcategories of possible results. In all cases, the triangles let you show or hide levels of detail, as seen in the picture below.

For example, Frequency Distribution analysis can produce summary tables, histograms, Z-score (standardized) histograms, and pie charts.

QC Subgroup Measurements is a more complex example. It has four categories of measurements (Xbar, R, S, and CUSUM Statistics) and a Summary Table. Each category produces several types of results: line charts, needle charts, bar charts, point charts, and results tables.

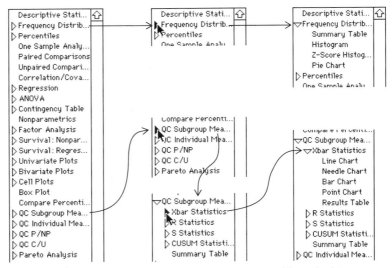

Let's work with Frequency Distribution to create a summary table and a histogram of Calories. These will help us determine whether the variable is normally distributed.

• Click somewhere in the white space of the view window to be sure no results are selected (This way, we avoid adopting variables from any analyses that are selected.)

• Click the triangle next to Frequency Distribution to show the detailed list

• Click and drag to select both Summary Table and Histogram

• Click Create Analysis

• Click OK to accept the default analysis parameters

Frequency Distribution

Number of intervals: `10`   ☐ Show normal comparison

Do you wish to enter your own interval information?

◉ no ○ yes width: ⬚   initial value: ⬚

Intervals indicate: [Count ▼]   include: [Lowest value ▼]

- -

Tables show: ⊠ Counts ☐ Percents ☐ Relative frequencies

Histograms show: [Counts ▼]

[Cancel] [**OK**]

- In the variable browser, select Calories and click Add

It looks like Calories is **bimodal**: the histogram has two humps. This is likely to be a problem in further analyses. (Dotted red lines indicate page breaks; we won't worry about them for now.)

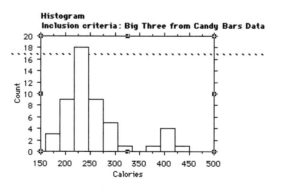

Frequency Distribution for Calories
Inclusion criteria: Big Three from Candy Bars Data

From (≥)	To (<)	Count
160.000	189.000	3
189.000	218.000	9
218.000	247.000	18
247.000	276.000	9
276.000	305.000	5
305.000	334.000	1
334.000	363.000	0
363.000	392.000	1
392.000	421.000	4
421.000	450.000	1
	Total	51

Histogram
Inclusion criteria: Big Three from Candy Bars Data

Quiz

If Calories are bimodal, perhaps it's because some candy bars have more fat or carbohydrates than most. **Are these variables bimodal as well?**   Clone the frequency distribution analysis with the other variables that are likely to be bimodal: Total fat g, Saturated fat g, and Carbohydrate g.

A glance at the histograms doesn't show bimodality in the fat and carbohydrate variables, although both Saturated fat g and Carbohydrate g seem to have small jumps at the high end. More information is needed.

What about when we include the smaller brands? Does increasing the sample size make any relationships more apparent? Turn off the Big Three criteria. Bring the dataset window forward by clicking it or selecting Candy Bars from the Window menu. From the criteria pop-up menu at the top of the window, select No Criteria.

Still no apparent bimodality except in Calories. Reselect the Big Three criterion to continue the analysis.

Create a new grouping variable

One way to cope with this problem in further study is to divide the candy bars into two groups: high calorie and low calorie. StatView's Recode feature lets you do this quickly.

- From the Manage menu, select Recode
- From the scroll list on the left, select Calories
- Click Continuous values to nominal groups

Since we're recoding a continuous variable (Calories) into a grouping variable, we need to choose a category for the groups. The only category defined thus far in the dataset is for Brand, which wouldn't work. Therefore, we need to define a new category with values "low" and "high."

- Click New

- Specify a name for the category: Category for Calorie Groups

- Specify the first Group label: Low
- Click Add
- Specify the second Group label: High
- Click Add
- Click Done

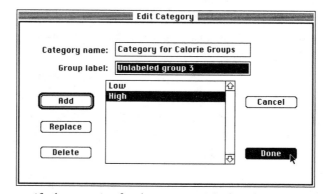

Now we need to specify the **cutpoint** for the groups—which Calories values go in the Low group, which in the High. The rectangular area represents the total range of Calories, from 125 to 450; we need to click some value below which values should be grouped "Low" and above which they are "High."

- Move the cross-hair cursor up and down until you find an appropriate cutpoint—some value in the "gap" between high and low values, like 360
- Click at that cutpoint

StatView shows the group assignments in pop-up menus to the right. Because we defined category groups in order from small to big, StatView's initial guesses were correct. (If we had not defined them "in order," we'd have to use the pop-up menus to fix the group assignments.)

- Click Recode

The dataset has a new variable showing Low and High group memberships.

- Click the dataset window to bring it forward, or select it from the Window menu
- Click the variable's name to select it

- Type a new name: Calorie groups
- Press Enter or Return

Grouped box plots

Now let's try to learn the reason for Calories' bimodality. In the quiz above, we determined that fat and carbohydrates were not clearly bimodal. However, their values could still differ between groups; or, other nutrients could be relevant. A grouped box plot is a quick way to examine several possibilities all at once.

Previously we grouped a box plot of Calories by brand name. This time, let's examine several variables at once and split it by calorie grouping.

- Click somewhere in the white space of the view window to be sure no results are selected
- In the analysis browser, double-click Box Plot
  (This is a shortcut for selecting Box Plot and then clicking Create Analysis.)
- In the variable browser, click and drag from Total fat g down to Protein g and click Add
- In the variable browser, click Calorie groups and click Split By

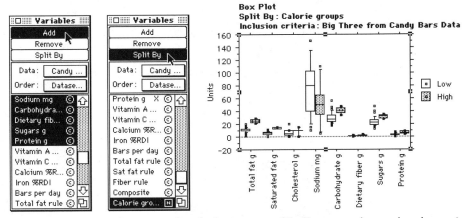

One thing we notice right away is that the large range of Sodium mg values makes the vertical scale too large for the other variables, which are squashed together in the lower half of the graph. Since sodium content probably doesn't contribute significantly to calorie content (sodium may be bad for people with high blood pressure, but it's not fattening). Let's remove it from the analysis.

- Make sure the analysis is still selected (has black handles); if not, click it
- In the variable browser, select Sodium mg and click Remove

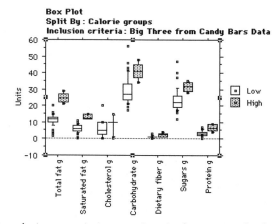

Now the most likely culprits are easier to examine. And sure enough, the fat content (both total and saturated), carbohydrates, sugars, and protein all seem to be greater for the high than for the low calorie candy bars.

Create an unpaired *t*-test

A statistical test for this conclusion is an unpaired *t*-test. A *t*-test tests the null hypothesis that the means of two groups are the same, and a significant *p* value (say, less than 0.05) means they are *not* the same. Let's just look at Total fat g for now.

- Click somewhere in the white space of the view window to be sure no results are selected
- In the analysis browser, double-click Unpaired Comparisons
- Click OK to accept the default parameters
  (The default options produce an unpaired *t*-test with a null hypothesis difference of 0.)

The note below the empty analysis objects says we need to add both a nominal and a continuous variable.

To complete this analysis, assign a continuous variable and a nominal variable using the variable browser Add Button.

- In the variable browser, Control-click (Windows) or Command-click (Macintosh) Total fat g and Calorie groups
- Click Add

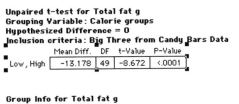

Unpaired t-test for Total fat g
Grouping Variable : Calorie groups
Hypothesized Difference = 0
Inclusion criteria : Big Three from Candy Bars Data

	Mean Diff.	DF	t-Value	P-Value
Low, High	-13.178	49	-8.672	<.0001

Group Info for Total fat g
Grouping Variable : Calorie groups
Inclusion criteria : Big Three from Candy Bars Data

	Count	Mean	Variance	Std. Dev.	Std. Err
Low	45	11.489	12.585	3.548	.529
High	6	24.667	9.067	3.011	1.229

We see that the mean difference is quite large, and the *p* value is well below 0.05. However, the groups are vastly different sizes (45 and 6), so we shouldn't take this result too seriously. Still, it seems apparent that the fat content between groups is significantly different, and it does make sense that candy bars with more fat would have more calories.

What about saturated fat?

If you took the quiz, you probably noticed that calories and total fat were, on average, pretty similar among the big three brands. However, the median lines in the box plots for saturated fat looked pretty different. In case you're skipping the quizzes, here's a plot you would have examined:

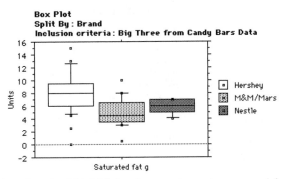

From the looks of this plot, the M&M/Mars bars are lower in saturated fat per serving than the Hershey and Nestle bars: compare the median lines in the middle of the boxes. However, the Nestle median falls inside the M&M/Mars box height, and all three boxes are overlapping with each other.

We can't be sure just by looking at box plots. The nutrition guidelines tell us to keep tabs on saturated fat, so let's look into this some more.

Create an ANOVA using a template

Let's do an analysis of variance (ANOVA) to see whether the numbers back up our visual interpretation. Our null hypothesis is that there is no significant difference in saturated fat content
between brand families, and the box plot suggests we'll be able to reject that hypothesis.

We could create an ANOVA by using the analysis and variable browsers, as we've been doing. In
fact, you can try that right now, if you like—you can probably figure it out quite easily.
Instead, though, we're going to look at one of StatView's most powerful features: **templates**. A
template is simply a way of saving a view of analysis and graph results—in any combination—
so that it can be recycled in a future analysis, with a twist: you can apply the template to *different datasets* and *different variables*. So, where other data analysis packages only allow you to
save batches of commands for repeating analyses *exactly*, StatView lets you repeat an analysis
strategy with completely different variables—no editing, no typing, no mistakes. What's
more, you can save all your annotations, layout, and color settings so that the template puts
together not just the analysis but your complete presentation.

StatView ships with dozens and dozens of pre-built templates that produce complete analyses—for example, the ANOVA template we'll use assembles an ANOVA table, a means table and a
bar chart of the effects, and even a Fisher's PLSD (Protected Least Significant Difference) post-
hoc test.

- From the Analyze menu, select the ANOVA and t-tests submenu and select ANOVA-factorial

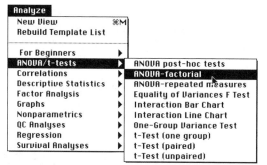

- Drag Saturated fat g to the Dependent Variable slot
- Drag Brand to the Factor(s) slot
- Click OK

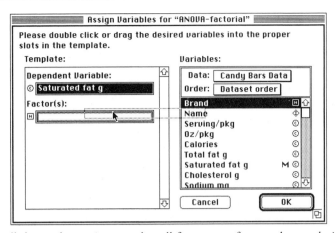

StatView does all the work, putting together all four parts of a complete analysis of variance. The ANOVA table is first. The *p* value is well under 0.05, so it looks like we can reject the null hypothesis.

ANOVA Table for Saturated fat g
Inclusion criteria: Big Three from Candy Bars Data

	DF	Sum of Squares	Mean Square	F-Value	P-Value
Brand	2	106.516	53.258	6.101	.0044
Residual	48	419.023	8.730		

Model II estimate of between component variance: 3.094

The next part of the output is a means table, showing that M&M/Mars has the smallest mean. You may examine the bar chart of means and confidence intervals and the post-hoc test for further details on the analysis. An "S" for "significant" marks the Fisher's PLSD *p* value for the Hershey, M&M/Mars combination: the *p* value is well under 0.05. (Since the count for Nestle is considerably smaller than for the other two, we shouldn't pay much attention to the other PLSD results.)

Means Table for Saturated fat g
Effect: Brand
Inclusion criteria: Big Three from Candy Bars Data

	Count	Mean	Std. Dev.	Std. Err.
Hershey	29	8.103	3.434	.638
M&M/Mars	16	5.000	2.338	.585
Nestle	6	5.833	1.169	.477

Fisher's PLSD for Saturated fat g
Effect: Brand
Significance Level: 5 %
Inclusion criteria: Big Three from Candy Bars Data

	Mean Diff.	Crit. Diff	P-Value	
Hershey, M&M/Mars	3.103	1.850	.0015	S
Hershey, Nestle	2.270	2.664	.0931	
M&M/Mars, Nestle	-.833	2.844	.5585	

(If you've forgotten what some of these statistics mean, you'll be relieved to know that the chapters in *StatView Reference* include discussions of the theories behind each type of analysis—and they give pointers on which tests to use, what you need to check first, how to interpret the numbers, and where to turn next.)

Finally, we get an interaction bar plot. This simply shows us the means and confidence intervals graphically.

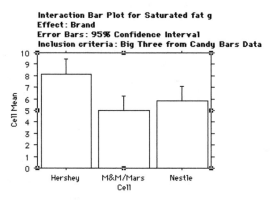

Notice that these results are no different from results created with the analysis browser. You can clone them, add variables, remove variables, reformat them—even resave them to be a new template!

Quiz

Are saturated fat values normally distributed? We should check that assumption before taking our results seriously. If we were doing an important analysis, we'd want to do more tests to be sure. For our purposes, it's reasonable simply to examine the histogram for Saturated fat g that we created earlier.

Can we predict calorie content from saturated fat content? Use the Regression - Simple template, specifying Calories as the Dependent Variable and Saturated fat g as the Independent Variable.

From total fat content? Use the Regression - Simple template, specifying Calories as the Dependent Variable and Total fat g as the Independent Variable.

From both total and saturated fat? Use the Regression - Multiple templates, specifying Calories as the Dependent Variable and both fat variables as Independent Variables. Notice that the Independent Variables slot grows to accommodate more than one variable.

How are these variables correlated? Use templates or browsers to create a correlation matrix and some bivariate scattergrams.

Since we never quite resolved the question of Calories' bimodality, among other reasons, it's probably best to refrain from drawing any major conclusions. We'll leave interpretation of these results up to you.

Save your work

Normally at this point in a data analysis project, you would want to save your work (if you haven't already).

Save a dataset

Since we've made some changes to the dataset (new variables and criteria), we should save:

- Make sure the dataset is the frontmost (active) window
  If not, click it or select Candy Bars Data from the Window menu.
- Select Save As from the File menu
- Type a filename: Candy Bars Data 2
- Click Save

StatView saves everything about the dataset: the values, the variable names, the attributes and summary statistics, the criteria (and whether one is in effect), and more. This way, you can resume working exactly where you left off.

Save a view

We also want to save our view full of graphs and tables.

- Make sure the view is the frontmost (active) window
  If not, click it or select Untitled View #1 from the Window menu.
- Select Save from the File menu
- Type a filename: Nutrition analysis
- Click Save

StatView also saves everything about a view: the analyses and graphs, variable assignments, the dataset(s) in use, etc. We can later reopen the view and continue our analysis, resuming right where we left off. All objects are still dynamic: you can still add and remove variables, change analysis parameters, and so forth.

For best results, always save datasets first, then views. Otherwise, when you reopen the view, StatView might have trouble locating its dataset(s).

Save a template

Now, suppose you have some candy bar data of your own—perhaps you've collected data on your own favorites. Perhaps you live in Japan and would prefer to study Japanese candy bars. Perhaps you prefer salty snacks, and want to do a similar analysis of potato chips, corn chips, pretzels, and crackers.

If you were to save your view in the Template (Windows) or StatView Templates (Macintosh) folder, you could use it as a template to redo this entire analysis on another dataset.

- Make sure the view is still the frontmost (active) window
  If not, click it or select Nutrition analysis from the Window menu.
- Select Save As from the File menu
- Navigate to the template folder inside the main StatView folder
- Create a new folder named My Projects
  (Windows 3.1 or Windows NT: before saving, use File Manager to create a new folder.)

Save View as   ? ☒

Save in: ☐ Template

☐ _For Beginners   ☐ Nonparametrics
☐ ANOVA and t-tests   ☐ QC Analyses
☐ Correlations   ☐ Regression
☐ Descriptive Statistics ☐ Survival Analyses
☐ Factor Analysis
☐ Graphs

File name: Nutrition analysis   Save
Save as type: ViewSet (*.SVV)   Cancel

Save View as

Save in: ☐ Template

☐ _For Beginners   ☐ Nonparametrics
☐ ANOVA and t-tests   ☐ QC Analyses
☐ Correlations   ☐ Regression
☐ Descriptive Statistics ☐ Survival Analyses
☐ Factor Analysis   ☐ My Project
☐ Graphs

☐ **StatView Templates** ▼   ☐ **Hard disk**
☐ **For Beginners**   Eject
☐ **ANOVA/t-tests**
☐ **Correlations**   Desktop
☐ **Descriptive Statistics**
☐ **Factor Analysis**   New ☐

Save View as: Cancel
Nutrition analysis   Save
File Format: StatView 4.1+ View ▼

Name of new folder:
My Projects
Cancel   Create

- Save in the new folder

Next, we rebuild the Analyze menu so that it offers your new folder and its template.

- From the Analyze menu, select Rebuild Template List

And here's the new, customized Analyze menu:

Analyze
New View   ⌘M
Rebuild Template List

 For Beginners   ▶
ANOVA/t-tests   ▶
Correlations   ▶
Descriptive Statistics ▶
Factor Analysis   ▶
Graphs   ▶
My Projects   ▶ Nutrition analysis
Nonparametrics   ▶
QC Analyses   ▶
Regression   ▶
Survival Analyses   ▶

Remember two things:

1. Saving a template is the same as saving a view, except that you put it inside the templates folder.

2. Using a template is the same as reopening a view, except that you can specify different datasets and/or different variables with a template.

Present results

So far we've just explored our data and done some analysis. It would probably be pretty hard to get anybody to pay much attention if we printed these analyses and tacked them up to a wall. Let's pull it all together into an eye-catching presentation!

Close the analysis browser

We're done analyzing these data, so let's make more room in the view window by closing its analysis browser pane.

• Double-click the split-pane control ([Σ])in the lower left corner of the view window

You can reopen the browser by double-clicking the control (now [▮→]) again.

Clean up results

First, let's straighten up these results, space them evenly, and move them off page breaks.

• From the Layout menu, select Clean Up Items
• Click Clean Up

Add some color

Now let's highlight those analysis objects that concern saturated fat. We can automatically select all those objects by working with the results browser. This browser is just like the analysis and variable browsers we've already seen, and it lets you work with analysis results.

• From the View menu (Windows) or Window menu (Macintosh), select Results browser
• In the results browser, select By Variable for the Order pop-up menu

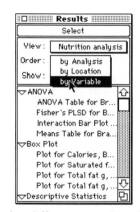

(Your list of results may be somewhat different, since "Quiz" sections are optional.)

- Resize the browser to make it wide enough for its entries
- Scroll down to the heading "Saturated fat g (Candy Bars Data 2)"
- Click this heading to select all its entries
(You may instead Control-click (Windows) or Command-click (Macintosh) individual entries underneath it, if you only want to highlight certain results.)
- Click the Select button

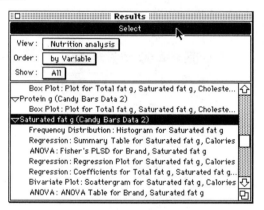

In the view window, all the analyses that involve the saturated fat variable are selected, so you can change them all at once. Next, we use StatView's drawing tools to make them red.

- Select Draw Palette from the View menu (Windows) or tear off the Draw palette from the Draw menu (Macintosh)
- At the bottom of the tool palette, click and hold the pen color tool (top rectangle)
- Drag and release to select red from the pop-up color palette

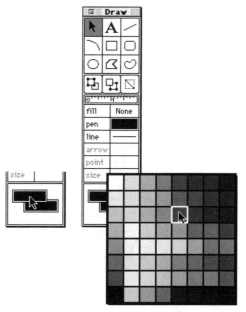

(Apologies for the gray "colors"!)

- Now the saturated fat results are red and eye-catching. (We won't bother to show the results here—a gray color palette looks silly enough!)

Art assignment

Call attention to the candy bar lowest in saturated fat per serving

- Use the results browser to find the box plot of saturated fat split by Brand
  (If you skipped the quizzes, make a box plot of Saturated fat g split by Brand now.)

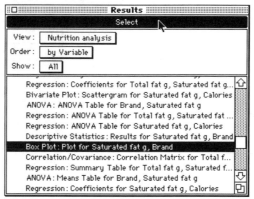

- Choose the line tool from the Draw palette

- Change the arrow to have an arrow head on the left end

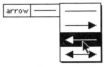

- Draw an arrow pointing to the lowest point
  (Click at the lowest point and drag to below the plot.)

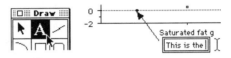

- Use the text tool to add a caption: This is the candy bar to eat!
  (Select the A tool, click where the arrow ended, and type a caption.)

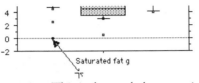

- Use the regular arrow cursor and Shift-click to select both the arrow and the caption

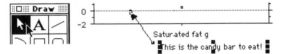

- Use the pen color tool to make the arrow and caption blue
  (Click the upper rectangle and drag to select blue from the palette.)

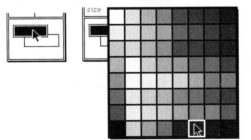

(Again, apologies for the gray depiction!)

You could continue to refine this plot, and the others, to your heart's content. We'll stop here.

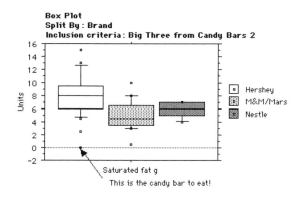

Print a presentation

After you've put the finishing touches on your presentation, you'll want to print it. If you have a color printer, you can print in full color.

- Make sure the view is the frontmost (active) window
  If not, click it or select Nutritional analysis from the Window menu.
- From the File menu, select Print
- Adjust the printing options and click OK (Windows) or Print (Macintosh)

Save a presentation

You'll want to save the view again, so that all your finishing touches are preserved.

- From the File menu, select Save

If your data change, StatView updates your analyses automatically. You don't have to repeat a single step. Suppose you discover the morning of your big presentation that someone entered a few data values wrong. (That never happens!) No need to panic. You just fix the values, and StatView does the rest—and your layout is preserved!

Save a template

You can also save this whole presentation—colors, annotations, and all—as a template. Then, you could apply all these analyses and artistic efforts to a completely different dataset in one simple step.

- From the File menu, select Save As
- Change to your My Projects folder inside the template folder
- Type a filename: Nutrition presentation
- Click Save

Notes

Where to go from here

Now you have a feel for data analysis the StatView way. The easy way.

There is much more to learn. Many more tools are available for helping you manage your data. Lots of drawing and layout tools give you complete control over every detail of your presentation. Scan through the remaining chapters of *Using StatView* to learn what's available.

StatView offers a broad range of statistical analyses and graphs—not just the sample we've used. A comprehensive *StatView Reference* devotes an entire chapter to each type of analysis you see in the browser.

Finally, as you get comfortable with StatView, you'll find countless shortcuts, tricks, and powerful variations for how to get your work done. These manuals, the Hints window, Balloon Help and Apple Guide (Macintosh only), and Windows Help (Windows only) are available to help you.

But, no matter where you concentrate your efforts, all the basic techniques you've just learned will serve you well. All of StatView's analyses work the same basic way, whether you use browsers or templates, whether you're using basic tables and graphs or specialized survival and quality control analyses.

Afterword

No candy bars were injured or mistreated in the making of this tutorial. All scenes involving candy bars were carefully supervised by humane, chocolate-loving professionals.

Datasets

The first step of any analysis is to get data into a dataset. StatView's dataset is a column-by-row spreadsheet-style window. This chapter discusses how to arrange datasets and how to enter and edit data in StatView.

This chapter also discusses in detail how to work with variable attributes—how to tell StatView what kind of data each column contains. The time you take in organizing your dataset pays big rewards when you analyze your data. StatView can guide you in building analyses with the appropriate kinds of data, and it can prevent you from using variables incorrectly.

Subsequent chapters discuss how to exchange data with other applications, how to manipulate data with formulas, and how to restrict analyses to data subsets by excluding cases manually or with logical expressions.

Dataset structure

Understanding the structure of your data is a very important first step in creating your dataset. To enter data properly, you must determine two things:

1. Data **class**: whether data are continuous or nominal. Continuous data are measurements that can assume any value within a given range; nominal data identify group memberships. Some analyses expect continuous data, some expect nominal data, and some expect both. (A third data class, informative, identifies cases in a dataset but is not used in analyses.)

2. Data **arrangement**: how to organize data into rows and columns properly for analysis in StatView.

We'll discuss each of these in detail after looking at an example.

Example

Suppose you're studying heart disease. Your data might include each patient's name, gender, age, weight, cholesterol levels, and alcohol use.

Class continuous or nominal? Names are informative—they merely identify each case. You can't do any statistical or graphical analyses on an informative variable.

Gender is nominal, since each patient belongs either to a male group or a female group.

Age is continuous, since each patient has an exact measurement that falls somewhere along the continuum between birth and death. Similarly, weight and cholesterol are continuous variables of exact measurements.

Alcohol use could be either continuous or nominal. You could record each patient's average daily number of drinks exactly in a continuous variable; or, you could group their daily averages into a nominal variable with several intervals—say, fewer than two, between two and six, and more than six. For a heart disease study, a nominal variable might make the most sense.

Arrangement? You would most likely arrange this dataset to have a row for each patient in the study and a column for each quantity measured, like this:

	Name	Gender	Age	Weight	Cholesterol	Alcohol use
1	J. Suds	male	22	138	197	2 - 6
2	T. Wilson	female	22	115	181	< 2
3	D.S. Quintent	male	22	190	190	< 2
4	R. Beal	female	22	115	131	2 - 6
5	R. James	male	25	160	172	2 - 6
6	S. Kaufman	male	22	150	233	< 2
7	M. Mubroid	male	23	154	194	< 2
8	L. Phote	male	24	185	155	< 2
9	C. Norman	male	23	178	234	2 - 6

This one-case-per-row arrangement is the most typical, and it is the arrangement usually expected by StatView. (Some analyses also accept other arrangements.)

Data class

The **class** of a variable is crucial to how it is used in an analysis. StatView interprets a variable differently depending on whether it is continuous or nominal.

Continuous data are measurements that can assume any numerical value over a given interval, such as weights of cars or batting averages of baseball players. **Nominal** data identify group memberships, such as the countries in which cars are built, or whether baseball players compete in the National League or American League. **Informative** data give case identifications, such as model names, player names, or jersey numbers.

Why do I need groups?

Many statistical and graphical analyses try to answer in various ways one basic question: *do measurements differ among groups of individuals?* For example, do husbands and wives vote for the same or different political candidates? How do American and National baseball league batting averages compare? Do men and women perform equally well on math tests? Do patients treated with a new drug have more or fewer heart attacks than patients not treated? Such analyses include unpaired *t*-tests, ANOVAs, unpaired nonparametric tests, contingency tables, cell plots, grouped box plots, and percentile comparison plots.

Therefore, these analyses require that data identify the group to which each observation belongs. If you set a variable to class nominal, StatView understands that its values represent various groups in the dataset. If you set a variable to class continuous, StatView understands that its values represents measurements that could fall anywhere along an interval. Because StatView understands these things in a properly-constructed dataset, it can make sure that you use variables appropriately in analyses.

In other words, your setting the correct class for each variable enables StatView to help you analyze your data. For each analysis, StatView coaches you to assign variables of the appropriate class and prevents inappropriate assignments.

Also, StatView can break down any analysis by groups. Suppose you are studying heart disease, but you want to study men and women separately. If you have a nominal gender variable, you can split all your analyses—you'll get separate results for men and for women.

Data types

One of StatView's most powerful features is that it allows you to set variables of any type to be nominal. For example, gender can be text with values such as Male and Female, or it could be numeric with values such as 0 and 1. Similarly, informative data can be any type (numeric or text). However, continuous data can only be numeric (real, currency, integer, long integer, or date/time).

To look at this (the relationship of type and class) the other way around, any numeric data can be continuous, nominal, or informative. However, text data (type string) can be either nominal or informative, and category data (type category) can only be nominal.

For more detail on data types, see "Type," p. 73.

Change classes

Another powerful feature is that you can easily change variables from continuous to nominal and vice versa. Sometimes the class of a variable is flexible or ambiguous.

Many variables could be either continuous or nominal, depending on how they are analyzed. For example, alcohol usage might be recorded as a nominal variable for a heart study, but if you're studying liver and stomach enzymes, it might be more appropriate to record exact (continuous) measurements of alcohol consumption. As another example, three levels of a drug (10, 25 and 50 i.u.) could be seen as three drug administration groups (nominal) or as three values along a range of possible values (continuous).

Class can be ambiguous. Many variables, although they are continuous in the strictest sense, are effectively nominal. For example, body weights are strictly continuous, because their values can fall anywhere within an interval if you measure them precisely enough. However, most people tend to report their weights rounded to the nearest five or ten pounds (or kilograms). You should assign the class that makes the most sense in the context of your research. Occasionally researchers will study variables both ways—for example, they'll use nominal weights in ANOVA tables but continuous weights in descriptive statistics tables.

Data arrangement

Typically, data are arranged so that each single row represents a single distinct case or individual, and each column contains a variable of measurements on each case. *Most datasets are arranged this way, and all StatView analyses can use data arranged this way.*

For example, we could record eye color and gender data for eight people like this:

	Eye Color	Gender
1	Brown	Male
2	Blue	Male
3	Blue	Female
4	Green	Male
5	Brown	Female
6	Blue	Male
7	Green	Female
8	Brown	Male

Each nominal variable is a separate column in the dataset. Each row represents one person, and the values in that row identify that person's eye color and gender— that is, the eye color and gender groups to which that person belongs.

This is the most typical data arrangement. Continuous variables can record other measurements for each individual—for example, this dataset could also have columns for weights, heights, and ages. Throughout all columns, though, one row in the dataset must represent one observation—one individual subject—one case.

Within this one-case-per-row arrangement, you can use a special **compact variable** structure, in which continuous values are recorded in separate columns representing groups of a nominal variable, and these columns are linked together (compacted) into a single structure within the spreadsheet. Repeated measures ANOVA *requires* that the levels of the within factor (the repeated measures) be stored in a compact variable. Elsewhere in StatView, compact variables are optional. For a complete discussion, see "Compact variables," p. 84.

This arrangement, with or without compact variables, is accepted by all analyses in StatView.

Other arrangements

A small number of analyses in StatView can also handle other data arrangements in addition to the usual one-case-per-row arrangement:

1. Contingency Tables also accept summary data and two-way table data.

2. Certain QC analyses accept summary data.

3. Factor Analysis can analyze correlation matrix data.

Summary data

Summary data show how many individuals fall in each combination of group memberships. The hair color and gender example would contain two nominal grouping variables in columns and an additional column with the count in each combination of groups (cell):

	Eye Color	Gender	Count
1	Blue	Female	1
2	Blue	Male	2
3	Brown	Female	1
4	Brown	Male	2
5	Green	Female	1
6	Green	Male	1

The dataset contains six rows, one for each possible combination of eye color and gender: blue eyes/female, blue eyes/male, brown eyes/female, and so on. Each combination is made up of entries in the nominal Eye Color and Gender columns. The count for each combination appears in the count column. Note that you cannot record information about individuals—you can only count how many individuals fall in a group.

You are not required to have as many rows as there are combinations. If duplicate combinations appear in your data, StatView sums the counts for that combination. Also, if a fractional value appears in a count column, the value is rounded to the nearest integer.

Only Contingency Tables analysis and certain QC analyses can analyze summary data.

Two way table

In a two-way table, each column is a column of the contingency table and each row a row of the table. The observed frequencies are entered in individual cells. There will be as many columns as groups in one nominal variable and as many rows as groups in the second nominal variable. Our example would look like this:

	Column 1	Column 2
1	2	1
2	2	1
3	1	1

The two columns represent the two gender groups: male and female. The three rows the three eye color groups: blue, brown and green. The values in each cell are the counts for the particular combination. Note that you cannot record information about individuals—you can only count how many individuals fall in a group.

Only Contingency Tables can analyze two-way table data.

Correlation matrix

A correlation matrix is a tabular arrangement of data with a correlation coefficient in each cell of the table. You can use Factor Analysis or Correlation/Covariance analyses to create a correlation matrix dataset. You can also enter a correlation matrix by hand.

Only Factor Analysis can analyze correlation matrix data.

Columns vs. variables

For most purposes, and in the most typical one-case-per-row data arrangement, the terms column and variable are interchangeable. However, we do make a distinction. Strictly speaking, a **column** is the vertical arrangement of cells in a dataset. A column usually contains a variable. A **variable** is the data contained within a column. Therefore, when we refer to a column in this chapter and throughout the manual, we are referring to the structure itself—not the data in it. When we refer to a variable, we mean the variable itself—not the cells it fills.

Columns and variables are *not* the same thing in the context of compact variables (see "Compact variables," p. 84).

Dataset windows

In this section, we discuss the windows you will use when working with StatView datasets: the dataset window and the variable browser.

The variable browser is useful with both dataset and view windows; we discuss how to use the variable browser with view windows in the chapter, "Analyses," p. 131.

StatView stores data in a special dataset window. Each dataset has its own window, and you can have thousands of datasets open at a time if enough memory is available. You can even analyze variables from several datasets at once.

The first step in creating a dataset is to open a new data window.

* From the File menu, select New

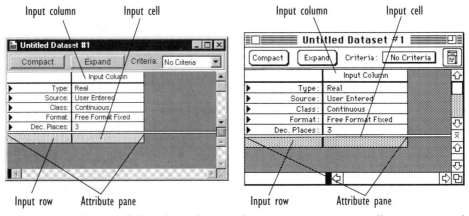

Input column   Input cell   Input column   Input cell

Input row   Attribute pane   Input row   Attribute pane

Each dataset window is a fully independent window. You can move it, scroll it, resize it, and close it like any other window in any other program.

The dimmed cell in the upper left corner of a new dataset represents both an input row and an input column. As soon as you enter a value into this cell, a new input row appears below it and a new input column appears to the right. You create columns (variables) by entering values into the input column and add rows by entering values in the input row. Each row represents a case and each column contains a variable.

A new input column appears when you start to fill the current input column or change its name. You can use Add Multiple Columns from the Manage menu to add several columns at a time; see "Add multiple columns," p. 62.

Here's what the window looks like with a dataset entered and the attribute pane closed:

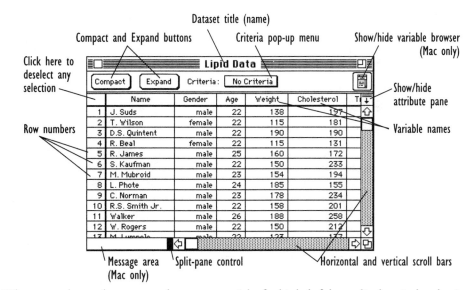

When your dataset has many columns, you might find it helpful to **split** the window horizontally into two **panes**, so you can visually compare columns that are far apart in the dataset. To split the dataset, click and drag or double-click the split-pane control (the black rectangle just to the right of the message area in the lower left corner). Double-clicking this control splits the dataset into two panes, and double-clicking again returns it to a single pane. When the dataset is split, you can use the scroll bars at the bottom to scroll either half of the dataset.

Dataset preferences

Preferences from the Manage menu allows you to set dataset preferences. You can choose defaults for decimal formatting, fonts, and which direction the cursor should move after you enter a cell—down to the next row of the same variable, or right to the next column of the same case. See "Dataset preferences," p. 227.

Variable browser

Variables in the dataset are listed in the variable browser, a floating window that appears alongside both dataset and view windows. When you are working in a dataset window, the variable browser allows you to:

1. Choose open datasets and open new datasets

2. Select variables

3. Create and expand compacted variables

To show or hide the variable browser, select Variable Browser from the View menu (Windows) or Variables from the Window menu (Macintosh). You can also show or hide the variable browser with the ▨ button in the toolbar (Windows) or the ▤ button in the upper right corner of the dataset and view windows (Macintosh). An Application Preference lets you choose whether the variable browser is shown or hidden by default; see "Application preferences," p. 225.

You can move the variable browser, resize it, or close it by using its window controls.

Buttons at the top of the browser change according to whether a view or dataset window is active. When a dataset window is active, its buttons let you Show, Compact, and Expand variables. When a view window (a window where you create analyses) is open, its buttons let you assign variables to play various roles in analyses.

| Dataset | View | Dataset | View |

In the middle part of the browser, a Data pop-up menu lets you open datasets and select among any datasets that are already open. The name of the currently active dataset is shown. Click on the menu to choose another open dataset, and choose Other to locate and open a previously saved dataset.

An Order pop-up menu lets you choose how to sort variable names in the scrolling list:

Dataset order	The order in which variables appear in the dataset's columns (left to right).
Alphabetical	Alphabetical order by variable name, with nonalphabetic names first.

Variable type	Grouped in order by continuous, nominal, and informative.
Usage	Ordered first by variable use in analyses and then in alphabetical order. When a dataset window is active, ordering is only alphabetical.

Variables are shown in a scrolling list. Icons next to variable names indicate their data class: ⓒ for continuous, Ⓝ for nominal, and ◇ for informative.

Compact variables (see "Compact variables," p. 84) are preceded by a triangle ▷ and followed by a ⓒ symbol. Click the triangle to tip it downward ▽ and display the category of the variable. These categories are marked nominal Ⓝ.

▷ Effectiveness ⓒ   ▽Effectiveness ⓒ
                              Time   Ⓝ

Show variables

The Show button selects a variable in the dataset and scrolls the dataset so the variable is visible. If you select more than one variable, Show scrolls the dataset to make the leftmost variable visible.

- Select one or more variable names
  To select one variable, click its name. To select several adjacent variables, click and drag or Shift-click their names. To select several nonadjacent variables, Control-click (Windows) or Command-click (Macintosh) their names.
- Click Show

A shortcut for Show: simply double-click a variable name. (The topmost button of any browser is always the default button; double-clicking an item has the effect of selecting the item and pushing the top button.)

Compact and expand variables

The Compact and Expand buttons let you create and expand compact variables directly from the variable browser, rather than by selecting the columns and using the Compact and Expand buttons in the dataset window itself.

- Select the variables to compact or expand
- Click Compact or Expand

For a discussion of compact variables, see "Compact variables," p. 84.

Enter data

The chapter "Tutorial," p. 1, presents a step-by-step exercise for entering a sample dataset. If you'd like to get a feel for the overall process of entering data and working with a dataset, the tutorial is a good place to start. This chapter discusses in more detail all the rules, variations, and shortcuts for entering and editing data, and it goes into more detail about what everything means.

Name variables

The default variable name is "Column *n*" where *n* is the number of the current column. It is better to give variables meaningful names, so it is easy to remember which variable is which when you are building analyses.

You can enter or edit variable names at any time.

- Click the cell containing the current name to select it
- Type a new name
  (Do this while the old name is selected and you have an I-beam cursor ⌶. To change only part of the name, select the part you want to change and correct it.)
- Press Enter or Return to store the new name
  (Or press Tab to select the next variable name.)

Analyses and graphs are labeled by the names of the variables in use, so you should use names that will be meaningful. You should capitalize and spell names in the dataset the way you'd like them to appear in results.

Variable names can be up to 80 characters long and can use any characters *except* colons (:) and quotation marks (" "). Each variable name must be unique within its dataset; you can have several datasets open at a time in StatView, and it is *not* a problem for variable names to be repeated among datasets.

Variable names should not begin with numerals, and they should not be the same as any function name (for example, "Log" is a function that computes the logarithm of a variable; "Log" should not be used as a variable name) or any group label defined in a category. You may break both rules if you need to, but StatView warns you with an error message.

For a complete list of function names, see "Formulas," p. 315 of *StatView Reference*. For more information about category group labels, see "Categories," p. 80.

Set attributes

Each column in the dataset has specific attributes that describe the variable you enter in the column. These attributes are data type, source, class, format, and number of decimal places. Each of these is discussed in detail in the section "Save datasets," p. 70.

You set variable attributes in a part of the data window called the **attribute pane**. The first five lines of this area are pop-up menus for each variable attribute. The input column of a new dataset begins with default attributes:

	Input Column
Type :	Real
Source :	User Entered
Class :	Continuous
Format :	Free Format Fixed
Dec. Places :	3

- Position the cursor over the cell of the attribute you want to change

The cursor changes to a pop-up menu icon: ▤.

- Click and hold the mouse button
- From the pop-up menu, select the correct attribute
- Release the mouse button

To change the attributes of several columns at once:

- Select all the columns you want to change
  Shift-click or click and drag to select adjacent columns. Control-click (Windows) or Command-click (Macintosh) to select nonadjacent columns.
- Make changes to any one of the selected columns

You should specify column attributes for each column *before* entering data. Doing so ensures that each column is set up appropriately for the data it is to contain. If you enter values that are not compatible with the attributes specified, StatView warns you that the values are incompatible.

Change attributes

You can change the attributes of a variable anytime *except*:

1. You cannot change the class of a variable that is in use in an analysis or formula definition.
2. You cannot change the type of a variable that is in use in an analysis or formula definition to category or string.
3. You cannot change any attributes for a compact variable except format and decimal places.
4. If the source of the variable is analysis generated, you cannot change the type or class.

Additional guidelines for changing each attribute are given under "Save datasets," p. 70.

View summary statistics

The variable attribute pane also contains a set of summary statistics for each variable. Usually, these statistics are hidden, but you can reveal them either by scrolling the attribute pane downward or by increasing the size of the attribute pane.

- Click and drag the attribute pane control $\boxed{\bar{x}}$ downward

```
┌─────────────────────────────── Lipid Data ═══════════════════════════════════┐
│ ┌─────────┐  ┌─────────┐                ┌──────────────┐                    ┌─┐│
│ │ Compact │  │ Expand  │   Criteria:    │  No Criteria │                    │▤││
│ └─────────┘  └─────────┘                └──────────────┘                    └─┘│
```

	Name	Gender	Age	Weight	Cholesterol	Triglyceri
▶ Type:	String	Category	Inte...	Integer	Integer	Integer
▶ Source:	User Entered	User Ent...	User...	User Ent...	User Entered	User Entere
▶ Class:	Informative	Nominal	Cont...	Continuo...	Continuous	Continuous
▶ Format:	●	●	●	●	●	●
▶ Dec. Places:	●	●	●	●	●	●
Mean:	●	●	24.3...	158.653	191.232	97.263
Std. Deviation:	●	●	3.269	28.389	35.674	60.946
Std. Error:	●	●	.335	2.913	3.660	6.253
Variance:	●	●	10.6...	805.931	1272.648	3714.387
Coeff. of Variation:	●	●	.134	.179	.187	.627
Minimum:	●	●	20	107	115	43
Maximum:	●	●	40	234	285	480
Range:	●	●	20.0...	127.000	170.000	437.000
Count:	●	95	95	95	95	95
Missing Cells:	●	0	0	0	0	0
Sum:	●	●	2310	15072....	18167.000	9240.000
Sum of Squares:	●	●	571...	2466970	3593733.000	1247864.00

1	J. Suds	male	22	138	197	
2	T. Wilson	female	22	115	181	
3	D.S. Quintent	male	22	190	190	
4	R. Beal	female	22	115	131	
5	R. James	male	25	160	172	
6	S. Kaufman	male	22	150	233	
7	M. Mubroid	male	23	154	194	
8	L. Phote	male	24	185	155	

For continuous variables, you see summary statistics: mean, minimum, maximum, standard deviation, standard error, variance, coefficient of variation, count, range, sum, sum of squares and number of missing cells. For nominal variables, only count and missing cells are calculated, and the other cells contain missing values. No statistics are shown for informative variables. When you open the attribute pane you always have complete, current summary information; the statistics update automatically whenever you make any change to your dataset. You can copy cells from the attribute pane and paste them into other windows or applications as needed. You cannot edit summary statistics or paste into their cells.

Control window panes

To hide the summary statistics, double-click the $\boxed{\bar{x}}$ control. To close the attribute pane completely, double-click it again. When the pane is closed, the pane control looks different ($\boxed{\downarrow}$). Double-click the control to reopen the attribute pane.

Opening, closing, and resizing the attribute pane does not affect the lower data pane of the window. Row 1 (or the input row in a new dataset) always starts right under the attribute pane. You can scroll the attribute and data panes independently.

Summary statistics are calculated only when the attribute pane is open. If you need to make many changes to your dataset, close the attribute pane to avoid delays from frequent recalculations.

Enter values

When you have set the attributes for a variable with the controls in the attribute pane, you are ready to enter the data for that variable in the dataset. The tutorial gives step-by-step instructions for entering a sample dataset; here we give general rules.

- Click a cell to select it
- Type a value
- Press Enter, Return, or Tab

	Column 1	Input Column
▶ Type :	Real	Real
▶ Source :	User Entered	User Entered
▶ Class :	Continuous	Continuous
▶ Format :	Free Format Fi...	Free Format Fixed
▶ Dec. Places :	3	3
1	1.682	

When you enter a value, a new input column appears to its right and a new input row appears below it, so you can enter another value. Also, the cursor moves to the next cell—either down to the next row, or right to the next column. Continue entering values in input cells until you complete one row or column.

Windows	Macintosh	Direction cursor moves
Enter on numeric keypad	Enter	Either down or to the right, depending on your Dataset Preferences.
Enter on main part of keyboard	Return	Down. From an input cell at the bottom of a column, the cursor moves to the top of the next row.
Tab	Tab	Right. From an input cell at the end of a row, the cursor moves down to the beginning of the next row.

Enter across

If you prefer to enter values across (filling in all the variables for one observation or case), you should name and set attributes for all your variables in advance. To begin a new row, either click the first cell for the row, or press Tab from the empty input cell at the end of the first row.

Enter down

If you prefer to enter values down (filling in all the cases for a variable), you might prefer naming and setting attributes for each variable individually. To begin a new column, either click the first input cell in the column, or press Return from the empty input cell at the bottom of the previous column.

Missing values

Sometimes you don't have a value for a given case of a variable. Perhaps a respondent didn't answer a question, or a doctor forgot to take a blood pressure reading for one patient, or perhaps a variable is simply not applicable to an observation for one reason or another. These cases are missing values. A **missing value** is exactly that: it's a data point that has no value. Cases with missing values on a particular variable are excluded from most analyses of the variable.

Do *not* enter 0 (zero) or any other number for missing values!

You can enter a missing value by simply leaving the cell blank. Missing values are displayed as periods (.). If you want, you can enter missing values in numeric variables by typing a period. For string data, simply leave an empty cell.

If you need to recode missing values to some specific value (perhaps for exporting to another application), use Recode from the Manage menu (see the chapter "Formulas," p. 315 of *Stat-View Reference*).

Manipulate columns and rows

You create one column at a time by entering a value in the input cell, pressing Tab, and repeating the process. You create a new row by entering a value in the input row, pressing Return, and repeating the process. Additional commands let you create several columns at one time as well as insert columns and rows between existing rows and columns.

Add multiple columns

You can add several columns at once using the Add Multiple Columns command in the Manage menu. This is especially convenient for adding several variables with the same attributes. To add several columns:

- Choose Add Multiple Columns from the Manage menu.
- In the dialog box, enter the number of columns you want to create
- Use the pop-up menus to set the attributes for these variables and click OK
  For more details on variable attributes, see "Variable attributes," p. 73.

The columns are appended to the right of existing columns. The default name for the nth variable to be created in a dataset is "Column n." You can use the Undo command in the Edit menu to delete the new columns if you make an error. You must select Undo immediately after adding columns, before taking any other action.

Insert columns

You can insert a column between two existing columns in the same dataset:

- Control-click (Windows) or Command-click (Macintosh) the border between two variable names
  Position the cursor between two variable names, over the vertical line separating the columns: the cursor changes to a cross-arrow ✛ shape. Hold the Control (Windows) or Command (Macintosh) key down: the cursor changes to a double-arrow ↦ shape. Click and release the mouse button. Release the key.

Gender	Age		Gender	Age		Gender	Column 26	Age
male	22		male	22		male	•	22
female	22		female	22		female	•	22
male	22		male	22		male	•	22

The newly inserted column has default variable attributes and is filled with missing values (.) until you enter data.

Repeat to insert additional columns.

Remove columns

You can remove a column at any time:

- Click the variable name to select the column
- Press the Delete or Backspace key *or* select Delete from the Edit menu

Insert rows

Inserting a row is similar to inserting a column:

- Control-click (Windows) or Command-click (Macintosh) the border between two row numbers
  Position the cursor between two row numbers, over the horizontal line separating the rows. Hold the Control (Windows) or Command (Macintosh) key down: the cursor changes to a double-arrow $\updownarrow$ shape. Click and release the mouse button. Release the key.
- In the dialog box, specify how many rows to add by typing a number

- Click Insert

Rows are added between the two rows where you clicked. Cells of the input rows contain missing values until you enter data. Repeat to insert additional columns.

Resize column widths

To increase or decrease the size of columns:

- Click and drag the border between variable names
  Position the cursor to the right of a variable name, on the vertical line separating columns: the cursor changes to a cross-arrow $\leftrightarrow$ shape. Click and drag to the left or right to make the column narrower or wider.

To resize several columns at once, select the columns and resize one of them. Shift-click or click and drag to select several adjacent columns. Control-click (Windows) or Command-click (Macintosh) to select several nonadjacent columns.

If a column is too narrow to display its data, pound signs (###) appear in place of numbers, and ellipses (...) appear in place of text data. Attributes and variable names in the attribute pane are similarly abbreviated.

Move and scroll

You can move the cursor from one cell to another by clicking or by using keyboard shortcuts.

Windows	Mac	Movement
Tab		Right (with wrap-around)
Shift-Tab		Left (with wrap-around)
Enter	Return	Down, except in input row (with wrap-around)
Shift-Enter	Shift-Return	Up (with wrap-around)
Enter on numeric keypad	Enter	Right or down, as set in Dataset Preferences
Shift-Enter on numeric keypad	Shift-Enter	Left or up, as set in Dataset Preferences
Page Up		Scroll up one page
Page Down		Scroll down one page
Home		Upper left corner of dataset
End		Lower right corner of dataset

Edit data

You can edit an individual value directly by clicking its cell and typing a new value.

You can also use the standard Cut, Copy, Paste, Clear, and Delete commands from the Edit menu on selected cells in a dataset. If you need to see what you have selected, choose Show Selection from the Edit menu to scroll the dataset to the highlighted section.

Datasets and views are dynamically linked, so if you make any changes to your data, StatView automatically recalculates graph and analysis results in the view.

Select data

The following tables tell you how to select cells, rows, and columns for editing.

Windows	Macintosh	Type of selection
Click the cell.		a single cell
Click one cell and drag vertically or horizontally to highlight all of them. Or, Shift-click the cells.		several adjacent cells

Control-click the cells	Command-click the cells.	several nonadjacent cells
Click the corner cell and drag diagonally to the opposite corner.		a small block of cells
Click a cell in one corner of the block. Scroll to the diagonally opposite corner of the block. Shift-click that corner cell.		a large block of cells
Select one block with either of the above techniques. Control-click and drag to select another block.	Select one block with either of the above techniques. Command-click and drag to select another block.	nonadjacent blocks of cells
From the Edit menu, choose Select All Rows or Select All Columns.		all rows or all columns
Click the row number. Be careful to single-click, not double-click; double-click is used for Include and Exclude; see "Include and exclude rows," p. 108.		an entire row
Click the variable name.		an entire column
Click a row number or variable name and drag over adjoining row numbers or variable names. To select a large block of data, click the first row or column, scroll to the row or column at the end of the group, and Shift-click.		adjacent rows or columns
Control-click the row numbers or variable names.	Command-click the row numbers or variable names.	nonadjacent rows or columns
Control-click criteria name in Criteria pop-up menu		rows that meet a criterion

To deselect any rows, cells or columns selected in the dataset quickly, click once in the empty rectangle above the row numbers and to the left of the first column heading.

Cut, clear, and delete data

You can remove entire columns or rows using Edit menu commands or your keyboard.

Windows	**Macintosh**	**Result**
Cut (Control-X)	Cut (Command-X)	Removes selected data to the Clipboard. If data do not constitute an entire row or column, the row or column remains in the dataset. Cells where data have been cut contain missing value symbols. If an entire row or column is selected (including row number or variable name), Cut completely removes the row or column from the dataset. Rows below a cut row move up, and columns to the right of a cut column move left.

Clear	Clear (Command-B)	Removes selected data and replaces them with missing values. Data are permanently cleared unless you immediately select Undo from the Edit menu or type Control-Z (Windows) or Command-Z (Macintosh). Clear does not remove rows or columns.
Delete (Backspace key)	Delete (Delete key)	If an entire row or column is selected, Delete removes it from the dataset. Deleted rows or columns are permanently removed unless you choose Undo immediately after deleting. With nonadjacent rows or columns, the dataset shrinks by the number of deleted rows or columns.

Copy data

You can Copy selected data to the Clipboard by selecting Copy from the Edit menu. You can Paste data from the Clipboard back into a selected area of any active StatView dataset. When you cut or copy numeric data to the Clipboard, they are converted to text when you switch to a different application. When data are converted from numeric to text format, only the number of decimal places currently displayed are saved. If you paste data outside of StatView, be sure to display enough decimal places before copying to preserve your data values.

A yin-yang cursor ☯ spins while data are converted to text. When you return to StatView, the information is in the Clipboard (assuming you have not placed anything there from another application).

You can merge data from different datasets using Copy and Paste commands. Then you can copy data from the source dataset and paste them into the empty cells of the target dataset. It is important to understand StatView's rules for pasting data, described next.

Paste data

\Pasting data into a dataset is much easier if you first familiarize yourself with the data you want to paste. You should also know the row-by-column size. You should consider the following things:

1. the size of the data relative to the size of the selected target area

2. the type of data to be pasted and the data type in the target area

3. the target location for the pasted data (such as the input row or the input column)

Size of the target area The selected area can have four basic sizes relative to the data in the Clipboard:

1. It can be the *exact* size of the data in the Clipboard. In this case, StatView pastes an exact copy of the data.

2. It can be *smaller* than the data in the Clipboard. In this case, StatView pastes as many values as it can, starting in the upper left cell and leaving out the additional data.

For example, if the Clipboard contains an array of numbers 3 columns wide and 3 rows deep, and the selected area is only 2 by 2, only the first four data points of the source data (2 by 2) are pasted. Paste does not shift cells to the right of the selected area further to the right, nor move the cells underneath the selected area down.

3. It can be *larger* than the data in the Clipboard, and an exact multiple. In this case, Stat-View duplicates the data as many times as necessary to fill the selected area.

4. It can be *larger* than the data in the Clipboard, but not an exact multiple. In this case, Stat-View copies the data only *once* and fills the remaining cells in the selected area with missing value symbols. This is a handy way to fill many cells with one value or several repeating values.

Data type to be pasted When you paste data into a dataset, the pasted data are converted to the selected area's data type, if the types are compatible. (Recall that you can set data types in the attribute pane.) When you paste data of one type into a selected area of a different type, the conversion in data type can cause a loss of data. See the data loss precautions in the section "Save datasets," p. 70.

Location of pasted data You can paste data into four areas of a dataset—the input row, the input column, the intersection of the input row and input column, or the body of the dataset.

When you paste data into the input row, the dataset grows to accommodate the new rows. However, if your source data have more columns than you have highlighted in the input row, the extra data are not pasted. To paste data into the input row of a dataset, highlight the entire row or as many cells across the input row as your source data occupy and choose Paste from the Edit menu.

When you paste data into the input column, the dataset grows to accommodate the new column(s). The type of the new column(s) is determined by the same procedures used in importing data. To paste data into the input column of a dataset, select the entire column or as many cells as your source data occupy and use Paste from the Edit menu. If you are pasting into a new dataset, simply highlight the input cell. The dataset adds the appropriate number of rows and columns to accommodate the data.

When you paste data into the intersection of the input row and the input column, the dataset grows to accommodate the new rows and columns. This is the one place where the dataset can grow to accommodate any number of pasted cells. To paste data into the intersection, highlight the single cell where the input row and input column meet and use Paste from the Edit menu.

You can paste columns of data, rows of data, or a block of data into existing dataset cells. In this case, data are only pasted into the highlighted area of the dataset. (See the earlier section, Size of the selected area.)

If you paste nonadjacent data into a dataset, be sure to paste rows into rows, columns into columns, and blocks into blocks the same size. StatView joins nonadjacent data in the Clipboard and cannot preserve the column/row structure of copied data unless they are pasted into areas the same shape as their origin. This capability is mainly useful for extracting subsets to a different dataset, or for replacing rows or columns in one dataset with nonadjacent (discontiguous) rows or columns from another. Pasting blocks of data into rows, columns, or blocks of different shapes should be done with caution.

Paste transposed data

Data in the Clipboard can be transposed while you paste. Use the Paste Transposed command to change entire rows into columns and entire columns into rows. For example, the following integers in a 3×3 section of a dataset transpose like this:

1	2	3
4	5	6
7	8	9

1	4	7
2	5	8
3	6	9

To transpose data, choose Paste Transposed from the Edit menu. The block of cells in the target dataset should be as wide as the data to be transposed are tall. For example, if you have a 3×8 set of data to be transposed, you need a block of cells 8×3 for the transposed data. To transpose the following data, you need to either select the cell at the intersection of the input row and column or an 8×3 pattern of target cells:

1	2	3
4	5	6
7	8	9
10	11	12
13	14	15
16	17	18
19	20	21
22	23	24

1	4	7	10	13	16	19	22
2	5	8	11	14	17	20	23
3	6	9	12	15	18	21	24

If the target dataset does not have enough rows or columns to hold the new data, either create enough rows or columns to hold the data or highlight the correct number of cells in the input row or input column. If you paste into the input row or input column, the dataset automatically enlarges to hold the transposed data.

Copy and Paste unusual selections

As we've described above, StatView lets you Copy and Paste data selections of any shape or size, and from one shape to a different one. Why would you want to Copy and Paste data from one cell to many, or from one nonadjacent selection to another of a different shape?

Suppose you are entering data for a typical factorial experiment:

	A	B	C
1	1	1	1
2	1	1	2
3	1	2	1
4	1	2	2
5	2	1	1
6	2	1	2
7	2	2	1
8	2	2	2

In real life, the factor levels would be more tedious to type than simple one-digit numbers, and you would have more cells to enter. Therefore, it could be handy to type the values one time each and then use clever Copy and Paste steps to finish the data entry. Here's one way we could enter these data:

- From the File menu, select New

- Create three columns by typing the variable names A, B, and C

- Select all three columns by clicking and dragging across the variable names

- In one of the column's variable attribute pane, select Integer for the Type (this changes the type for all three columns in one step)

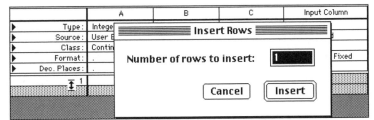

- Enter the value 1 for the first row of A
- Control-click (Windows) or Command-click (Macintosh) the border under the row number label for the first row, then specify 7 more rows to insert
  (This technique is detailed under "Insert rows," p. 63.)

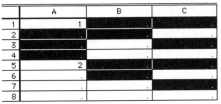

- Double-click the split-pane control to close the attribute pane
- In row 5 for A, enter the value 2
- Select the cell with the 1, and from the Edit menu select Copy
- Control-click (Windows) or Command-click (Macintosh) to select all the other cells that should have a 1

	A	B	C
1	1		
2			
3			
4			
5	2		
6			
7			
8			

- From the Edit menu, select Paste
- Now select the cell with the 2, and from the Edit menu select Copy
- Control-click (Windows) or Command-click (Macintosh) to select all the other cells that should have a 2

	A	B	C
1	1	1	1
2	1	1	
3	1		1
4	1		
5	2	1	1
6		1	
7			1
8			

- From the Edit menu, select Paste

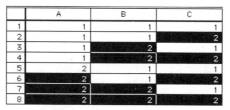

You're done! If you keep StatView's selection flexibility in mind, you'll find many similar opportunities to save time when entering and editing your datasets.

Save datasets

You can save changes to any active dataset by selecting Save from the File menu. If you want to save the changed dataset under a different name and preserve the original dataset unchanged, choose Save As from the File menu. If the file is untitled when you choose Save, a dialog box prompts you to name it.

Choose the file format you want from the choices listed at the bottom of the dialog box.

(Windows only) The normal format that StatView uses is DataSet. You can also choose Excel or Text for exporting data to other applications.

(Macintosh only) The normal format that StatView uses is StatView 4.1+ Data. You can also choose Excel or text (for exporting data to other applications), Old StatView Data (for exporting to versions of StatView earlier than version 4.1) or SuperANOVA Data (for exporting to SuperANOVA). It is best to save files as StatView 4.1+ Data unless you plan to transfer data to another application or to earlier versions of StatView. When you save as StatView 4.1+ Data, you retain all information about the dataset including formula definitions, criteria, the current selection, which rows are currently included, and so on. SuperANOVA format is useful for transferring data to StatView versions 4.0, 4.01, and 4.02, because it retains formula and criteria definitions.

See update documentation for other formats that might be available in your version of Stat-View. For more information about the Excel file format, see "Importing and exporting," p. 99.

Exchange datasets between Windows and Mac versions of StatView

The DataSet Transfer format is a cross-platform dataset format that can be read by both Windows and Macintosh versions of StatView. The DataSet Transfer format preserves all data, formula definitions and values, and criteria definitions. It does *not* preserve the current selection, the current inclusion and exclusion of rows, or custom column widths. DataSet Transfer files have the filename extension .SSD (Windows). Note that DataSet Transfer files save data values in double precision, which may cause slightly different results for FPU and NOFPU Macintosh versions of StatView, which operate in extended precision. Datasets that are opened or saved in DataSet Transfer format remain in that format, and you might want to use DataSet Transfer as your usual format if you routinely exchange data between Mac and Windows versions of StatView.

Moving a dataset from Mac to Windows

In StatView for Macintosh:

- Open the dataset
- From the File menu, select Save As
- From the File Format list, select DataSet Transfer
- Type a filename ending with the extension .ssd
  (Including the .ssd extension identifies the file to Windows as a StatView dataset in the DataSet Transfer format.)
- Click Save

Use PC Exchange or another utility to copy the file onto a floppy disk formatted for Windows (DOS), or copy it to a Windows volume by using a network connection. Then, in StatView for Windows:

- From the File menu, select Open
- Locate the file
  (If you didn't include the .ssd extension, you must choose All Files (*.*) from the Files of Type list.)
- Click Open

Moving a dataset from Windows to Mac

In StatView for Windows:

- Open the dataset
- From the File menu, select Save As
- From the Files of Type list, select DataSet Transfer
- Type a filename ending in the .ssd extension
  (Including the .ssd extension identifies the file to PC Exchange as a StatView dataset in the DataSet Transfer format.)
- Click Save

Copy the file onto a floppy disk and use PC Exchange or another utility to read the disk with your Macintosh, or copy it to a Macintosh volume by using a network connection. Then, in StatView for Macintosh:

- From the File menu, select Open
- Locate the file
- Click Open

If you would like to be able to open DataSet Transfer (.ssd) files automatically on Macintosh by double-clicking them, open the PC Exchange control panel and add an assignment matching .ssd files to StatView:

- Open the PC Exchange control panel
- Click Add
- Type the extension: .ssd
- Select the application: StatView
- Select the document type: svdx
- Click OK
- Close the control panel

Close datasets

Close a dataset by clicking the close box in the upper left corner of the dataset or by selecting Close from the File menu. StatView prompts you to save any changes made since last saving the dataset.

If you attempt to close a dataset whose variables are used in an open view, you will be alerted to this fact. If you continue and close the dataset without closing the view first, all of the variables from the dataset will be removed from the view. We advise you to close views that use the variables of a dataset *before* closing the dataset. In addition, if you close an Untitled dataset (one not yet saved or a text file that has not been saved as a StatView document) and do not save it, StatView will not able to match the dataset with any view(s) that use the variables of that dataset.

Open datasets

To open an existing dataset, select Open from the File menu.

You can choose which types of files are shown in the dialog box from the pop-up menu at the bottom of the dialog box. Supported Files (Windows) or All Available (Macintosh) displays files of any format that StatView can read or import. Other choices are any types of files that can be imported on the current platform. The various dataset types are discussed under "Save datasets," p. 70.

See the chapter "Importing and exporting," p. 99, for more information on importing.

Print datasets

To print a dataset, make it the active (frontmost) window and select Print from the File menu. If the attribute pane is open, attribute settings and summary statistics print along with the data. The entire dataset is printed, even if it does not all fit in the window. Row numbers and variable names always appear on printouts.

Variable attributes

Here we discuss in detail the five variable attributes and how to change them. Please pay particular attention to the consequences of changing variable attributes.

Type

Data **type** specifies whether a variable contains real numbers, integers, long integers, strings, date/time values, currency values, or categories. The default type for a new column is real.

Type	Examples	Description
Real	9.8765 1.2E34 3.141592...	Numbers with fractional parts. Set the number of decimal places to display in the dataset with the Decimal Places pop-up menu. (Full precision is stored and used in all calculations.)
Integer	1 −756 7,142	Whole numbers between 32,767 and -32,767, inclusive.
Long Integer	−98,765 3 348,920	Whole numbers between 2,147,483,647 and -2,147,483,647, inclusive.
String	John Doe 436-39-9976 Patient #28A	Alphanumeric (text) data. Entries in string columns can be as long as 255 characters.
Date/time	7/ 8/08 July 8, 1908 10:20:13	Points in time. Many display formats are available. Regardless of the format used, date/time values are an exact time: a specific hour, minute, and second of a specific day, month, and year.
Currency	$142,213.00 £ 113.88 ¥872.543	Real data displayed in one of many international currency formats. Set the number of decimal places to display in the dataset with the Decimal Places pop-up menu.
Category	Female 2 Group 1	Alphanumeric (text) data recording group memberships for individual observations or cases. You must choose an existing category definition or create a new one.

Values for each type must fall within the following ranges. All numerical computations are performed in the fullest precision of the platform you are using, so the ranges of acceptable values for real numbers vary among platforms. Macintoshes based on 680x0 processors with a numeric coprocessor (FPU) perform calculations in 96 bit extended precision. Macintoshes based on 680x0 processors without numeric coprocessors (noFPU) perform calculations in 80 bit extended precision. Power Macintoshes (PPC) and Windows machines (Win) perform calculations in 64 bit double precision.

Type	CPU	Minimum	Smallest fraction	Maximum
Real	FPU	−1.1E4932	±1.9E−4951	1.1E4932
	noFPU			
	PPC	−1.7E308	±5.0E−324	1.7E308
	Win			
Long integer		−2,147,483,647		2,147,483,647
Integer		−32,767		32,767
Date/time		Friday, January 1, 1904 0:00:01		Monday, February 6, 2040 6:28:15

Categories

Sometimes your data identify particular groups rather than signifying quantities. Data like this are nominal. You can set any data type to nominal, but category data can be used *only* in a nominal variable. When you set a variable's type as category, you are prompted to provide information about the groups that make up the variable. For example, to enter the gender of patients in a study, you define a category in which Gender has exactly two group labels: Male and Female. The only data that can be entered into this column are Male and Female.

Using a category to enter your nominal data offers you specific advantages over other data types. The advantages are explained under "Class," p. 78. See "Categories," p. 80, for more information.

Date/time values

It is important to understand the following rules about date and time values:

1. Any dates outside the valid time range are invalid. (However, you can type 0 in a date/time data cell to get the current date at midnight.) If you attempt to enter or create by formula any date value outside this range, you get either an error message or a missing value.

2. If you specify only a date without a time, StatView assumes you mean exactly midnight of that day. If you specify a time without a date, StatView assumes the current day, month, and year. If you specify only a partial date or time, StatView assumes you mean the very beginning of that time; for instance midnight of the first day, if you specify a month; midnight of the first day of the first month, if you specify only a year; etc.

3. StatView works with the current date and time set for your system. Be sure you have set the correct time, date, time zone, etc.

4. If you enter an ambiguous date/time value, such as 8/11 (which could mean either August 11 or 8 November), StatView warns you. A dataset preference lets you suppress this warning; see "Silently accept ambiguous values," p. 227.

If you are unsure how StatView interprets a value, choose a date/time format that shows more detail.

Change types

Exercise caution when changing variable types if you have already entered data in the column. Some changes in data type cause data loss. For example, changing real variables to integers rounds values to the nearest integer, e.g. 1.456 becomes 1. If you then change type back to real, you get integers with zero fractional values, e.g. 1.000.

If you ever change a data type by mistake, immediately select Undo from the Edit menu to avoid permanent data loss.

Following are the possible consequences of changing data types:

New type	Result of changing from other types
Real	Integers are unharmed. Long integers are unharmed. Strings that are real numbers are unharmed (except that numbers exceeding 19 significant digits lose precision). Other strings are converted to missing. Date/time values are interpreted as an exact integer number of seconds since the earliest possible date (varies according to platform). Currency values are unharmed. Categories are converted to their underlying codes (indices) 1, 2, 3, ...
Integer	Reals are rounded up or down to the nearest integer, e.g. 1.234 becomes 1. Values outside range $-32{,}767 \leq x \leq 32{,}767$ are converted to missing. Long integers outside the range $-32{,}767 \leq x \leq 32{,}767$ are converted to missing. Strings that are valid integers are unharmed. Other strings are converted to missing. Date/time values are interpreted as an exact number of seconds since the earliest possible date (varies according to platform). Values greater than 32,767 are converted to missing. Currency values are rounded up or down to the nearest integer, e.g. ¥1.234 becomes ¥1. Values outside the range $-32{,}767 \leq x \leq 32{,}767$ are converted to missing. Categories are converted to their underlying codes (indices) 1, 2, 3, ...
Long Integer	Reals are rounded up or down to the nearest integer, e.g. 1.234 becomes 1. Values outside the range $-2{,}147{,}483{,}647 \leq x \leq -2{,}147{,}483{,}647$ are converted to missing. Integers are unharmed. Strings that are valid long integers are unharmed. Other strings are converted to missing. Date/time values are interpreted as an exact number of seconds since the earliest possible date (varies according to platform). Values greater than 2,147,483,647 are converted to missing. Currency values are rounded up or down to the nearest integer, e.g. ¥1.234 becomes ¥1. Values outside the range $-2{,}147{,}483{,}647 \leq x \leq -2{,}147{,}483{,}647$ are converted to missing. Categories are converted to their underlying codes (indices) 1, 2, 3, ...
String	Reals are converted to their current text representation as set by Format and Decimal Places; this can result in loss of precision. Integers are unharmed. Long integers are unharmed. Date/time values are converted to their current text representation as set by Format. Currency values are converted to their current text representation as set by Format; this can result in loss of precision. Categories are converted to their group names as given by the current category definition.

Date/time	Reals are rounded to an exact integer number of seconds after the earliest possible date (varies by platform). Values outside the range $0 \leq x \leq 4,294,967,295$ are converted to missing.
	Integers are interpreted as an exact number of seconds after the earliest possible date (varies by platform). Negative values are converted to missing.
	Long integers are interpreted as an exact number of seconds after the earliest possible date (varies by platform). Negative values are converted to missing.
	String values that match valid date/time formats (see the Formats menu) are interpreted accordingly. Other string values are converted to missing.
	Currency values are rounded to an exact integer number of seconds after the earliest possible date (varies by platform). Values outside the range $0 \leq x \leq 4,294,967,295$ are converted to missing.
	Category values that match valid date/time formats (see the Formats menu) are interpreted accordingly. Other string values are converted to missing.
Currency	Reals are reformatted (with no loss of data) according to the currency format chosen.
	Integers are reformatted (with no loss of data) according to the currency format chosen.
	Long integers are reformatted (with no loss of data) according to the currency format chosen.
	String values that match valid currency formats (see the Formats menu) are interpreted accordingly. Other string values are converted to missing.
	Date/time values are interpreted as an exact number of seconds since the earliest possible date (varies according to platform) and are reformatted according to the currency format chosen.
	Categories are converted to their underlying codes (indices) with the currency units chosen for Format, e.g., $1, $2, $3, …
Category	Reals are changed to initial group names that are "Group for" and the character representation of the real numbers according to the Format and Decimal places settings, e.g. "Group for 1.234." Underlying values (indices) are assigned according to increasing numeric value. Categories can have at most 255 levels.
	Integers are changed to initial group names that are "Group for" and the integer values, e.g. "Group for 57." Underlying values (indices) are assigned according to increasing numeric value.
	Long integers are changed to initial group names that are "Group for" and the long integer values, e.g. "Group for −57,689." Underlying values (indices) are assigned according to increasing numeric value. Categories can have at most 255 levels.
	Strings are converted to initial group names that are the unique values appearing in the variable. Underlying values (indices) are assigned in alphabetic order. Categories can have at most 255 levels. Categories can have at most 255 levels.
	Date/time values are changed to initial group names that are "Group for" and the date/time values, e.g. "Group for 5/10/63." Underlying values (indices) are assigned according to increasing numeric value. Categories can have at most 255 levels.
	Currency values are changed to initial group names that are "Group for" and the current representation of the currency values according to the Format and Decimal places settings, e.g. "Group for 1.234." Underlying values (indices) are assigned according to increasing numeric value. Categories can have at most 255 levels.

Source

Data **source** identifies the origin of data in the variable. It can be user-entered, created by a formula, or generated by an analysis.

User Entered	Data you enter by hand or import; this is the default.
Dynamic Formula	Data created with Formula or Recode commands. A dynamic formula variable updates if the variables it uses change, or if there are other changes (e.g. sorting, row insertion) in the dataset.
Static Formula	Data created by choosing the Static Formula pop-up or Series or Random Numbers commands. Such formulas do not recalculate automatically, although they can be updated manually. Changing a dynamic formula to static stops dynamic recalculation of the formula, but you can change it back to dynamic at any time.
Analysis Generated	Data generated by an analysis: residuals, fitted and predicted values from a regression, factor scores from a factor analysis. Factor Analysis, Correlation/Covariance, Survival: Nonparametric, and Survival: Regression can create a new dataset containing a correlation matrix. See the appropriate analysis chapter for a discussion of analysis generated variables.

Change sources

Be careful when changing the source of variables that already have data values. Some changes in source can cause loss of information. For example, changing Formula variables to User Entered retains the current data values but discards permanently the formula definition.

New source	Result of changing from other sources
User Entered	Values from Dynamic Formulas are saved but the formula definition is lost. Values from Static Formulas are saved but the formula definition is lost. Changing from Analysis Generated to User Entered breaks the variable's link with the analysis that created it and allows you to save the variable with the dataset (An immediate Undo can restore the link).
Dynamic Formula	Changing User Entered to Dynamic Formula replaces all data with values generated by the formula. Changing a static formula to dynamic forces values to recalculate when changes to the dataset occur, but you can change it back to static at any time. Changing from Analysis Generated to Dynamic Formula breaks the variable's link with the analysis that created it and new values are computed by the formula. (An immediate Undo can restore the link.)
Static Formula	Changing User Entered to Static Formula replaces all data with values generated by the formula. Changing a Dynamic Formula to Static stops dynamic recalculation of the formula, but you can change it back to dynamic at any time. Changing from Analysis Generated to Static Formula breaks the variable's link with the analysis that created it and new values are computed by the formula. (An immediate Undo can restore the link.)
Analysis Generated	You cannot change any other source to Analysis Generated. Only StatView analyses can create Analysis Generated variables.

Class

Data **class** describes the information contained in a variable. You can assign variables a nominal, continuous or informative data class. (The differences between nominal and continuous variables are crucial and are discussed under "Data class," p. 50.) Class defaults to continuous unless type is category or string, in which case class defaults to nominal.

Continuous	Continuous data are measurements that have magnitude and rank and can assume any numerical value over a given interval, such as weights of cars or batting averages of baseball players. The default class, unless type is category or string. Real, integer, long integer, currency, and date/time type variables can be continuous.
Nominal	Nominal data identify group memberships, such as the countries in which cars are built, or whether baseball players compete in the National League or American League. The default when type is category or string. Any type variable can be nominal.
Informative	Informative data give case identifications, such as model names, player names, or jersey numbers. Any type variable can be informative. Informative variables are useful only when viewing the dataset. They cannot be used in analyses or formulas; change class to nominal or continuous if you need to use the data in formulas or analyses.

Change classes

You can change data class for a variable at any time unless the variable is currently used in an analysis or formula. Only data class choices compatible with the current data type selection can be made. Other choices are dimmed (inactive) in the Class pop-up menu.

Changing data class from continuous to nominal can be meaningful for some variables; this flexibility is discussed in more detail under "Data class," p. 50. Analyses use variables differently according to their class. When you change a variable from continuous to nominal, groups are sorted in increasing numerical or alphabetical order.

Although you can use any data type as a nominal variable, category data offer some special advantages. If you plan to use the variable as both nominal and continuous, choose a non-category type and change the data class. See "Categories," p. 80 for more information.

Format

Data **format** specifies how to display real, currency, and date/time data. The format you choose affects only the display of the data, not its contents. Values are stored and computations are performed to the fullest precision of your platform, always.

Real	Free Format Fixed	Displays real numbers using Fixed Places format unless the column is not wide enough to display the entire number. If that occurs, the number is displayed in scientific notation.
	Free Format	Ignores trailing zeroes to the right of the decimal point without regard to the number of decimal places specified.
	Fixed Places	Displays the data using the number of decimal places specified. Data are not displayed in scientific notation.
	Scientific	Displays data in scientific notation using the specified number of decimal places.
	Engineering	Displays the numbers in scientific notation using exponents that are multiples of e3 and e-3.
	Enhanced Free Fixed	Displays real numbers like Free Format Fixed, with the enhancement that it switches to scientific notation whenever doing so results in a more accurate representation of the number.
Currency	StatView supports most major international currency formats. Examine the pop-up menu to see the choices available to you. Your choices vary according to platform, operating system, and international configuration.	
Date/time	StatView supports most major international date/time formats. Examine the pop-up menu to see the choices available to you. Your choices vary according to platform, operating system, and international configuration. Regardless of format chosen, date/time values are always stored and interpreted as a complete date—an exact number of seconds since the earliest possible date (which varies by platform).	

Change formats

Feel free to choose the format most convenient for the moment. Values are always stored and used in computations to the fullest precision of the platform you are using. Your format choice affects only the *display* of values. Therefore, changing formats is usually harmless. However, when you exchange data with other applications through the clipboard or text files, be sure to choose formats that display values in sufficient precision.

We recommend that you choose date/time formats that are complete enough to reveal exactly how values you enter or compute are interpreted. All date/time values are stored as an exact time on an exact date, regardless of the format used. Many of the date/time formats hide this exactness from you. For example, the format "Jan 04" shows the exact time Monday, 6 February 2040 06:28:15 as "Feb 40."

If you enter an ambiguous date/time value, such as 8/11 (which could mean either August 11 or 8 November), StatView warns you. a dataset preference lets you suppress this warning; see "Silently accept ambiguous values," p. 227.

If you are unsure how StatView interprets a value, choose a date/time format that shows more detail.

Decimal places

The Decimal Places attribute specifies how many digits after the decimal point to display for real numbers. Values are always stored in the fullest precision of the platform you are using. Your choice affects only the *display* of values.

Changing the number of decimal places to display is always harmless.

Categories

A **category** is a special variable type that makes nominal data entry faster and more accurate. The category type allows you to define a named set of labels for the **groups** of one or more variables. (Other common terms for groups are **cells** and **levels**.) Once you associate a variable with a category, each value you enter in the column must be one of that category's defined group labels. This prevents data entry mistakes. Also, you can use shortcuts to enter group labels quickly.

For example, you might create a category definition called Color that has the group labels Red, Yellow, Green, and Gray (in that order) to use for any variables that record color groups. You cannot enter any other values—such as Redd, Blue, or 4.3—in those variables. You can enter Red by typing R, r, or 1. You can enter Yellow by typing Y, y, or 2. You can enter Green by typing GRE, gre, or 3. You can enter Gray by typing GRA, gra, or 4. (Since Green and Gray both begin with GR, it is necessary to type a third letter.)

You are not required to use the category type for nominal data. Remember, variables of any type (real, integer, long integer, string, date/time, currency, or category) can have class nominal. However, categories offer several advantages:

1. You can enter data faster. Type the first letter or two of a group name, and StatView finishes the name for you. Or, type the number of the group—1 for the first group label in the definition, 2 for the second group, etc.—and StatView fills in the label.
2. You can prevent data entry errors. StatView won't let you enter a value that isn't defined in the category.
3. You can save memory and disk space.

You might not want to use the category type for all your nominal class variables. Categories have three disadvantages:

1. You might not have an exhaustive list of all the group levels you'll need in advance; in this case, a string variable might be more convenient.
2. Category definitions are limited to 255 groups. If your variable has more groups than that, you'll need to use another type.
3. Variables with type category can *only* have class nominal or informative. If you might also want to use the variable as a continuous variable, you should use another type.

You *must* use categories in two cases:

1. When you recode a continuous variable to nominal (using cutpoints to group ranges of values together), you must define a category or choose an existing category. See "Continuous data to nominal groups," p. 118.

2. When you create compact variables, you must use a category to define its groups. See "Compact variables," p. 84.

Finally, whenever possible you should re-use the same category definition with variables that share the same group names; this reduces storage space and eliminates naming conflicts. (Using the same labels in two separate category definitions can lead to problems with formulas, criteria, and other data manipulations.)

Create category definitions

Whenever a category is needed (for a category variable, compact variable, or when recoding continuous data to nominal groups) you see a dialog box:

The scrolling list contains all defined categories. These are categories used in the active dataset and any other open datasets. You can choose an existing category from this scrolling list or create a new category. To choose an already existing category, select it and click OK.

For an example of how you might define and use a category, see tutorial chapter, p. 5. Here we give general directions.

• Choose an open dataset from the Window menu, or select New from the File menu

• If the attribute pane is hidden, double-click the ⬇ control above the vertical scroll bar

• Select Category from the Type pop-up menu in the attribute pane for the column

The Choose Category dialog box appears. If categories are listed, you can choose one and click OK to apply it to the column. If no categories are listed, it means you have not defined any for this or another open dataset. You must click New to create a new category. The Edit Category dialog box appears:

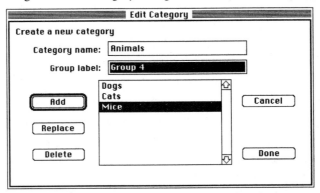

- Type the first group level for the category
- Click Add
- Repeat these steps until you have named all the group levels you need

Group labels can be as long as 255 characters. They appear in the cells of your dataset (and as sub-headings below compact variable names), and they are used to label analysis and graph results for their groups. Type the name exactly as you want to see it in the dataset and in analysis results.

- Enter Dogs in the Group label box and click Add or press Return. Dogs appears in the scrolling list.
- Type a name for the category

Category names can be as long as 255 characters. The name you give appears only in the Choose Category dialog box; it is never visible in your dataset or view windows.

When you are through, the Edit Category dialog box shows your list of group labels.

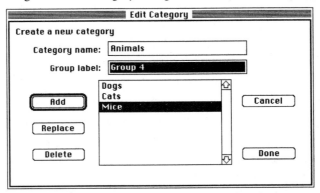

To replace or rename a label, select the group label in the scrolling list, type a new name in the Group label box, and click Replace. To delete a group label, select the group label in the scrolling list and click Delete.

- Click Done to save the category definition

Enter category data

You have two ways to enter data in a column with type category:

1. Type the first letter of a group label. If the first letter is unique, StatView completes the label for you. If several labels begin with the same letter, type as many letters as necessary for a unique match. If no group labels begin with the letter(s) you type, StatView alerts you to your error.

2. Type the number of the group label—1 for the first label, 2 for the second, and so on—according to the order in which you defined the labels. StatView fills in the label for you.

For example, suppose you defined group levels Low, Medium and High. You could enter a Low value by typing L, l, or 1. You could enter Medium by typing M, m, or 2. You could enter High by typing H, h, or 3. If you typed another letter or number, StatView would alert you to your error.

Define category levels in the order in which you want results to appear, if such an ordering exists for your variable; for example, Low, Medium, and High; or Monday, Tuesday, Wednesday, …

Edit category definitions

You can edit categories with the Edit Categories command from the Manage menu.

• From the Manage menu, select Edit Categories

• In the Choose Category dialog box, select the category you want to change

• Click Edit

The Edit Category dialog box appears. This dialog box is exactly like the dialog box used to create a new category.

• Select the label you want to change

• Type a new value in the Group label box

• Click Replace

To delete a group label, select the group label in the scrolling list and click Delete.

You should only delete group labels that have no data associated with them. If you delete a group label from a category that is in use, the group does not disappear. Instead, it is *replaced* with the next group label and all groups adopt the label of the following group—all the labels "slide up" one group. The last group label is replaced by a generic "Unlabeled Group #." For example, a category called Color contains four group labels: Green, Blue, Red and Black. If all the group labels are used in a variable, and you delete the group label Red using the Edit Categories dialog box, every occurrence of Red is replaced with Black and every occurrence of Black is replaced with "Unlabeled group 4."

See also "How can I reorder category variables?," p. 238. For more information on how Stat-View uses group ordering in graphs and analyses, see "How does StatView use ordering in nominal variables?," p. 238.

Delete unused categories

You can create a category and later delete the variable that used the category. Doing so does not delete the category definition itself; it is still available for use with other variables.

To delete an unused category definition:

- Open the dataset that contains the category
- From the Manage menu, select Edit Categories
- Select the category you wish to delete
- Click Delete
- Click Done

You can delete only categories that are not used by any dataset. If you try to delete a category that is being used, an error message appears.

Compact variables

Recall our discussion of "Data arrangement," p. 51, in which we introduced the most typical way to arrange data: one row in the dataset represents one case. For example, we could record cholesterol readings and gender data for eight people like this:

Gender	Cholesterol
male	127
male	232
male	224
female	193
male	197
female	181
male	191
female	194

The principal advantage of this data arrangement is that one row always represents one case. Every cell in any column across one row describes one individual. We could record weights, ages, and names and know that each value in a row corresponded to that person.

However, sometimes it is easier to visualize groups when their members fill separate columns, like this:

Cholesterol readings	
Male	Female
127	193
232	181
224	194
197	•
191	•

You can easily see which readings are male, which are female. Now you identify a cholesterol reading's group by its *column*, not its row.

The advantages of this other arrangement are even more apparent when you have several nominal variables creating subgroups. Here is the usual way to arrange such data:

Smoking	Gender	Cholesterol
Smoker	male	127
Nonsmoker	male	232
Nonsmoker	male	224
Smoker	female	193
Smoker	male	197
Nonsmoker	female	181
Smoker	male	191
Nonsmoker	female	194

Quick! How many male nonsmokers do we have? How many female smokers? It's not easy to tell. This arrangement helps:

Cholesterol readings			
male		female	
Smoker	Nonsmoker	Smoker	Nonsmoker
127	232	193	181
197	224	•	194
191	•	•	•

Now it's easy. We have two male nonsmokers and one female smoker. This arrangement is also more compact. What took 8 rows and 3 columns now takes only 3 rows and 4 columns.

StatView lets you record data this way if you prefer. Not surprisingly, StatView's special structure is called a **compact variable**, because it expresses the same information in fewer cells.

There are several advantages to using compact variables:

1. Compact variables help you see which values of a continuous variable fall into which nominal group or subgroup.

2. Sometimes raw data are arranged this way, and it is easier to enter data into StatView using the same arrangement.

3. Compact variables are visually smaller: they take up fewer cells.

4. For repeated measures ANOVA, StatView requires that your within factor be coded this way.

Please note, though, that there are disadvantages:

1. Compact variables violate the usual assumption of data arrangement: that values on a single row correspond to a single case (observation, subject, patient, individual). The correspondence between values of different continuous variables is lost.

For example, we cannot necessarily enter Ages and Weights for male and female smokers and nonsmokers and then match up one male smoker's cholesterol reading with his weight and his age, unless we were careful to enter the subjects' numbers in the same order for each compact variable.

However, this is *not always* a disadvantage. Sometimes you *need* to break the one-case-per-row connection between two variables. Suppose that you want to perform a Kolmogorov-Smirnov test to compare a variable against a variable that is known to be normally distributed; i.e., you want to test whether your variable is normally distributed. You don't want to compare the variables case for case. Putting the actual and ideal values in two columns of a compact variable lets you get around that problem. (In fact, the Normality Test in the Dataset Templates folder uses exactly this trick; see "Normality Test," p. 233.)

Note that when compact variables store within factors for repeated measures ANOVA, the compact variable *must* conform to the one-case-per-row rule: each value must belong to the individual case represented in that row of the dataset. *All other analyses* interpret the data in compact variables as though they were stored in the usual "long and skinny" continuous and nominal variable columns.

2. You cannot use the nominal portion of a compact variable in an analysis unless you also use its continuous portion.

3. The nominal portion of a compact variable *must* have type category. Usually nominal variables can have any type.

4. You cannot change the type, source, or class of a column that is part of a compact variable; you must expand the variable, change the attributes, and then recompact the columns.

5. You cannot compact columns of differing types, sources, or classes. You must set matching attributes before compacting.

If you have not already done so, please read the section "Categories," p. 80. The following discussions assume you understand categories.

Build compact variables

You already know how to enter data in the usual row-and-column arrangement: you create a nominal variable in one column, and you enter group names down the column for each case. Then you create a continuous variable in a second column and enter measurements down the column for each case. If you have several nominal variables, you simply create more columns and fill them with grouping variables.

However, if you want to enter data in a compact variable, you need to follow special steps so that StatView understands that the columns are actually different groups of a single variable.

In this section, we present two exercises, in which you learn step-by-step how to enter the compact variables we examined above. First, we'll enter the simple example: the one with just one grouping variable (Gender). Then we'll enter the complex example: the one where values are broken down both by Gender and by Smoking

Simple compact variable

Entering a **simple compact variable** (a compact variable with only one nominal variable) is a two-step process.

1. First, you create a column for each group (in this case, male and female).

2. Second, you compact the two columns into a single variable.

We'll start this exercise with a new, empty dataset. (This isn't necessary. You can also add compact variables to an existing dataset. If you do, though, please remember that the cells in your compact variable cannot necessarily be read the way other cells are—they might or might not belong to the cases that fill each row. Only repeated measures ANOVA interprets the values as belonging to their rows; for other analyses, case memberships are assigned as though the separate columns were stacked on top of each other in a single column.)

- From the File menu, select New

Now we name two variables, one for each group.

- Click the cell that reads "Input Column"
- Type a new variable name: Male
- Press Tab to move to the next variable name
- Type a new variable name: Female

All our cholesterol readings are whole numbers, so we give both columns type integer:

- Shift-click both variable names to select both columns
- From the Type pop-up menu for one column, select Integer

	Male	Female	Input Column
▶ Type:	Integer	Integer	Real
▶ Source:	User Entered	User Entered	User Entered
▶ Class:	Continuous	Continuous	Continuous
▶ Format:	●	●	Free Format Fixed
▶ Dec. Places:	●	●	3

Now we can enter the values.

- Click the first input cell
- Type the first male value: 127
- Press Enter

Continue entering all the values. Your dataset should look like this:

	Male	Female
▶ Type:	Integer	Integer
▶ Source:	User Ente...	User Ente...
▶ Class:	Continuous	Continuous
▶ Format:	●	●
▶ Dec. Places:	●	●
1	127	193
2	232	181
3	224	194
4	197	●
5	191	●

Since we have fewer female values than male, the female column has missing values at the bottom.

Now we can compact the two columns into one variable:

- Shift-click both variable names to select both columns
- Click the Compact button in the top left corner of the window

(Or, you can select the two names in the variable browser, and then click the Compact button in the variable browser.)

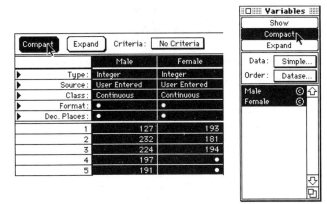

- In the Compact Variables dialog box, type a variable name: Cholesterol readings
- Click Compact

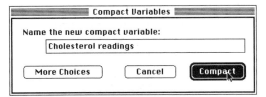

- Double-click the attribute pane control $\boxed{\overline{x}}$ to close the attribute pane

| | Cholesterol readings | |
	Male	Female
1	127	193
2	232	181
3	224	194
4	197	•
5	191	•

That's all there is to it. Now take a look at the variable browser. Notice that it shows a single variable, Cholesterol, with a little triangle ▷ in front of it. The triangle indicates that Cholesterol is a compact variable.

- Click the triangle to tip it downward ▽ and reveal the nominal variable within
- Widen the browser so you can read the full variable names

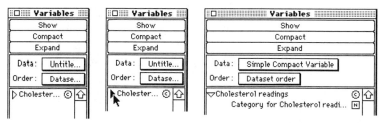

Notice that Cholesterol readings and Category for Cholesterol readings both look like regular variables. Cholesterol readings has a ⓒ class marker for continuous, and Category for Cholesterol readings has an N class marker for nominal. They *look* like regular variables in the browser because they *work* like regular variables in the browser. We'll learn in "Expand compact variables," p. 94, that the "parts" of a compact variable each act the way regular variables do. You select them and apply them to analyses the same way as regular variables.

First, let's save the dataset:

- From the File menu, select Save
- Specify a filename: Simple Compact Variable
- Click Save

Complex compact variable

Entering a **complex compact variable** (a compact variable with more than one nominal variable) follows basically the same two step process:

1. First, you create a column for each *sub*group; in this case, male smokers, male nonsmokers, female smokers, and female nonsmokers.

2. Second, you compact the columns into a single variable. However, you must also assign category definitions for each grouping distinction: a gender category with labels male and female, and a smoking category with labels smoker and nonsmoker.

Again we'll start with a new, empty dataset.

- From the File menu, select New

Name four variables, one for each group.

- Click the cell that reads "Input Column"
- Type a new variable name: Male Smokers
- Press Tab to move to the next variable name
- Type a name: Male Nonsmokers
- Press Tab
- Type a name: Female Smokers
- Press Tab
- Type a name: Female Nonsmokers

All our cholesterol readings are whole numbers, so we give all columns type integer:

- Shift-click (or click and drag) all variable names to select all columns

- From the Type pop-up menu for one column, select Integer

		Male Smoker	Male Nonsm...	Female Smoker	Female Nonsm...	Inp
▶	Type :	Integer	Integer	Integer	Integer	Real
▶	Source :	User Entered	User Entered	User Entered	User Entered	User En
▶	Class :	Continuous	Continuous	Continuous	Continuous	Continu
▶	Format :	•	•	•	•	Free Fo
▶	Dec. Places :	•	•	•	•	3

Now we can enter the values.

- Click the first input cell
- Type the first male value: 127
- Press Enter

Continue entering all the values. Your dataset should look like this:

		Male Smoker	Male Nonsm...	Female Smoker	Female Nonsm...
▶	Type :	Integer	Integer	Integer	Integer
▶	Source :	User Entered	User Entered	User Entered	User Entered
▶	Class :	Continuous	Continuous	Continuous	Continuous
▶	Format :	•	•	•	•
▶	Dec. Places :	•	•	•	•
	1	127	232	193	181
	2	197	224	•	194
	3	191	•	•	•

Since we have fewer female values than male, the female column has missing values at the bottom.

Now we can compact the two columns into one variable:

- Shift-click or click and drag all the variable names
- Click the Compact button in the top left corner of the window

(Or, select all the names in the variable browser, and then click the Compact button in the variable browser.)

Compact	Expand	Criteria :	No Criteria		
		Male Smoker	Male Nonsm...	Female Smoker	Female Nonsm...
▶	Type :	Integer	Integer	Integer	Integer
▶	Source :	User Entered	User Entered	User Entered	User Entered
▶	Class :	Continuous	Continuous	Continuous	Continuous
▶	Format :	•	•	•	•
▶	Dec. Places :	•	•	•	•
	1	127	232	193	181
	2	197	224	•	194
	3	191	•	•	•

- Type a variable name: Cholesterol readings
- Click More choices

Now we see the More choices version of the Compact Variables dialog box:

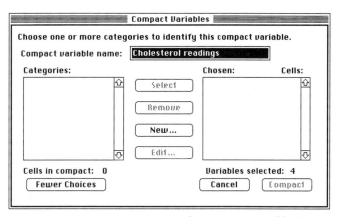

You must assign categories to structure your complex compact variable. (For simple compact variables, StatView takes care of this for you.) For a complete discussion of category variables, see "Categories," p. 80.

The Categories scroll list on the left shows the names of categories that have been defined in any open datasets. The Chosen scroll list on the right shows the categories that are currently selected to identify this compact variable (none, yet). "Variables selected" below the "Chosen" shows the number of variables being compacted. "Cells in compact" below the Categories list shows how many group labels are defined for any category you select. This is important.

Recall that each column represents one group. Therefore, we need to choose a category with as many group labels. Or, we need to choose several categories whose group labels combine to make as many subgroups. (The product of the numbers of cells must equal the number of variables selected.) Our example has four columns, and they represent four subgroups produced by combining gender and smoking. (2 groups × 2 groups = 4 subgroups.)

The buttons in the middle create categories and move them from one list to another as follows:

Control	Description
Select	Adds the selected category from the Categories list to the Chosen list.
Remove	Removes selected categories from the Chosen scrolling list. If you select a category by mistake, click Remove to remove it from the definition of the compact variable.
New	Lets you create a new category which is added to both scrolling lists. Use New to build a compact variable when categories describing its structure do not already exist. For more details, see "Create category definitions," p. 81.
Control-click (Windows) or Command-click (Macintosh) New	Builds a category definitions for a simple compact variable from the names of the selected columns. (The Fewer choices dialog box does this transparently for simple compact variables.)
Edit	Lets you edit a selected category in the Categories list. For more details, see "Edit category definitions," p. 83. If you make a mistake in creating a category, use Edit to correct it.

Since we don't have any categories defined yet, we must create two: one for gender, and one for smoking. First we define a gender category:

- Click New
- Type a Category name: Gender
- Type a Group label: Male
- Click Add
- Type another Group label: Female
- Click Add
- Click Done

Repeat the process for smoking:

- Click New
- Specify a Category name: Smoking status
- Specify a Group label: Smoker
- Click Add
- Specify another Group label: Nonsmoker
- Click Add
- Click Done

Now "Cells in compact" and "Variables selected" both say 4, indicating that we have successfully assigned categories for the correct number of subgroups (see the picture below). Notice that we defined the categories in order (gender then smoking) and also defined their groups in order (male then female, smoker then nonsmoker). This is simpler than it might seem—just read from left to right in your columns.

- Click Compact

```
┌──────────────────────────────────────────────────────┐
│▦▦▦▦▦▦▦▦▦▦▦ Compact Variables ▦▦▦▦▦▦▦▦▦▦▦│
│ Choose one or more categories to identify this compact variable.│
│ Compact variable name:  [Cholesterol readings        ]│
│ Categories:                    Chosen:        Cells:  │
│ ┌──────────────────┐  ┌────────┐ ┌──────────────────┐│
│ │Untitled        ⇧│  │ Select │ │Gender          ⇧││
│ │Gender          │  └────────┘ │Smoking status   ││
│ │Smoking status  │  ┌────────┐ │                  ││
│ │                │  │ Remove │ │                  ││
│ │                │  └────────┘ │                  ││
│ │                │  ┌────────┐ │                  ││
│ │                │  │ New... │ │                  ││
│ │                │  └────────┘ │                  ││
│ │              ⇩│  ┌────────┐ │                ⇩││
│ └──────────────────┘  │ Edit...│ └──────────────────┘│
│                        └────────┘                    │
│ Cells in compact:  4           Variables selected:  4│
│ ┌──────────────┐          ┌────────┐ ┌════════╗      │
│ │ Fewer Choices│          │ Cancel │ ║Compact ║      │
│ └──────────────┘          └────────┘ ╚════════╝      │
└──────────────────────────────────────────────────────┘
```

- Click the variable name (Cholesterol readings) to select all four columns
- Click and drag the borders between group names to make the columns narrower
- Double-click the attribute pane control $\boxed{\bar{x}}$ to close the attribute pane

	Cholesterol readings			
	Male		Female	
	Smoker	Nonsmoker	Smoker	Nonsmoker
1	127	232	193	181
2	197	224	•	194
3	191	•	•	•

Again the variable browser shows a single variable, Cholesterol, with a triangle ▷ indicating that it is a compact variable.

- Click the triangle to reveal the nominal variables within

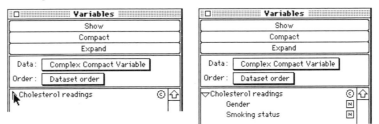

The nominal variables have the names we gave to their category definitions, and they appear in the same order as we chose them. Again, Cholesterol readings and its nominal components all look like regular variables. Cholesterol readings has a ⓒ class marker for continuous, and Gender and Smoking status have ⓝ class markers for nominal.

Again, let's save the dataset:

- From the File menu, select Save
- Specify a filename: Complex Compact Variable
- Click Save

Expand compact variables

Sometimes you might want to unpack compact variables back into simple, regular columns. Removing the compact structure is easy.

Simple compact variable

For a simple compact variable, all you do is select the compact variable and click the Expand button. You can do this either in the dataset window or the variable browser.

- From the Window menu, select Simple Compact Variable
  (If you closed the dataset, use File/Open to reopen it.)

- Select Cholesterol readings (click its name) in either the dataset or the variable browser

- Click the Expand button in either the dataset or the variable browser

	Cholesterol readings	
	Male	Female
1	127	193
2	232	181
3	224	194
4	197	•
5	191	•

Variables
Show
Compact
Expand
Data: Simple Compact Variable
Order: Dataset order
Cholesterol readings

You're back to the original two columns:

	Male	Female
1	127	193
2	232	181
3	224	194
4	197	•
5	191	•

Complex compact variable

Expanding a complex compact variable takes several steps.

- From the Window menu, select Complex Compact Variable
  (If you closed the dataset, use File/Open to reopen it.)

- Select Cholesterol readings (click its name) in either the dataset or the variable browser

- Click the Expand button in either the dataset or the variable browser

You've unpacked the Smoking levels. Now you need to expand each gender level.

- Select Cholesterol readings Male in either the dataset or the variable browser

- Click Expand in either the dataset or the variable browser

- Select Cholesterol readings Female in either the dataset or the variable browser

- Click Expand in either the dataset or the variable browser

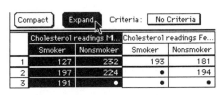 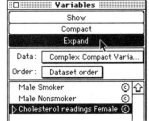

And you're done.

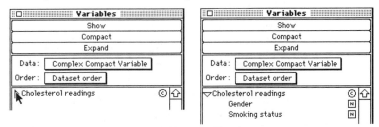

If you expand a compact variable by mistake, select Undo from the Edit menu.

Analyze compact variables

Now we learn how to work with compact variables in analyses. We assume that you already know the basics of working with analysis objects in a view window. If not, either review the chapter "Tutorial," p. 1, or skip ahead to the chapter "Analyses," p. 131.

If you closed your Simple Compact Variable and Complex Compact Variable datasets, reopen them now.

- From the File menu, select Open
- Select a dataset
- Click Open

We've already seen that compact variables look like regular variables in the variable browser, except that their nominal components are indented underneath their continuous components. Small triangle controls ($\triangleright$ and $\triangledown$) let you show or hide the built-in nominal parts.

You can select any part of a compact variable by clicking it just as you would a regular variable. You can Add or Remove its parts the same way you would Add or Remove regular variables. You can Split By the groups of a nominal part.

Let's try a few simple analyses with Simple Compact Variable.

Add both parts

- From the Analyze menu, select New View

- From the analysis browser, double-click Descriptive Statistics
- Choose Basic Statistics and click OK
- In the variable browser, select Simple Compact Variable from the Data pop-up menu (if it is not already chosen)
- Shift-click or click and drag to select both Cholesterol readings and Category for Cholesterol readings
  (If you don't see Category for Cholesterol readings, click the triangle control ▷)
- Click Add

Descriptive Statistics

	Cholesterol readings
Mean	192.375
Std. Dev.	31.622
Std. Error	11.180
Count	8
Minimum	127.000
Maximum	232.000
# Missing	2

Nominal Descriptive Statistics

	# Levels	Count	# Missing	Mode
Category for Cholesterol re...	2	10	0	•

Because we Added both variables, both are treated as X variables. We could instead Split By the nominal part (after we Remove it from its current X role).

- Make sure the analysis object is still selected (still has black handles)
- In the variable browser, select Category for Cholesterol and click Remove
- Click Split By

Descriptive Statistics
Split By: Category for Cholesterol readings

	Cholesterol readings, Total	Cholesterol readings, Male	Cholesterol readings, Female
Mean	192.375	194.200	189.333
Std. Dev.	31.622	41.385	7.234
Std. Error	11.180	18.508	4.177
Count	8	5	3
Minimum	127.000	127.000	181.000
Maximum	232.000	232.000	194.000
# Missing	2	0	2

We can work with the Complex Compact Variable similarly. Let's look at box plots of Cholesterol readings, split by both nominal parts.

- Click in the white space of the view to deselect the tables
- From the analysis browser, double-click Box Plot
- In the variable browser, select Complex Compact Variable from the Data pop-up menu
- Select Cholesterol readings, Gender, and Smoking
  (If you don't see the nominal parts, click the triangle control ▷. Shift-click or click and drag to select all three parts.)
- Click Add

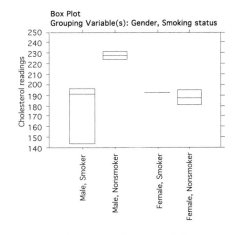

You might want to try removing the nominal parts and then reassigning them to the analysis as Split By variables. The results convey the same information in a different way:

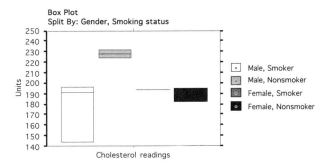

For information on using compact variables in analyses, see "Compact variable," p. 40 and "Repeated measures ANOVA," p. 82 of *StatView Reference*.

Importing and exporting

StatView can read and write several file types directly, and it can import data saved by other applications in plain ASCII text files. StatView automatically lists any files it can read in the Open dialog box. If you prefer to see only a certain file type, select that type for List Files of Type (Windows) or Show (Macintosh).

StatView imports each file into a new dataset. If you need to combine several imported files in one dataset or add imported data to an existing dataset, you can do so by importing the data, copying it into the clipboard, and pasting it into the other dataset.

To prevent accidental file loss, the default name for an imported file is the original filename plus " (imported)." You can change the name yourself with Save As; be sure to supply a unique name to avoid replacing the original file by mistake.

You can also exchange data with other applications through the clipboard: Copy data from one application and Paste it into the other. StatView interprets data in the clipboard using the same algorithms it uses for importing files.

For transferring data among Windows and Macintosh versions of StatView and StatView for SAGENT, use the DS Transfer format. DataSet Transfer preserves all data, formula definitions and values, and criteria definitions. It does *not* preserve the current selection, the current inclusion and exclusion of rows, or custom column widths.

Microsoft Excel

StatView can read and write Excel data files directly. Importing and exporting are as simple as opening and saving StatView files. See your online documentation for the latest versions of Excel supported by StatView.

Read Excel files

- From the File menu, select Open
- For List Files of Type (Windows) or Show (Macintosh), select Excel
- Select the Excel file
- Click Open

StatView reads the entire Excel worksheet into a single StatView dataset. StatView reads only the values in each cell—it does not import macros, links, or functions, although it *does* import the current *results* of functions. Variable names and types are handled the same way for Excel import as they are for text import; see "How StatView imports data," p. 102.

StatView can read all built-in Excel formats and many custom formats and it assigns imported variables to the nearest equivalent variable types in StatView. Any unrecognized formats are converted to type real or string. You may change these by using the variable attribute pane; see "Variable attributes," p. 73.

Write Excel files

- From the File menu, select Save As
- Choose Excel file type
- Specify a filename and folder location
- Click Save

StatView writes the entire dataset as a single Excel worksheet. StatView writes only the values in each cell—it does not export formulas or criteria. Currency data are written with zero or two decimal places, depending on the current display in StatView. All other data types are converted to the nearest equivalent format in Excel.

ASCII text

Most applications can open and save documents in a plain ASCII text file format for exchange with other applications. If you are not sure how to save plain text files from an application, consult its documentation. In most cases, a Save As or Export command is available in the File menu. If you have troubles importing, examine the ASCII text file with a text editor or word processor. Be sure to display all special characters and formatting symbols, and if you need to make corrections, remember to save as plain ASCII text.

Import text

StatView expects data in text files to be organized in rows and columns, with each row (case) on a single line and with values separated by one or more separator (delimiter) characters such as a tab, comma, or space. By default, StatView expects tab-delimited columns. Values that contain the delimiter characters should be enclosed in double quotation marks (" ").

(Macintosh) StatView expects carriage returns at the end of each line. To import a text file created on another platform, you must first use a utility such as Apple File Exchange to replace linefeeds (LF) or carriage returns and linefeeds (CR/LF) with just carriage returns (CR).

- From the File menu, select Open
- Choose Text file type
- Select a file

- Click Open
- Set importing options appropriate for your file
- Click Import

The default settings are appropriate for most files; most Windows and Mac applications use the tab-delimited format for text files. Many older DOS programs and programs on other platforms use commas and/or spaces. When in doubt, use a text editor to examine your file.

Items may be separated StatView recognizes tabs, spaces, commas, returns or any user-entered character as separator characters. If you use returns as separators, you must specify the number of variables.

Convert small integers to Categories If your source application uses integers rather than text values to code the levels of groups, you might want to use this option. For example, a variable containing the values 1 and 2 to represent Male and Female can be converted to a category with two groups, Group 1 and Group 2. After importing, you can edit the category definition to change its labels to Male and Female. Integer variables are converted to categories only if the integer variable contains fewer than 255 unique elements and the smallest value falls between 0 and 6.

Import non-numeric data as type string This option is a safeguard and is checked on by default. By default, text values are imported with type string. However, you may turn the option off to import text variables containing repeated group names with type category.

Make variables with errors have type string If your imported dataset has missing values (.) you don't expect, you might want to import again using this option. Often missing or incorrect separator characters can cause values to shift to columns where their type is inappropriate, which causes error messages or missing values. Any variables with errors are imported as string variables; this way, all data values are displayed and you can investigate and correct the problems.For more information about data types, see "Type," p. 73 and "How StatView imports data," p. 102.

Export text

StatView can export data to plain ASCII text files for use in other applications. Before exporting, you should investigate the format your target application expects (consult its documentation), so you can make the appropriate choices in StatView's export dialog box.

When you save data as text, only the actual displayed values are saved. Be sure to adjust Decimal Places settings before exporting so that real values are saved with sufficient precision.

- Open your dataset in StatView
- From the File menu, select Save As
- Choose Text file type
- Specify a filename
- Click Save
- Choose an appropriate separator character
- Specify whether to include variable names, whether to enclose text values in quotation marks, and whether to save category values as integer codes

- Click Export

End lines (Windows only) Most Macintosh and UNIX applications expect lines in a text file to have just carriage returns (CR), while most DOS and Windows applications expect both carriage returns and line feeds (CR/LF). This option lets you choose which line ending characters to use for the exported file.

Missing values Some applications require a particular code for missing values. You can replace StatView's missing value symbols (.) in one of two ways. Either recode missing values in StatView with Recode from the Manage menu, or use a text editor to perform a global search and replace on the exported text file.

How StatView imports data

The following sections provide more detail about how StatView interprets data it imports. These rules apply to all file formats alike.

Variable names

StatView can import variable names directly only if every variable name contains nonnumeric characters. (No variable names can be strictly numbers. For example, Year1975 is okay but 1975 would cause problems.)

If variable names are not unique, StatView numbers occurrences after the first to ensure that all names are unique.

Data types

StatView assigns each variable the most appropriate data type based on the number of values of each type found in the column. (Types are discussed under "Type," p. 73.) Most variables contain values of a single type, and StatView assigns that type. When variables contain values of more than one type, StatView counts how many values have each type and then uses the following rules:

1. If any numeric type has the highest count, and there is at least one real value, the type is real. If there is no real value but there is at least one long integer value, the type is long integer. If there are no real or long integer values, the type is integer.

2. If more than half the values are currency or date/time, that type is assigned. If fewer than half the values are currency or date/time, the type with the next highest count is used.

3. If strings have the highest count, type is string unless there are repeated values. If there are repeated values and fewer than 256 distinct strings, type is category with group labels in alphabetical order.

Sometimes, data entry errors or missing separator characters shift different types of data into a single column. When a data point is incompatible with its column's type, it is replaced with a missing value (.)If a variable has many unexpected missing values, use the import option Make variables with errors have type string. String variables can contain any data point, so you can examine the variable to investigate the problem.

Missing values

StatView imports two adjacent separator characters as a missing value. Consider the row:

  1 [Tab] 3 [Tab] 5 [Tab] 7 [Tab] [Tab] 11

StatView would import these values as:

  1 3 5 7 . 11

However, multiple *space* separators are not read as multiple missing values, because many applications use as many spaces as necessary to align columns. Rather, multiple spaces are read as a single space and a single separator. For example:

  38 [space] 4 [space] 12 [space] [space] [space] 19

You might expect the three consecutive spaces to translate as two missing values in six variables:

  38 4 12 . . 19

Instead, the spaces are treated as one separator character, leaving four variables:

  38 4 12 19

Category definitions

Categorical variables with the same levels (group names) share the same category definition. For example, if two columns both use only the values Mouse, Dog, and Cat, StatView assigns the same category definition to both. This way you can easily Copy and Paste between the columns.

Example

The following example illustrates data type assignment and the effectiveness of the Convert small integers to categories choice in the Import dialog box.

Examine the Text File Example in a text editor such as Microsoft Word. Notice that it contains no variable names. (If you save, be sure to save as plain text.)

```
1  12/1/87  $1  1  1  red  Charlie
2  12/2/87  $10,001  2    blue  Parker
3  12/3/87  $20,001  3  3  1  Miles
2  12/4/87  $30,001  4  4  yellow  Davis
3  12/5/87  $40,001  5.1  5  red  John
2  12/6/87  $50,001  5.2    red  Coltrane
1  12/7/87  $60,001  5.3  7  blue  Roscoe
2  12/8/87  $70,001  5.4  8  green  Mitchell
3  12/9/87  $80,001  5.5  9  10  23.7
1  12/10/87  $90,001  5.6    red  Ra
```

In StatView, import Text File Example using default settings.

Column 1	Column 2	Column 3	Column 4	Column 5	Column 6	Column 7
Integer	Date/Time	Currency	Real	Integer	String	String
User Ent...	User Ent...	User Ent...	User Ent...	User Ent...	User Ent...	User Ent...
Continuous	Continuous	Continuous	Continuous	Continuous	Nominal	Nominal
●	1/ 1 /04	($1,234...	Free For...	●	●	●
●	●	0	1	●	●	●
1	12/ 1/87	$1	1.0	1	red	Charlie
2	12/ 2/87	$10,001	2.0	●	blue	Parker
3	12/ 3/87	$20,001	3.0	3	1	Miles
2	12/ 4/87	$30,001	4.0	4	yellow	Davis
3	12/ 5/87	$40,001	5.1	5	red	John
2	12/ 6/87	$50,001	5.2	●	red	Coltrane
1	12/ 7/87	$60,001	5.3	7	blue	Roscoe
2	12/ 8/87	$70,001	5.4	8	green	Mitchell
3	12/ 9/87	$80,001	5.5	9	10	23.7
1	12/10/87	$90,001	5.6	●	red	Ra

The following table shows how StatView assigns each variable type:

Variable	Type	Reason
Column 1	Integer	All values are integer.
Column 2	Date/Time	All values are date/time.
Column 3	Currency	All values are currency.
Column 4	Real	Although many values are integer, the variable does contain one real value.
Column 5	Integer	All values are integer. The three missing values do not affect data type.

Column 6	String	Eight out of ten values are string. There are repeated strings (red and blue), but we did not turn off the option to Import non-numeric data as type string.
Column 7	String	Nine out of ten values are string and none are repeated. The number 23.7 is merely another string.

You can transfer more of the information from the text file by importing again with different options.

- Choose Open from the File menu
- Choose Text file type
- Select Text File Example and click Open
- Uncheck Import non-numeric data as type string (turn the option off)
- Check Convert small integers to Categories (turn the option on)
- Click Import

Column 1	Column 2	Column 3	Column 4	Column 5	Column 6	Column 7
Category	Date/Ti...	Currency	Real	Category	Category	String
User Entered	User Ent...	User Ent...	User Ent...	User Entered	User Ent...	User Ent...
Nominal	Continuo...	Continuo...	Continuo...	Nominal	Nominal	Nominal
●	1/ 1/04	($1,234...	Free For...	●	●	●
●	●	0	1	●	●	●
Unlabeled group 1	12/ 1/87	$1	1.0	Unlabeled group 1	red	Charlie
Unlabeled group 2	12/ 2/87	$10,001	2.0	●	blue	Parker
Unlabeled group 3	12/ 3/87	$20,001	3.0	Unlabeled group 3	blue	Miles
Unlabeled group 2	12/ 4/87	$30,001	4.0	Unlabeled group 4	yellow	Davis
Unlabeled group 3	12/ 5/87	$40,001	5.1	Unlabeled group 5	red	John
Unlabeled group 2	12/ 6/87	$50,001	5.2	●	red	Coltrane
Unlabeled group 1	12/ 7/87	$60,001	5.3	Unlabeled group 7	blue	Roscoe
Unlabeled group 2	12/ 8/87	$70,001	5.4	Unlabeled group 8	green	Mitchell
Unlabeled group 3	12/ 9/87	$80,001	5.5	Unlabeled group 9	●	23.7
Unlabeled group 1	12/10/...	$90,001	5.6	●	red	Ra

Columns 1, 5, are now category variables with simple group labels. You can change group labels for categories so they are more informative (see "Edit category definitions," p. 83). Column 6 is also category; notice that in row 3 the value 1 is interpreted as blue, the first group in the category, and in row 9 the value 10 is missing, since the category has only four groups.

Older StatView products (Macintosh only)

Many StatView users also use SuperANOVA or older versions of StatView. You can open and save SuperANOVA and Old StatView data files directly with StatView, or you can exchange data through intermediate text files.

Text

When you save data as text, only the actual displayed values are saved. Be sure to display enough decimal places to meet your needs. Formula, Recode, Series, and Criteria definitions are not saved.

Old StatView data

Files saved as StatView 4.1+ Data cannot be read by StatView II, StatView SE+Graphics, or StatView 512+. To export data to any of these packages, save the files in Old StatView Data format.

All numeric data are saved in full precision. Formula, Recode, Series, and Criteria definitions are lost. Data class and format attributes are lost. Compact variables are saved in expanded format. Date/time and Currency variables can only be saved if they are first converted to type string.

SuperANOVA data

If you save a dataset in SuperANOVA format, nearly all information is kept intact. We recommend using SuperANOVA as an intermediate format to transfer data to StatView versions 4.00–4.02.

Any current selection (highlighting) of cells, rows, or columns is lost. Row inclusion/exclusion settings are lost; all rows become included. Certain functions used in formulas are not available in SuperANOVA, although they are interpreted correctly in any version of StatView that supports them.

If your formulas contain functions that SuperANOVA does not recognize, SuperANOVA opens the Formula dialog box with the dataset and highlights the unknown function. You have two choices in this situation:

1. Click Cancel in the Formula dialog box. This retains the computed values in the formula column. If you save this dataset, you can read it back into StatView with all formula information intact.

2. Change the formula column from Dynamic Formula to User Entered. This removes the formula definition but preserves its current values. If you save this dataset and read it back into StatView, the formula definition is lost.

IMPORTANT

REGISTRATION NUMBER

STV 04520   **STV 04520**

Please affix this number to your registration card. Duplicate stickers are provided for your convenience. You *must* return your registration card *with sticker attached* in order to receive free technical support for one year via one of the following options:

E-mail: support@sas.com

World Wide Web: www.sas.com/ts/

Phone: 919-677-8008 **Fax:** 919-677-4444

Managing data

StatView's Manage menu offers numerous ways to manage your dataset.

1. Include Row, Exclude Row let you choose which cases (rows) are used in statistical and graphical analyses.

2. Create Criteria and Edit/Apply Criteria let you define logically which cases (rows) are used for analyses, e.g., all cases with Weight values less than 200 and Age values greater than 20.

3. Formula, Series, and Random Numbers create new variables by definitions using StatView's mathematical expression language. For example, you could create a variable of Celsius temperatures from one of Fahrenheit temperatures with a formula like this:

   (Temperature − 32)*5/9.

4. Sort reorders cases (rows) according to the values of one or more key variables.

5. Recode creates new variables by grouping the values of continuous variables into nominal values or by replacing missing values with a specific value.

The other Manage menu commands are discussed elsewhere.

1. Edit Categories lets you change category definitions for group labels and is discussed under "Edit category definitions," p. 83.

2. Add Multiple Column enables you to add any number of empty columns to the dataset in a single step and is discussed under "Manipulate columns and rows," p. 62.

3. Preferences let you customize StatView's behavior to suit the way you work and are discussed in "Tips and shortcuts," p. 221.

Manage multiple datasets

If a dataset window is active (frontmost) when you select a Manage menu command, the command takes action on that dataset. If a view window is active and several datasets are open, you must choose which dataset to change.

- Select the dataset you want to manage
- Click Use

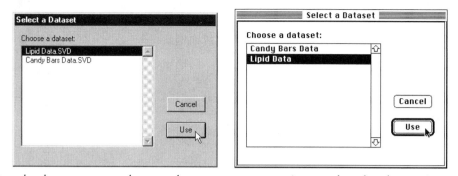

To make changes to more than one dataset, repeat your actions on the other datasets in turn. You can also Copy and Paste formula definitions between datasets.

Include and exclude rows

When you use a variable in an analysis, all the values in that variable are included in the analysis unless you exclude some rows (cases). All rows are included in analyses by default. If you prefer to restrict your analyses to a subset of the rows in a dataset, you can use Include Row and Exclude Row commands, Criteria commands, or both. Criteria are discussed separately under "Create criteria," p. 124 and "Edit/Apply Criteria," p. 129.

Use Include Row and Exclude Row to restrict analyses to certain rows. When you exclude rows or include rows that were excluded, any analysis results in any open view window using those data automatically recalculate to show the new results (unless you turn Recalculate off; see "Control recalculations," p. 138).

- Select the row(s) by clicking row number(s)
  To select multiple adjacent rows, Shift-click or click and drag their numbers. To select non-adjacent rows, Control-click (Windows) or Command-click (Macintosh) their numbers. To select all rows, use Select All Rows from the Edit menu.

- From the Manage menu, select Include Row or Exclude Row

You can tell whether a row is included or excluded by its row number. Included row numbers appear in regular, dark type. Excluded row numbers are dimmed or grayed. These characteristics are also visible if you print your dataset.

Shortcut Double-click any row number to toggle the row between included and excluded.

Caution Many columnwise functions have a final argument that controls which rows of the column are used for computations: AllRows, OnlyIncludedRows, or OnlyExcludedRows. When you use the latter two arguments, be aware that any Include Row, Exclude Row, and Criteria commands you use will cause these formula variables to recalculate.

Include and Exclude vs. Criteria

Include Row and Exclude Row commands are most useful when you are exploring your data. For example, you might temporarily exclude a few cases that seem to be outliers. You can easily adjust which rows are included until you begin to make sense of your data. At that point, or when you want to work with subsets systematically according to logical rules (e.g., all rows with Weight values between 100 and 300), it is better to use criteria commands. Criteria are also preferable when you need to preserve subsets for future use.

Formula

Formula creates variables through algebraic definitions called formulas. For example, you can create simple formulas to sum two variables or to log a variable. Or, you can write a complex formula with many arguments.

Formula variables are dynamically linked to the variables used to define them, so if those variables change, the formula variable automatically updates. (You can turn this link off by switching the source from Dynamic Formula to Static Formula.) *Warning:* if you change the names of variables used in formulas, you must fix the formulas yourself.

- From the Manage menu, select Formula
- Use the browsers and keypad to build an expression
  (Or type an expression directly into the text box.)
- Click Compute

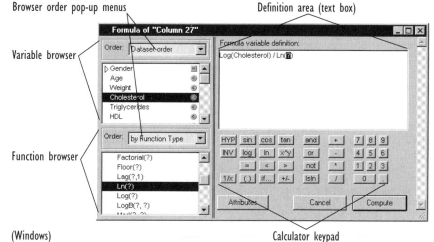

(Windows)

The Formula dialog has a variable browser, a function browser, and a calculator keypad for building expressions interactively. You can also type formulas directly into the definition area, and as StatView recognizes the variable or function name you are typing, it completes the name and supplies all the needed parameters.

Window controls

This dialog box behaves like a regular window: you can resize it, use Cut, Copy, and Paste on the text, change fonts, and move the window behind or in front of other windows.

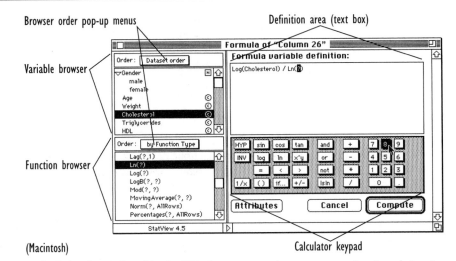

Browser order pop-up menus   Definition area (text box)

Variable browser

Function browser

(Macintosh)   Calculator keypad

A Formula dialog box is listed in the Window menu, where you can select it to bring it to the front. You can double-click the top area beneath the title bar to bring its dataset to the front. Select Print from the File menu to print a formula definition.

(Macintosh only) The triangle ▷ at the bottom of the dialog box is a split-pane control; click and drag it to resize or close the browser pane. If you drag it all the way to the left, the variable and function areas disappear; you can still type and use the keypad to create formulas.

Use Attributes if you want to specify variable names and attributes before clicking Compute. You can adjust attributes afterward in the dataset window if you prefer. See "Variable attributes," p. 73.

Variable browser

The variable browser lets you choose variables from the current dataset.

Use the Order pop-up menu to choose how to sort variable names in the scrolling list:

Dataset order	The order in which variables appear in the dataset's columns (left to right).
Alphabetical	Alphabetical order by variable name, with nonalphabetic names first.
Variable type	Grouped in order by nominal, continuous, and compact.
Usage	Ordered first by variable use in analyses and then in alphabetical order. When a dataset window is active, ordering is only alphabetical.

As in the main variable browser, variables appear in a scrolling list. Icons next to variable names indicate their data class: ⓒ for continuous and Ⓝ for nominal (informative variables cannot be used). Nominal variables have triangle ▷ controls. Click a triangle to tip it downward ▽ and reveal group labels. This mechanism provides an easy way to enter a group label from a nominal variable into a formula, which is particularly useful in formulas with if…then…else statements.

Compact variables are shown as several continuous variables; for example, a compact variable of Male and Female Weight values is listed as two continuous variables, Male Weight and Female Weight.

To insert a variable name (or a nominal value) in a formula definition, double-click it in the variable browser.

Function browser

The function browser offers an array of date/time, logical, mathematical, probabilities, random numbers, series, special purpose, statistical, text, and trigonometric functions you can use for creating variables. You can use the Order pop-up menu to sort functions alphabetically or by type.

When you order functions by type, each type has a triangle ▷ control. Click the triangle to tip it downward ▽ and reveal its functions.

Function type	Functions discussed
Date/Time	Date, DateDifference, Day, DayOfYear, Hour, Minute, Month, Now, Second, Time, Weekday, WeekOfYear, Year
Logical	<, <= or ≤, =, >= or ≥, >, <> or ≠, AND, ElementOf, IS, ISNOT, OR, XOR, false, if...then...else, IsMissing, IsRowExcluded, IsRowIncluded, NOT, true
Mathematical	+, −, *, /, (), ^, +, −, Abs, Average, AverageIgnoreMissing, Ceil, Combinations, CumProduct, CumSum, CumSumSquares, Difference, Div, DotProduct, e, Erf, Factorial, Floor, Lag, Ln, Log, LogB, Mod, MovingAverage, Norm, Percentages, Permutations, Pi, π, Remainder, Round, Sqrt, Sum, SumIgnoreMissing, Trunc
Probabilities	ProbBinomial, ProbChiSquare, ProbF, ProbNormal, Probt, ReturnChiSquare, ReturnF, ReturnNormal, ReturnT
Random Numbers	RandomBeta, RandomBinomial, RandomChiSquare, RandomExponential, RandomF, RandomGamma, RandomNormal, RandomPoisson, RandomT, RandomUniform, RandomUniformInteger
Series	BinomialCoeffs, CubicSeries, ExponentialSeries, FibonacciSeries, GeometricSeries, LinearSeries, QuadraticSeries, QuarticSeries, RowNumber
Special Purpose	{ }, (:), [:], (:], [:), <, <= or ≤, >= or ≥, >, ChooseArg, VariableElement
Statistical	BoxCox, CoeffOfVariation, Correlation, Count, Covariance, GeometricMean, Groups, HarmonicMean, LogOdds, MAD, Maximum, Mean, Median, Minimum, Mode, NumberMissing, NumberOfRows, OneGroupChiSquare, Percentile, Range, Rank, StandardDeviation, StandardError, StandardScores, SumOfColumn, SumOfSquares, TrimmedMean, Variance
Text	Concat, Find, Len, Substring
Trigonometric	ArcCos, ArcCosh, ArcCot, ArcCsc, ArcSec, ArcSin, ArcSinh, ArcTan, ArcTanh, Cos, Cosh, Cot, Csc, DegToRad, RadToDeg, Sec, Sin, Sinh, Tan, Tanh

Note that:

1. Trigonometric functions evaluate arguments or return results in radians (there are 2π radians in 360˚). See "DegToRad(?)," p. 372 and "RadToDeg(?)," p. 405 of *StatView Reference* for help converting between radians and degrees.

2. For logical functions, 0 is false; 1 or any nonzero, nonmissing value is true; and missing is missing. You can use IsMissing, IS, and ISNOT for special handling of missing values.

3. For the statistical functions, unless otherwise indicated, the first argument must be a variable name and remaining arguments can be any value. Many functions let you specify which rows of the dataset to use in the calculation: AllRows (the default), OnlyIncludedRows, or OnlyExcludedRows. See "Row inclusion," p. 325 of *StatView Reference*.

To insert a function in a formula definition, double-click it in the function browser.

Calculator keypad

The calculator keypad offers the most frequently used operators and functions, including the arithmetic operators +, −, *, and /, and the trigonometric functions sin, cos, and tan.

Button	Function	INV function	HYP function	INV HYP function
sin	sin(?)	arcsin(?)	sinh(?)	arcsinh(?)
cos	cos(?)	arccos(?)	cosh(?)	arccosh(?)
tan	tan(?)	arctan(?)	tanh(?)	arctanh(?)
and	? AND ?	NOT(? AND ?)		
+	? + ?	? + ?		
log	log(?)	10 ^ ?		
ln	ln(?)	e ^ ?		
x^y	? ^ ?	? ^ (1/?)		
or	? OR ?	NOT(? OR ?)		
−	? − ?	? − ?		
=	? = ?	? ≠ ?		
<	? < ?	? ≥ ?		
>	? > ?	? ≤ ?		
not	NOT(?)	?		
*	? * ?	.		
1/x	1/?	?		
()	(?)	.		
if...	if ? then ? else ?	.		
+/−	− ?	+ ?		
IsIn	? ElementOf ?	NOT(?ElementOf?)		
/	? / ?	.		

To insert an operator or function in a formula definition, click its button. Click first the INV button and then another button to insert an inverse functions. Click HYP and a trig button to insert an hyperbolic trig functions, and click INV, then HYP, then a trig button to insert inverse hyperbolic functions.

Mathematical expression language

The functions found in the browser and keypad constitute a complete mathematical expression language, which is detailed in the chapter "Formulas," p. 315 of *StatView Reference*. Consult that chapter for a comprehensive discussion of how expressions are evaluated, how each function works, and myriad examples.

To see a quick definition for a function, open the Hints window and select the function.

Build definitions

Functions and variables appear in the definition area as you double-click them in the browsers, click them in the keypad, or type them. To insert an element in a particular part of a formula, first click the I-beam cursor Ɪ in that location.

Most functions require that you supply arguments for the functions. These are represented by question marks ? in the formula definition area (and the function browser). **Arguments** are the objects of operators and functions. When you enter a function into a formula definition, you need to replace the "?" with the desired argument.

For example, if you click the Log button or double click Log(?) in the function browser, "Log(?)" appears and "?" is selected (highlighted) in the definition text box. Replace a selected ? with the desired argument by typing it or selecting it from the keypad or a browser. To select the next ? for replacement, press Tab. To select the previous ? for replacement, press Shift-Tab.

Arguments to a function can be constants, variables, or expressions. For example, the function Sum(Weight, Ln(Age), 10) adds for each row the value of the Weight variable, the natural log of the Age value, and the number 10. Some functions contain default arguments which you can change, such as LinearSeries(1, 1), which accepts two arguments. When you enter it into a formula it appears with a 1 for each of its arguments. You can change these default arguments to any values you want. Arguments are discussed in detail in "Arguments," p. 323 of *StatView Reference*.

Many functions can take a varying number of arguments. Functions of this type contain ellipses (…) to indicate that they allow any number of arguments. After supplying as many arguments as you need, you must remove the trailing ellipsis (…).

To learn what is expected for each argument of a function, open the Hints window and select the function. For a complete discussion of each function and its arguments (and some general rules), look up the function in the chapter "Formulas," p. 315 of *StatView Reference*.

Compute, Save, Cancel

Click the Compute button to create a new variable defined by the formula. Click Cancel, press Escape, or press Control-Period (Windows) or Command-Period (Macintosh) to cancel a formula and close the dialog box. If you are editing an existing formula variable, Cancel reverts to the original definition and Compute recomputes the variable.

New variables are appended at the right side of the dataset. To move a variable, Copy or Cut the data, insert an empty column elsewhere in the dataset (see "Insert columns," p. 62), and Paste the data into the empty column. To create a formula variable in another location, insert a column and change its source to Static Formula or Dynamic Formula.

To edit an existing formula, select Dynamic Formula from the variable's Source pop-up menu.

Some examples

The following are all valid formula expressions:

```
-3
1+2
1 + (2 - 10)
3 (4+6)
4^2
log(100)
```

The expression 3 (4+6) means "3 times the quantity 4 plus 6," and it returns 30. The expression log(100) means "evaluate the base 10 logarithm of the value 100," and it returns 2.00.

A formula can also operate on variables in the same dataset:

```
Age / 2
Log(Weight)
```

A formula of this type is evaluated on a row-by-row basis. For example, the expression "Age / 2" is first evaluated for row number 1 of the dataset, then row number 2, then 3 and so on. If the Age value in row number 1 is 10, the resulting formula for row number 1 is 5 (10 divided by 2).

Logical formulas can be created with the if…then…else function, such as:

```
if Age > 1
  then 10
  else Age
```

The result of this formula is 10 for each row of the Age variable with a value greater than 10. Otherwise the result is the existing value of the Age variable in that row.

Consult the "Formulas," p. 315 of *StatView Reference*, for more examples and further discussion.

Exercise

Here we create a new formula variable to average two variables, Triglycerides and Trig-3yrs.

- Open Lipid Data from the Sample Data folder
- From the Manage menu, select Formula
- Start typing a variable name: Triglycerides

As soon as you type "Trigl" the rest of the variable name is filled in. You type as few characters as are needed to distinguish a variable from all others.

• Click + on the keypad

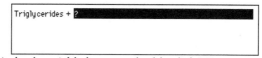

• In the Formula window's variable browser, double-click Trig-3yrs

The selected "?" is replaced by the variable name. The formula now reads:

Triglycerides + "Trig-3yrs"

Variable names, dates, and nominal levels of a category appear in quotation marks if they are not purely alphabetic or contain spaces. For rules, see "Quotation marks," p. 325 of *StatView Reference*.

• Select the entire formula
• Click the ( ) button on the keypad

The entire expression is enclosed in parentheses, so the formula now reads:

(Triglycerides + "Trig-3yrs")

• Click in the blank area of the text box to deselect the expression
• Click the / operator and then 2 the keypad

The formula is now complete. It reads:

(Triglycerides + "Trig-3yrs")/2

• Click Compute

The new variable, the average of Triglycerides and Trig-3yrs, appears at the right of your dataset, to the left of the input column.

Shortcuts

As you observed in the exercise, StatView automatically creates placeholders for arguments and anticipates the rest of a formula or function when you start typing. In a similar way, Stat-View anticipates arguments for the mathematical operators +, −, *, and /. For example, if you double-click a variable and then click the + operator, the definition area highlights a ? to indicate that it is ready to take the second argument:

In addition, if any part of a formula is already selected when you insert a function name, the selection is interpreted as the first argument of any function that can take arguments. For example, if you select Weight in the formula definition, and click the Sin button you see:

sin(Weight)

When you type variable names or functions in the formula definition, you have to type only enough characters to identify the word uniquely. For example, if you type "we" and you have a variable named Weight, the remaining characters are automatically entered. However, if you have a variable named "Weight" and a variable named "Weight1," you have to type the whole word, since the letters "we" are not unique. When you begin to type the name of a function, the function is inserted, along with any arguments, and the first argument of the function is selected. If StatView anticipates a term incorrectly, simply delete any incorrect character

Errors in formula

If you make an error in a formula definition, you get a warning after you click Compute. The Hints window advises you about your error, and the formula window highlights the problematic area. Formulas do not compute until their expressions can be interpreted unambiguously.

Most errors involve invalid arguments (e.g., constants where variables are expected), a wrong number of arguments, missing parentheses, or misspelled function or variable names. Many common errors can be prevented simply by using the browsers and the keypad to build formulas rather than trying to type formulas by hand.

Any formula with an error will not compute. For a new formula, missing values fill the column until the formula can be computed. If you edit the formula for an existing, valid formula variable and cause an error, the original definition and its values remain.

For help solving common formula errors, see "Formulas and criteria," p. 240.

Dynamic vs. static formulas

Formula variables use dynamic formulas by default. If you change data associated with a dynamic formula, the formula automatically recalculates.

You can change the source of a formula variable from Dynamic Formula to Static Formula in the attribute pane. Changing formulas to *static* prevents recalculation. Changing to User-Entered deletes the formula information completely but saves the values. You cannot edit the data in a Dynamic or Static Formula variable unless you first change it to User Entered. See "Change sources," p. 77.

If you delete a variable that is used in a formula, you are alerted to the fact that the variable is used in a formula definition. If you continue and delete the variable, the formula changes automatically to static and retains its current values. You can then change the column to user-entered or redefine the formula.

Sort data

Sort reorders the rows of a dataset in either ascending or descending order according to the values of one or more **key** variables in the dataset. For example, when you sort the rows of Lipid Data on the values of Cholesterol in ascending order, the subject with the lowest cholesterol value appears in the top row and the one with the highest in the bottom row. Any subjects with missing cholesterol values appear at the end.

- From the Manage menu, select Sort
- Select a variable and click Make Key
  (Or select and click Make Key for several variables in order.)
- For each key, click the arrow icon to choose ascending(⇧) or descending (⇩) order
- Click OK

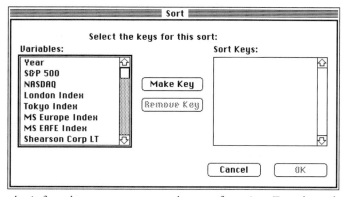

"Ascending" order is from lesser to greater numbers, or from A to Z, and numbers come before letters. Case and accent marks are ignored when sorting text. Missing values are sorted as if they were the largest values in a variable. Nested sorts (sorts with more than one key variable) order cases with matching values on the first variable according to values of a second variable, etc.

Only complete datasets are sorted; if you want to sort only a few rows or a few columns, you must first extract them to another dataset.

Caution You can unsort data only by immediately selecting Undo from the Edit menu or typing Control-Z (Windows) or Command-Z (Macintosh). Otherwise you cannot unsort data unless you took precautions to preserve the order before sorting. For tips on how to preserve a sorting order permanently, see "RowNumber," p. 417 of *StatView Reference*.

Recode data

Recode creates new variables two different ways: by grouping the values of continuous variables into nominal values, or by replacing missing values of a nominal or continuous variable with a specific value. The original variable is unchanged. You cannot recode informative variables or compact variables. (To recode a nominal variable into a different nominal variable, use a formula; see "if ? then ? else ?," p. 341 and "ChooseArg(?)," p. 359 of *StatView Reference*.)

Grouping values of continuous variables lets you derive nominal variables from continuous data. For example, ranges of temperatures in degrees recode into hot, temperate, or cold; response times in seconds convert to slow, medium and fast. Date/time data with day/month/year values can be grouped into seasons.

Recoding missing values is useful for preparing a dataset for export to a data analysis package that expects missing values to be coded a certain way; for example, some packages expect missing values to be coded –99.

- From the Manage menu, select Recode
- Select a variable
- Choose which way to recode

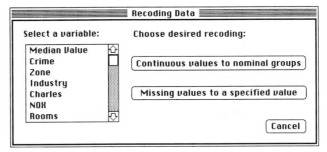

Continuous data to nominal groups

When you choose Continuous values to nominal groups, you must specify a category to define the group labels to be used for the recoding. You can either select an existing category or click New to define a new one. Assigning categories in order from least to greatest simplifies later steps in recoding. For help with categories, see "Categories," p. 80.

After you create or choose a category, you must specify how to divide the range of continuous values into groups. A value bar represents the range of data; its top and bottom edges correspond to the variable's maximum and minimum values.

- Either click breakpoints in the value bar or enter values in the text box
- Use pop-up menus to correct group label assignments
  StatView automatically assigns group labels in order according to the category definition. If your category definition orders labels from least to greatest, Recode assigns groups correctly.
- Click Recode

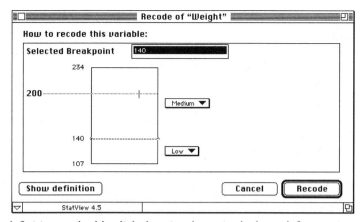

Click Show definition or double-click the triangle ▽ in the lower left corner to open a pane showing the formula definition for the recode. You can then drag the triangle to resize the split pane. Click Hide definition or double-click the triangle to close the split pane. Select Print from the File menu to print the definition. You cannot edit the formula definition directly.

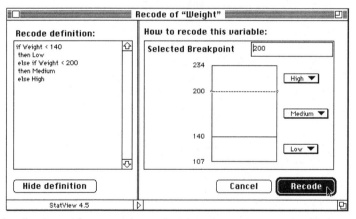

To change a breakpoint, either move it or select it and enter a new value in the text box.

A Recode dialog box is listed in the Window menu, where you can select it to bring it to the front. You can double-click the top area beneath the title bar to bring its dataset to the front. Select Print from the File menu to print a formula definition.

If you prefer, you can use Formula to build your own recoding formula; Recode is a shortcut. Either way, you can use the variable's Source pop-up menu to view and edit a formula defini- tion, or to change from static formula to dynamic formula or user entered. See "Change sources," p. 77. By default, recoded variables are based on dynamic formulas, which means that changes or additions to the original variable automatically change the recoded variable.

New variables are appended at the right side of the dataset. To move a variable, Copy or Cut the data, insert an empty column elsewhere in the dataset (see "Insert columns," p. 62), and Paste the data into the empty column. To create a recode variable in another location, insert a column and change its source to Static Formula or Dynamic Formula.

Missing values to a specified value

Recoding missing values to a specific value works by building an if…then…else formula. You must supply a value in place of its question mark (?) placeholder. The value you specify can be a number, a string, or some other function, such as the mean of the variable.

You can choose any function from the browser at the left. For more information about each function, refer to the chapter "Formulas," p. 315 of *StatView Reference* or examine the Hints window: when you click a function, the Hints window describes the function and its parameters briefly.

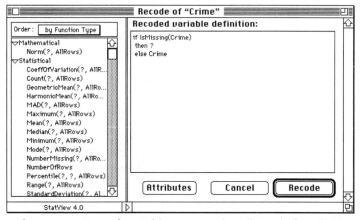

Use Attributes if you want to specify variable names and attributes before clicking Create. You can adjust attributes afterward in the dataset window if you prefer. See "Variable attributes," p. 73.

A Recode dialog box is listed in the Window menu, where you can select it to bring it to the front. You can double-click the top area beneath the title bar to bring its dataset to the front. Select Print from the File menu to print a formula definition.

If you prefer, you can use Formula to build your own recoding formula; Recode is a shortcut. Either way, you can use the variable's Source pop-up menu to view and edit a formula definition, or to change from static formula to dynamic formula or user entered. See "Change sources," p. 77. By default, recoded variables are based on dynamic formulas, which means that changes or additions to the original variable automatically change the recoded variable.

New variables are appended at the right side of the dataset. To move a variable, Copy or Cut the data, insert an empty column elsewhere in the dataset (see "Insert columns," p. 62), and Paste the data into the empty column. To create a recode variable in another location, insert a column and change its source to Static Formula or Dynamic Formula.

Exercise

In this exercise, you create a variable that categorizes the risk of heart attack in patients as high, medium, or low, depending on their measured HDL-Cholesterol values. The lower the

HDL-cholesterol values, the higher the risk of heart attack. Values below 35 denote high risk, between 35 and 60 medium risk, and 60 and above low risk.

- Open Lipid Data from the Sample Data folder
- From the Manage menu, select Recode
- Select HDL and click Continuous values to nominal groups
- Click New
- Define a category called HDL risk with three group labels, High risk, Medium risk, Low risk, in order
- Click Done
- Type the value 35 and press Enter (Windows) or Return (Mac)
- Type the number 60 and press Enter (Windows) or Return (Mac)
- Click Show Definition to see the corresponding formula

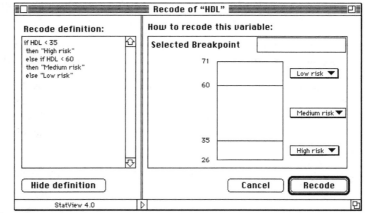

- Click Recode

The recoded variable is appended to the right side of the dataset. Recoded variables are based on dynamic formulas, which means that changes or additions to HDL automatically change the recoded variable.

Series

Series generates new variables with values based on common types of series. Series variables are based on static formulas, and you can edit them the same way you edit formulas. You can also use Formula to generate series with dynamic formulas.

- From the Manage menu, select Series
- Double-click a series in the scroll list
- Replace any ? arguments and edit any default parameters to suit your needs
- Specify the number of rows and columns to create
- Click Create

This dialog box behaves like a regular window: you can resize it, use Cut, Copy, and Paste on the text, and change font. You can double-click the top area beneath the title bar to bring its dataset to the front. Select Print from the File menu to print a formula definition.

(Windows only) You can move a Series window behind or in front of other windows. It is listed in the Window menu, where you can select it to bring it to the front.

You can create any number of rows and columns of the same series. By default, Series creates one variable with the number of rows currently present in the dataset. If you specify a larger number of rows, rows are added to all columns and filled with missing value symbols (.) in the other columns unless they are formula variables whose definition specifies otherwise.

Use Attributes if you want to specify variable names and attributes before clicking Create. You can adjust attributes afterward in the dataset window if you prefer. See "Variable attributes," p. 73.

For more information about each series, refer to the chapter "Formulas," p. 315 of *StatView Reference*, or examine the Hints window: when you click a series, the Hints window describes the function and its parameters briefly.

Use the variable's Source pop-up menu to view and edit a formula definition or to change from static formula to dynamic formula or user entered. See "Change sources," p. 77.

New variables are appended at the right side of the dataset. To move a variable, Copy or Cut the data, insert an empty column elsewhere in the dataset (see "Insert columns," p. 62), and Paste the data into the empty column. To create a series variable in another location, insert a column and change its source to Static Formula or Dynamic Formula.

Exercise

This exercise creates a new dataset with five variables and one hundred observations.

- From the File menu, select New
- From the Manage menu, select Series
- Double-click CubicSeries(1,0,0,1)
- Specify the number of rows: 100

- Specify the number of variables: 5
- Click Create

Five new variables are added to your dataset.

Random numbers

Random Numbers lets you create new variables whose values are generated from a commonly used distribution. Random Numbers variables are static formula variables and can be edited accordingly. You can also use Formula to generate random numbers with dynamic formulas.

- From the Manage menu, select Random Numbers
- In the function browser on the left, double-click a distribution
  (Or type a distribution name directly into the definition area.)
- Replace any ? arguments and edit any default parameters to suit your needs
- Specify the number of rows and columns to create
- Click Create

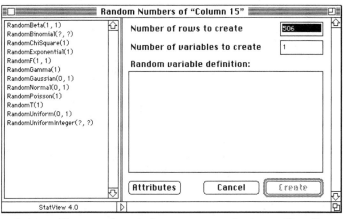

This dialog box behaves like a regular window: you can resize it, use Cut, Copy, and Paste on the text, change fonts, and move the window behind or in front of other windows. You can double-click the top area beneath the title bar to bring its dataset to the front. Select Print from the File menu to print a formula definition.

(Windows only) A Random Numbers dialog box is listed in the Window menu, where you can select it to bring it to the front.

You can create any number of rows and columns of random numbers from the same distribution. By default, Random Numbers creates one variable with the number of rows currently present in the dataset. If you specify a larger number of rows, rows are added to all columns and filled with missing value symbols (.) in the other columns unless they are formula variables whose definition specifies otherwise.

Use Attributes if you want to specify variable names and attributes before clicking Create. You can adjust attributes afterward in the dataset window if you prefer. See "Variable attributes," p. 73.

For more information about each distribution, refer to the chapter "Formulas," p. 315 of *Stat-View Reference*, or examine the Hints window: when you click a distribution, the Hints window describes the function and its parameters briefly.

Use the variable's Source pop-up menu to view and edit a formula definition or to change from static formula to dynamic formula or user entered. See "Change sources," p. 77.

New variables are appended at the right side of the dataset. To move a variable, Copy or Cut the data, insert an empty column elsewhere in the dataset (see "Insert columns," p. 62), and Paste the data into the empty column. To create a random variable in another location, insert a column and change its source to Static Formula or Dynamic Formula.

Create criteria

When you use a variable in an analysis, all the values in that variable are included in the analysis unless you exclude some rows (cases). All rows are included in analyses by default. If you prefer to restrict your analyses to a subset of the rows in a dataset, you can use Include Row and Exclude Row commands, Criteria commands, or both. Include Row and Exclude Row are discussed separately under "Include and exclude rows," p. 108.

Use Criteria to specify algebraically which cases to include in calculations. When you apply a criterion, any analysis results in any open view window using those data automatically recalculate to show the new results (unless you turn Recalculate off; see "Control recalculations," p. 138).

You can tell whether a row is included or excluded by its row number. Included row numbers appear in regular, dark type. Excluded row numbers are dimmed or grayed. These characteristics are also visible if you print your dataset.

Caution Many columnwise functions have a final argument that controls which rows of the column are used for computations: AllRows, OnlyIncludedRows, or OnlyExcludedRows. When you use the latter two arguments, be aware that any Include Row, Exclude Row, and Criteria commands you use will cause these formula variables to recalculate.

Criteria can be as simple or complex as you like. Criteria are saved when you save the associated dataset. A list of all defined criteria appears in the dataset's Criteria pop-up menu.

There are four ways to select and define new criteria:

1. From the Manage menu, select Create Criteria
2. From the Manage menu, select Edit/Apply Criteria and click New
3. From the dataset Criteria pop-up menu, select New
4. From the dataset Criteria pop-up menu, select Random

Any method leads you to a Criteria dialog box (except the fourth, which leads you to a random criterion dialog box).

```
┌─────────────────────────────────────────────────────────────────┐
│ ▤□▰▰▰▰▰▰▰▰▰▰▰ Criteria 1 of "Investment returns" ▰▰▰▰▰▰▰▰▰□▤ │
│  Criteria name:  │ Criteria 1                            │        │
│  Criteria definition:                                            │
│  ┌───────────────────────────────────────────────────────────┐  │
│  │                                                           │  │
│  │                                                           │  │
│  └───────────────────────────────────────────────────────────┘  │
│                        Select a variable                         │
│              ┌─────────────────────────────────┐                │
│              │ Year                        ⊗ ⇧ │                │
│              │ S&P 500                     ⊗   │                │
│              │ NASDAQ                      ⊗   │                │
│              │ London Index                ⊗   │                │
│              │ Tokyo Index                 ⊗   │                │
│              │ MS Europe Index             ⊗   │                │
│              │ MS EAFE Index               ⊗   │                │
│              │ Shearson Corp LT            ⊗ ⇩ │                │
│              └─────────────────────────────────┘                │
│                 ┌────────┐  ┌────────┐  ┌────────┐              │
│                 │  Save  │  │ Select │  │ Apply  │              │
│                 └────────┘  └────────┘  └────────┘              │
└─────────────────────────────────────────────────────────────────┘
```

This dialog box behaves like a regular window: you can resize it, use Cut, Copy, and Paste on the text, change fonts, and move the window behind or in front of other windows.

A Criteria dialog box is listed in the Window menu, where you can select it to bring it to the front. You can double-click the top area beneath the title bar to bring its dataset to the front. Select Print from the File menu to print a formula definition.

A criteria definition consists of three parts: a variable, a comparison operator and a value. You choose these three parts from the scrolling list below the definition area. The scrolling list coaches you through each step of the definition process by showing you first a list of variables, then a list of comparison operators, and finally either a list of the levels of a nominal variable or a value bar for a continuous variable.

To create a complex criterion (one using AND, OR, or XOR), click in the definition area after the expression and then select a logical conjunction from the list. You may use the logical NOT by editing the definition.

You can edit definitions by clicking in the part of the definition you want to change. Again, the scroll list coaches you: it changes to the type of list you need to edit that part of the definition.

You can type a definition directly into the definition box if you prefer. You can print a criterion definition by choosing Print from the File menu.

Define criteria

Defining a criterion is a four-step process: name the criterion, select a variable, choose a comparison operator, and set a value or range of values.

Name the criterion

The default name is "Criteria *n*." You should supply a more meaningful name, because you select and apply criteria by name from the Criteria pop-up menu and the Edit/Apply Criteria. Also, the name of any criterion in effect appears automatically in the titles of statistical analyses and graphs as a reminder that results are based on a subset of the data.

Select a variable

Double-click a variable from the list (or type its name) to select it. A criterion can be based on any continuous or nominal variable in the dataset. Select the variable whose values determine whether cases are included or excluded from analyses. For example, if you want to analyze only those cases whose Weight value is greater than 160, select Weight.

Choose a comparison operator

Next, choose a comparison operators. For example, if you want to analyze only those cases whose Weight value is greater than 160, select > for "greater than."

<	less than
=	equal to
>	greater than
< > or ≠	not equal to
<= or ≤	less than or equal to
>= or ≥	greater than or equal to
ElementOf	is an element of
IS	equal to, or both are missing values
ISNOT	not equal to, or one value missing and the other is not

For a detailed discussion of StatView's logical operators, see the chapter "Formulas," p. 315 of *StatView Reference*.

What you see for the final step varies according to the variable you select in the first step. For a continuous variable, you see a value bar; for nominal, a list of its levels (group labels).

Set a value or range with a value bar

A value bar is a linear representation of the range of the variable from its minimum to its maximum. Both extrema are labeled.

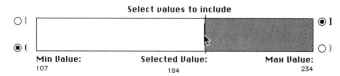

The number below Selected value changes as you move the cursor across the bar.

To define a range, click endpoints in the value bar and choose brackets or parentheses at each end of the value bar to specify closed or open intervals. Brackets [ ] indicate closed intervals, which include their endpoints. Parentheses ( ) indicate open intervals, which exclude their endpoints. For example, if a variable contains integers between 1 and 10, the range [4:6] contains the values 4, 5, 6, the range (4:6] contains the values 5 and 6 and (4:6) only contains the value 5.

To specify a single value, click in the value bar. To change a value, click the vertical line and drag it to its new location. To specify an interval, click and drag between endpoints.

For =, <> or ≠, IS or ISNOT, which take a single value, a vertical line indicates that value.

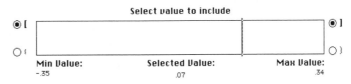

For <, >, >= or ≥, or <= or ≤ , which take a range, a bracket or parenthesis and a gray fill pattern indicate the included range.

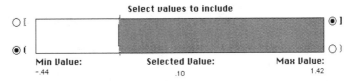

For ElementOf, which takes an interval of a continuous variable, brackets or parentheses and a gray fill pattern indicate the included range.

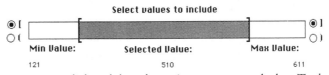

To move an existing range, click and drag the entire range across the bar. To change one of the endpoints of a range, click drag the endpoint to the new position. You can also change the range values by typing the ranges into the criterion definition.

Choose a level or levels

When the variable is nominal, you see a list of its group labels instead of the value bar.

Select a category group

Mammal
Bird
Reptile
Amphibian

Double-click one or more group label to select one or more groups. If you need to define a criterion that includes only those cases with or without a missing value for a certain variable, use IS or ISNOT and a missing value (.).

Complex criteria

If you click inside the definition area at the end of a definition, the scrolling list presents a list of Boolean operators. You can combine as many criteria as you like using AND, OR or XOR. To enter a Boolean operator, double-click it or type its name. You can group expressions by inserting parentheses into the definition.

Parentheses, AND, OR, and XOR are discussed in detail in the chapter "Formulas," p. 315 of *StatView Reference*.

Apply, Save, and Select

The buttons at the lower right corner of the Criteria dialog box give you three options when you are finished creating or editing criteria. All three buttons save the criterion with the dataset, add it to the Criteria pop-up menu, and bring the dataset to the front.

Save	Save the criterion and include it in the Criteria pop-up menu.
Apply	Evaluate the criterion, save it, and apply it: include in analyses only those rows that evaluate to true.
Select	Evaluate the criterion, save it, and select (highlight) those rows that evaluate to true. Do not apply the criterion.

If the criterion definition is incorrect, you cannot apply or save it until you correct the error.

Criteria pop-up menu

The Criteria pop-up menu at the top of the dataset lists all criteria defined for the dataset. A criterion is dimmed if it has not been saved or applied, if its dialog box is open for editing, or if it has become invalid because the variable it is based upon has been deleted or renamed.

- Select No Criteria to turn off criteria (to include all rows)
- Select New to define a new criterion
- Select Random to define a random criterion
- Select a criterion to apply it
- Control-select a criterion to select in the dataset rows that would be included by the criterion

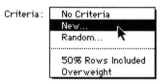

No Criteria is the default, indicating that all dataset rows are included in any analysis.

Random criteria use the following dialog box:

Enter a percentage between 0 and 100 for each row to be included. Click OK to create a criterion named "*n*% Rows Included" and apply it to the dataset. A new random sample is included each time you select or define a random criterion. If you need to do more complicated random inclusions, see "RandomInclusion(?)," p. 409 of *StatView Reference*.

A special dialog box lets you create complex random criteria. For example, you might want to include a random number generator seed so that a random inclusion can be reproduced. See "RandomInclusion(?)," p. 409 of *StatView Reference*.

When you close a dataset that contains random criteria, their definitions are saved, but an exact row inclusion is only saved if the random criterion is in effect (applied) when you save.

Edit/Apply Criteria

You can *apply* an existing criterion two ways.

1. From the Manage menu, select Edit/Apply Criteria, choose a criterion, and click apply.

2. From the Criteria pop-up menu in a dataset, select the criterion.

You can *edit* existing criteria with Edit/Apply Criteria only.

• From the Manage menu, select Edit/Apply Criteria

• Select one or more criteria

• Click Edit

Selecting any criterion shows a preview of its definition.

In a criterion's dialog box, you can either edit a definition directly in the text box, or you can select part of the definition and make another choice from the scrolling list or value bar. If you edit a criterion currently applied to the dataset, the dataset immediately reflects the change.

You can also *delete* criteria so that they are no longer saved with a dataset

• From the Manage menu, select Edit/Apply Criteria

• Select one or more criteria

• Click Delete

You can *turn criteria off* two ways.

1. From the Manage menu, select Edit/Apply Criteria, select No Criteria, and click Apply.

2. From the Criteria pop-up menu in a dataset, select No Criteria.

Exercise

In this exercise, you create two criteria: one to include only men in analyses, and one to include only men with low lipid counts.

- Open Lipid Data from the Sample Data folder
- From the Manage menu, select Create Criteria
- Double-click Gender
- Double-click =
- Double-click Male
- Name the criterion Men
- Click Apply

You have just created a criterion to include only those data for male subjects. Now we create one that includes only men with low lipid counts.

- From the Criteria pop-up menu, select New
- Double-click Gender
- Double-click =
- Double-click Male
- Click after the end of the definition
- Double-click AND
- Double-click Cholesterol
- Double-click ≤
- Click in the value bar when the Selected Value is 200
- Name this criterion Low Lipid Males
- Click Apply
- From the Criteria pop-up menu, select Men

Only those rows in the dataset with values for men are included. The rest have dimmed row numbers.

- From the Criteria pop-up menu, select Low Lipid Males

Notice how the included rows change. If you were using this dataset in some analyses, the tables and graphs in the view would change as you selected different criteria from the pop-up menu.

Analyses

StatView provides two ways of creating statistical analyses (tables and graphs):

1. You can choose analyses from the analysis browser and use the variable browser to assign variables to roles in the analyses.
2. You can select templates from the Analyze menu and assign variables to them. Templates are preassembled sets of analysis results.

This chapter discusses the first method: using analysis and variable browsers to construct analyses directly. We discuss the second method in the next chapter, "Templates," p. 161. That chapter also shows how to use browsers to build your own templates for the statistics and graphs you use most frequently.

Once you have created an analysis—either with browsers or with templates—you can change its parameters or its variable assignments, adopt its variable assignments for another type of analysis, and clone it into an analysis of different variables. You can split an analysis into separate analyses for each group in a nominal variable, or each subgroup formed by crossing several nominal variables. You can restrict your analyses to a subset of your dataset by including and excluding rows or by defining criteria for which rows to include.

These techniques apply equally to results created with templates. A result is a result, no matter how you create it. You can mix both templates and your own analyses in a single view.

Finally we discuss how to print views and how to save views as documents or templates.

Overview

There are several ways to build analyses in the view.

1. **Create** an empty analysis object with the analysis browser; then, use the variable browser to assign variables to the empty object. (Or, assign variables first and then create the analysis.)
2. **Adopt** the variable assignments from one analysis to use with a new analysis you choose from the analysis browser.
3. **Clone** a completed analysis to analyze new variables you choose from the variable browser.

Exercise

A simple exercise shows how this works. This diagram shows the basic sequence of steps.

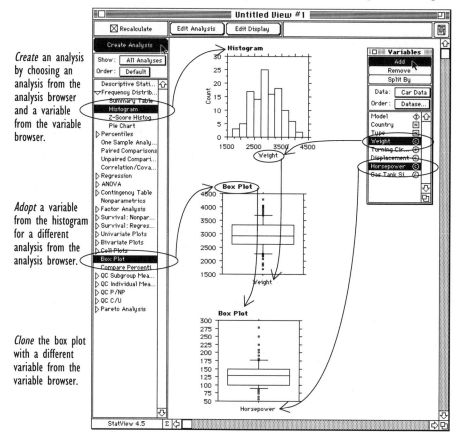

Create an analysis by choosing an analysis from the analysis browser and a variable from the variable browser.

Adopt a variable from the histogram for a different analysis from the analysis browser.

Clone the box plot with a different variable from the variable browser.

First we *create* a new analysis.

- Open Car Data from the Sample Data folder
- From the Analyze menu, select New View
- In the analysis browser under Frequency Distribution, select Histogram and click Create Analysis
- Accept the default parameters for the histogram by clicking OK
- In the variable browser, select Weight and click Add

Shortcut You can instead select an analysis in the analysis browser, assign variables in the variable browser, and *then* click Create Analysis. For large datasets or complex computations, waiting to click the Create Analysis button last can save time, because you don't have to wait for calculations after adding each variable.

Second, we *adopt* the variable assignment (Weight) from this histogram simply by leaving the analysis selected while we create another analysis—this time a box plot.

- Be sure the histogram is still selected (has black selection handles); if not, click to select it

- In the analysis browser, select Box Plot and click Create Analysis

Third, we *clone* the box plot to analyze another variable, Horsepower.

- Be sure the box plot is still selected (has black selection handles); if not, click to select it
- In the variable browser, select Horsepower and Control-Shift (Windows) or Command-Shift-click (Macintosh) the Add button

As you can see, result objects help you generate new analyses. They retain the information used to create them: the analysis you chose, the variables you assigned, and even the parameters you specified (for example, in the histogram above we accepted the default parameters for how to divide the variable into intervals, and we chose not to add a normal curve). When a result (object) is selected, this information passes directly to your next analysis, saving steps you would otherwise have to repeat.

Important All results know which kind of analysis produced them, which parameters were set, and which variables were involved. If any result is selected when you create another result, it passes that knowledge to the new result.

To prevent new results from learning such things from old results—i.e., to create completely different analyses—you must be sure that existing results are not selected (do *not* have black selection handles). Click in the empty space of a view to deselect objects.

Determine whether results are selected

Because information from a selected result passes to new results, it is always important to know whether any results are selected. You can find out three ways:

1. Look at the objects. If they have black selection handles, they are selected. If they do not, they are not selected.

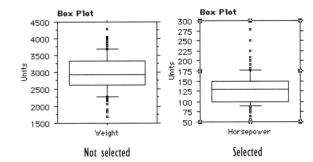

Not selected   Selected

2. Look at the Results Selected note in the upper right corner of the view.

If no results are selected, this area is blank.

3. Look at the Results browser, and choose Show Selection
   To open the Results browser, select Results Browser from the View menu (Windows) or select Results from the Window menu (Macintosh)

Edit Analysis

Each analysis presents its own dialog box in which you set **analysis parameters**: choices you make to control how the analysis is performed. For example, when you create a histogram, you can specify how to divide the range into intervals, whether intervals show counts or cumulative counts, etc. (Since histograms are only one possible result from a Frequency Distribution analysis, the dialog box also has options that apply to the other types of output.)

After the histogram is created, you can click Edit Analysis to return to this dialog box and change the parameters.

- Select one or more analysis results
- Click Edit Analysis
- Change the parameter settings
- Click OK

The Edit Analysis dialog box for any analysis is the same one you see when you first create the analysis. Some analyses have no parameters, so Edit Analysis has no effect.

If you change the parameters of an analysis, any other results associated with that analysis also change. For example, if you create a frequency distribution analysis with both a table and a histogram, changing the number of intervals of the frequency distribution updates both the summary table and the histogram.

If you select more than one type of analysis and click Edit Analysis, you see a series of dialog boxes, one for each type of analysis. Not all analyses have parameters you can change; for these, Edit Analysis has no effect.

Each analysis has different parameters, so each has its own unique dialog box. For details on any analysis' parameters, see its chapter in *StatView Reference*. Also, take advantage of online help; see "Help (Windows only)," p. 222 and "Hints window," p. 222.

Shortcut Alt-double-clicking (Windows) or Option-double-clicking (Macintosh) an analysis has the same effect as selecting it and clicking Edit Analysis. (Note that double-clicking an analysis is the same as selecting it and clicking Edit Display. However, a view preference lets you switch these shortcuts. See "View preferences," p. 232.)

Edit Display

You can also edit how each result is displayed. While Edit Analysis changes the parameters—and therefore the results—of an analysis, Edit Display changes how the results are presented. For example, you can edit any table to have double borders and format numbers with only one decimal place. Or, you can transpose a graph (flip it sideways) and give it a different axis frame. Not all results' displays can be edited.

- Select one or more analysis results
- Click Edit Display
- Change the display option settings
- Click OK

For more on editing graphs and tables, see "Customizing results," p. 179.

Shortcut Double-clicking an analysis has the same effect as selecting it and clicking Edit Display. (Note that Alt-double-clicking (Windows) or Option-double-clicking (Macintosh) an analysis is the same as selecting it and clicking Edit Analysis. However, a view preference lets you switch these shortcuts. See "View preferences," p. 232.)

Multiple and compound results

You can assign as many variables to an analysis as you want. The way StatView handles extra variables varies according to the analysis.

For some analyses, assigning more variables changes simple graphs or tables into **compound** tables or graphs that show results for all the variables at once. For example, assigning two variables to a Descriptive Statistics table breaks the table into a compound table with a row for each variable. Similarly, assigning two variables to a box plot changes it to a compound box plot, where a single graph frame contains boxes for each variable.

Descriptive Statistics

	Mean	Std. Dev.	Std. Error	Count	Minimum	Maximum	# Missing
Weight	158.653	28.389	2.913	95	107.000	234.000	0
Cholesterol	191.232	35.674	3.660	95	115.000	285.000	0

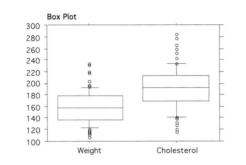

Box Plot

For other analyses, assigning more variables causes StatView to produce **multiple** analyses. For example, assigning two variables to a frequency summary table produces two separate tables, and assigning two variables to a histogram produces separate histograms for each group.

Frequency Distribution for Weight

From (≥)	To (<)	Count
107.000	119.700	8
119.700	132.400	13
132.400	145.100	10
145.100	157.800	16
157.800	170.500	12
170.500	183.200	18
183.200	195.900	11
195.900	208.600	3
208.600	221.300	2
221.300	234.000	2
	Total	95

Frequency Distribution for Cholesterol

From (≥)	To (<)	Count
115.000	132.000	4
132.000	149.000	6
149.000	166.000	11
166.000	183.000	19
183.000	200.000	21
200.000	217.000	15
217.000	234.000	10
234.000	251.000	2
251.000	268.000	4
268.000	285.000	3
	Total	95

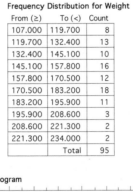

Histogram

Histogram

Similarly, you can assign as many Split By variables to an analysis as you want. The way Stat-View handles extra variables varies according to the analysis.

For some analyses, Split By changes simple tables or graphs into **compound** tables or graphs that show results for all the groups at once. For example, adding a Split By variable to a Descriptive Statistics table breaks the table into a compound table with a column for each group. Similarly, adding a Split By variable to a box plot changes it to a compound box plot, where a single graph frame contains boxes for each group.

Descriptive Statistics
Split By: Gender

	Weight, Total	Weight, male	Weight, female
Mean	158.653	169.282	127.208
Std. Dev.	28.389	23.288	16.208
Std. Error	2.913	2.764	3.308
Count	95	71	24
Minimum	107.000	107.000	110.000
Maximum	234.000	234.000	190.000
# Missing	0	0	0

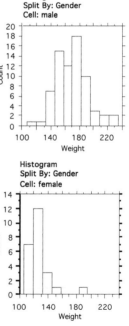

For other analyses, Split By produces **multiple** tables or graphs for each group. For example, adding a Split By variable to a frequency distribution analysis produces separate summary tables and histograms for each group.

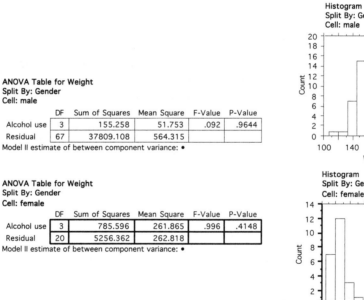

ANOVA Table for Weight
Split By: Gender
Cell: male

	DF	Sum of Squares	Mean Square	F-Value	P-Value
Alcohol use	3	155.258	51.753	.092	.9644
Residual	67	37809.108	564.315		

Model II estimate of between component variance: •

ANOVA Table for Weight
Split By: Gender
Cell: female

	DF	Sum of Squares	Mean Square	F-Value	P-Value
Alcohol use	3	785.596	261.865	.996	.4148
Residual	20	5256.362	262.818		

Model II estimate of between component variance: •

For information on how each analysis uses split-by variables, see the *StatView Reference* chapter for that analysis.

Control recalculations

Analysis results and their data are dynamically linked, and results update immediately to reflect any changes you make to the dataset. You can turn this link off temporarily by turning off (unchecking) the Recalculate control in the upper left corner of the view window.

When recalculate is on (checked), all tables and graphs are recalculated when:

1. you change the value of a variable in use

2. you delete a variable in use

3. you add, delete, or clear data rows

4. you apply a criteria to the dataset

5. you add or remove variables

6. you change the sort order of the dataset (only affects certain analyses)

If you plan to make several changes to analyses or variables, it is a good idea to turn off recalculation. This way, you can make your changes without waiting for recalculation after each change.

Force recalculation

Uncheck (turn off) and then Control-click (Windows) or Command-click (Macintosh) the Recalculate checkbox to force recalculation of *all* analyses. Ordinarily, turning on Recalculate just recalculates those results whose data have changed.

Cancel calculations

Anytime the cursor is a spinning yin-yang (☯), you can cancel the operation by typing Esc (Windows) or Command-Period (Macintosh).

Recalculate in the background

You can use other applications while your analysis calculates. StatView can perform calculation in the background, so you can switch to another application.

Placeholder results

StatView ensures that all results appearing on the screen are consistent with the current analyses, variables and state of the dataset. If recalculate is on and the analysis or data are changed, all tables and graphs are updated. However, if recalculate is not on and the analysis or data change, tables and graphs are replaced with placeholders until you turn recalculate on. A placeholder is an empty graph or a box with an X in it.

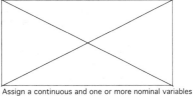

ANOVA Table for <None>

Assign a continuous and one or more nominal variables
using the variable browser Add button.

Analysis windows

In this section, we discuss the windows you will use when analyzing data in StatView: the view window, the variable browser, and the results browser. Each of these windows has controls for creating and changing analyses.

View window

StatView builds and displays analyses in a special view window. A **view window** is a living document window for both graphs and text tables, with an analysis browser for creating analyses on the left and Edit Analysis and Edit Display buttons for modifying results along the top. The document area scrolls both vertically and horizontally to provide as much room as you need for a complete presentation.

For a self-guided tour of the view window:

• From the Analyze menu, select For Beginners/View Window Intro

Or, to open a new, empty view window:

• From the Analyze menu, select New View
(Or in any open dataset, double-click the empty rectangle before the first variable name.)

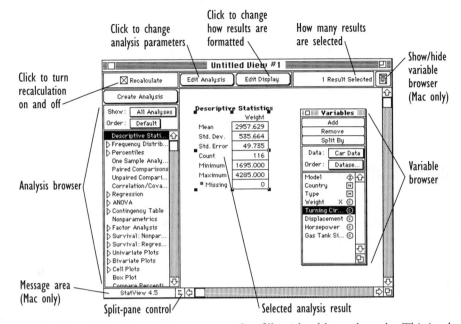

Click to change
analysis parameters

Click to change
how results are
formatted

How many results
are selected

Show/hide
variable
browser
(Mac only)

Click to turn
recalculation
on and off

Analysis browser

Variable
browser

Message area
(Mac only)

Split-pane control

Selected analysis result

Most of the view window is an empty page area that fills with tables and graphs. This is where you'll build statistical analysis tables, draw graphs, and put together presentations. Think of this part of the view window as your paper.

View window controls

The view window is a normal window. You can move it, resize it, and scroll it the same way as any other window.

The Recalculate button at the top of the window lets you control how results **recalculate**, or update to reflect changes in the dataset. Recalculate is checked on by default. If you want to suspend calculations temporarily (perhaps you need to edit several variables and don't want to wait for dozens of tables and graphs to recalculate), just uncheck Recalculate—click it to turn it off; see "Control recalculations," p. 138.

The Edit Analysis button lets you change the parameters of an analysis; see "Edit Analysis," p. 134. The Edit Display button lets you change how results are formatted and drawn; see "Edit Display," p. 135.

Near the upper right corner, a note tells you whether any results are selected and, if so, how many. If no results are selected, the area is blank. Knowing whether results are selected is important when you are creating new analyses, because new analyses adopt variable assignments from any selected results; see "Determine whether results are selected," p. 133.

The status bar (Windows) or the area underneath the analysis browser tells what StatView is doing at the moment.

View window preferences

You can set preferences to customize view windows to suit your style of working. See "View preferences," p. 232.

Analysis browser

StatView's analyses are listed in the **analysis browser.** The analysis browser lets you create analyses.

The sigma $\boxed{\Sigma}$ in the lower left corner of the view window is a split-pane control; click and drag it to resize the browser pane. Double-click it or click and drag $\boxed{\Sigma}$ all the way left to close the analysis browser pane. When closed, the split-pane control is a right arrow $\boxed{\rightarrow}$; double-click or click and drag $\boxed{\rightarrow}$ to reopen the browser pane. A preference lets you choose whether the analysis browser pane is open or closed by default; see "Application preferences," p. 225.

To create an analysis, just select the analysis from the analysis browser, then click the Create Analysis button.

Analyses with triangle controls ($\triangleright$) can produce more than one type of **results** or output. Click a triangle to tip it downward ($\triangledown$) and reveal a list of possible results. Some even have subcategories of possible results. The triangle controls let you show or hide levels of detail, as seen in the picture below.

For example, Frequency Distribution analysis can produce summary tables, histograms, Z-score (standardized) histograms, and pie charts.

QC Subgroup Measurements is a more complex example. It has four categories of measurements (Xbar, R, S, and CUSUM Statistics) and a Summary Table. Each category produces several types of results: line charts, needle charts, bar charts, point charts, and results tables.

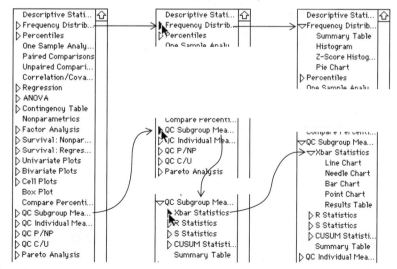

Control-click (Windows) or Command-click (Macintosh) any triangle to tip all triangle controls up or down in one step.

If you select the heading of an item with a triangle control, you get the default results for that analysis. (To determine what those results are, just tip the triangle downward and see what is highlighted when you select the heading.)

Show

In the middle part of the browser, a Show pop-up menu lets you select which types of analyses to show in the browser. All analyses are shown by default.

Basic Statistics and Graphs Only simplify the most common analyses by reducing clutter. They also speed the process by automatically using the default analysis parameters rather than presenting a dialog box for you to specify parameters. You can still change the parameters with Edit Analysis button; see "Edit Analysis," p. 134.

Survival Analysis and Quality Control restricts your choices to those analyses, since specialists using those analyses may not need StatView's more general routines.

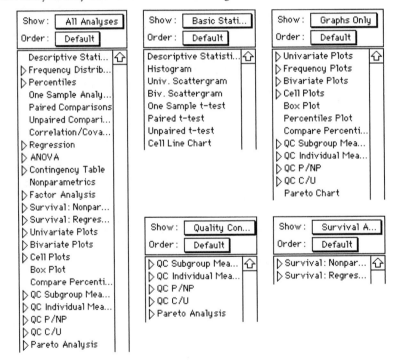

Order

An Order pop-up menu lets you choose how to sort analysis items in the scrolling list. Your Order choice has no effect on how analyses are created.

Create analysis

For multiple-results items (items with triangle controls), you can select any combination of one or more results. Click an analysis heading (a triangle item) to select the default results for that analysis; it doesn't matter whether the list is shown or hidden. Shift-click or click and drag to select several adjacent results items. Control-click (Windows) or Command-click (Macintosh) to select several nonadjacent items.

You can even select items from completely different types of analyses, e.g., you could Control-click (Windows) or Command-click (Macintosh) to select Histogram from Frequency Distribution and Line Chart from QC Subgroup Measurements/Xbar Statistics.

To perform an analysis, select it in the browser and click the Create Analysis button, or double-click the item in the browser. Most selections are followed by a dialog box in which you set parameters for the analysis; if you know you want the default parameters, you can bypass the dialog box by Right-clicking (Windows) or Control-clicking (Macintosh) Create analysis. Another way to bypass the dialog box is to choose Basic Statistics or Graphs Only from the Show pop-up menu, but doing so also limits you to those analyses.

Variable browser

Variables in the dataset are listed in the variable browser, a floating window that appears alongside both dataset and view windows. When you are working in a view window, the variable browser allows you to:

1. Choose variables from open datasets and open new datasets
2. Assign variables to analyses (and specify what role they should play in analyses)
3. Remove variables from analyses
4. Split analyses into separate results for each group in a nominal variable

To show or hide the variable browser, select Variable Browser from the View menu (Windows) or select Variables from the Window menu, or click the 📑 button in the upper right corner of the dataset and view windows(Macintosh). A preference lets you choose whether the variable browser is shown or hidden by default; see "Application preferences," p. 225.

In the middle part of the browser, a Data pop-up menu lets you select among open datasets or open other datasets. Click on the menu to choose another open dataset, and choose Other to locate and open a previously saved dataset.

The Order pop-up menu lets you choose how to sort variable names in the scrolling list:

Dataset order	The order in which variables appear in the dataset's columns (left to right).
Alphabetical	Alphanumeric order by variable name.
Variable class	Grouped in order by continuous, nominal, informative.
Usage	Ordered first by variable use in analyses and then in alphabetical order. When a dataset window is active, ordering is only alphabetical.

Variables are shown in a scrolling list. Icons next to variable names indicate their data class: ⓒ for continuous, Ⓝ for nominal, and ◇ for informative.

Compact variables are preceded by a triangle ▷ and followed by a ⓒ symbol. Click the triangle to tip it downward ▽ and display the category of the variable. These categories are marked nominal Ⓝ.

▷ Effectiveness ⓒ   ▽Effectiveness ⓒ
                              Time   Ⓝ

Assignment buttons

Each analysis requires certain variables before it can calculate. Notes below empty (placeholder) results tell you what is expected. For example, a box plot coaches you, "To complete this analysis, assign at least one continuous variable using the variable browser Add Button." *StatView Reference* chapters detail the variable requirements of each analysis.

Add assigns variables to analyses and **Remove** removes them.

The buttons at the top of the variable browser change according to the analysis you choose. For most analyses, you use these three buttons:

```
┌─░░░░ Variables ░░░░─┐
│ ┌─────────────────┐ │
│ │      Add        │ │
│ ├─────────────────┤ │
│ │    Remove       │ │
│ ├─────────────────┤ │
│ │    Split By     │ │
│ └─────────────────┘ │
└─────────────────────┘
```

For most analyses, StatView determines each variable's role from its class—continuous or nominal. For example, you add both continuous and nominal variables to an ANOVA, and StatView knows that the continuous variable should be the dependent variable and the nominal variables are independent variables (or "factors"). StatView's ability to assign roles automatically is one of the many benefits of setting attributes for each variable in the dataset; see "Set attributes," p. 58.)

However, some analyses have buttons that assign variables to specific roles in an analysis. For example, for bivariate plots, you need to assign an **X Variable** for the horizontal axis and a **Y Variable** for the vertical axis. For regressions, you need to specify a **Dependent** variable and one or more **Independent** variables. Otherwise, StatView would have no way of knowing what you intend. These and other specialized buttons are discussed for each type of analysis in *StatView Reference*.

Split By shows results separately for each group of a nominal variable, or each subgroup defined by two or more nominal variables. You can split any analysis. For example, if you have a Gender variable that divides your dataset into male and female groups, assigning Gender as a Split By variable in a box plot produces separate boxes for males and females (in many cases it also produces results for the total sample). You can Remove a Split By assignment to stop analyzing groups separately.

Assign variables

All variable browser buttons work the same way.

• Select one or more variables

• Click the appropriate button to assign the variable(s)

Shift-click or click and drag to select several adjacent variables. Control-click (Windows) or Command-click (Macintosh) to select several nonadjacent variables.

Shortcut Double-click a variable to assign it to the default role—this is equivalent to clicking the topmost button, whatever that may be. See the Shortcuts card for tips on making other types of variable assignments.

Usage markers

When a variable is assigned to an analysis, and that analysis is selected in the view, a usage marker in the variable browser indicates which role the variable is playing. For example, this browser shows that in the selected analysis, Age is the Y variable, Weight is the X variable, and the analysis is split by Gender groups. Other variables have no usage markers because they are not involved in the analysis.

```
Name            ◈
Gender       S  N
Age          Y  ©
Weight       X  ©
Cholesterol     ©
Triglycerides   ©
HDL             ©
```

If you select a different result in the view, the usage markers change accordingly. Following are some common usage markers you might see:

X	A continuous variable in any analysis
	An independent variable or covariate in a regression
	An X (horizontal axis) variable in a bivariate plot
	A nominal variable in a frequency distribution or descriptive statistics
Y	A dependent variable in a regression or ANOVA
	A Y (vertical axis) variable in a bivariate plot
G	A grouping or factor variable
S	A Split By variable
F	An independent variable or covariate forced into a stepwise regression
C	An item count variable for QC P/NP charts
	A unit count variable for QC C/U charts
	A censor variable for Survival analysis
T	A time to event variable for Survival analysis
#	A stratification variable for Survival analysis
!	A variable playing multiple roles (usually because more than one result is selected)

If no result is selected in the view, any usage markers indicate any preassignments for a pending analysis (where you select an analysis in the analysis browser and then assign variables in the variable browser before clicking Create Analysis in the analysis browser).

Number of variables

Some analyses can handle any number of variables. Some accept only a specific number. Still others can handle multiple variables with one usage, but only a single variable of another usage. The number of variables an analysis requires is the determining factor in what happens when new variables are assigned to an existing analysis.

For example, an unpaired *t*-test requires a single continuous and a single nominal grouping variable. What happens if you assign another continuous variable to the analysis? A new, separate analysis is generated that performs a t-test on the new continuous variable using the groups identified by the original nominal variable. The result appears as an additional table in the view. On the other hand, a descriptive statistics table and a correlation matrix analyze multiple variables. As you assign new variables, the tables simply expand to include the new variables. For examples of how this works, see "Multiple and compound results," p. 135

To understand what will happen when you assign new variables to an analysis, you need to know the number and class of variables it requires. See the *StatView Reference* chapter for the data requirements of each analysis.

You can force additional variables to appear in their own tables or graphs by cloning an analysis (see below) rather than simply adding variables to an existing analysis.

Clone analyses

One shortcut for creating subsequent analyses is to **clone** an analysis: to make another set of results using the same analysis parameters but different variables. To clone an analysis:

- Select a result in the view
- Select one or more variables in the browser
- Control-Shift-click (Windows) or Command-Shift-click (Macintosh) the appropriate browser button, such as Add

An example of this appears earlier in the chapter; see "Exercise," p. 132.

Shortcut Control-Shift-double-click (Windows) or Command-Shift-double-click (Macintosh) variables to clone an analysis with default (topmost button) roles.

Analyze variables in several datasets

The variable browser's Data pop-up menu lets you choose among several open datasets. Using this pop-up menu, you can assign variables from several different datasets to a single analysis. If you assign variables of different lengths (i.e., if you assign variables from datasets with different numbers of rows), StatView does the following to compensate:

- Variables with fewer values are padded with missing values at the end so that all variables have the same number of cases.
- The excluded rows are the union of the excluded rows for the datasets which contain the variables. For example if variable A comes from dataset A with rows 3 and 4 excluded, and variable B comes from dataset B with rows 7 and 8 excluded, rows 3, 4, 7 and 8 will be excluded from each analysis that uses both variables.

Two analyses are exceptions to these rules—descriptive statistics and one sample analyses (only if you do not have split-by variables assigned). For these two analyses, no missing values are padded and the exclusion applies to each variable individually. If you do have split-by variables assigned, they calculate the same as other analyses.

Results browser

Results in the view window are listed in the results browser, a floating window that appears alongside the view window. If a view contains a great deal of output or you are working with several views at once, the results browser makes it easy to keep track of what you have done, what is currently selected and where particular results are located. The results browser allows you to:

1. Choose open views and open saved views

2. Locate graphs and tables by location, analysis, or variable

3. Select results one or many at a time

The results browser is closed by default. To open it (if it is closed) or bring it to the front (if it is hidden), select Results Browser from the View menu (Windows) or select Results from the Window menu (Macintosh). A preference lets you choose whether the results browser is shown or hidden by default; see "Application preferences," p. 225.

The View pop-up menu lets you select among open views or open other views. The name of the currently active view is shown. Click on the menu to choose another open view, and choose Other to locate and open a previously saved view.

The Order pop-up menu lets you choose how to sort result names in the scrolling list. By Analysis sorts results according to the type of analysis. By location sorts results by page, in order of appearance in the view. By variable sorts results according to the variables assigned to them (analyses involving more than one variable are listed multiple times in the browser—once for each variable). Changing browser order has no effect on the order of objects in the view itself.

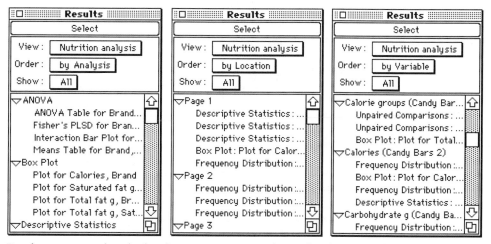

Results are grouped under headings appropriate to the Order chosen. Each heading has a triangle control ($\triangledown$). Click a triangle to tip it upward ($\triangleright$) and hide its results. Control-click

(Windows) or Command-click (Macintosh) any triangle to tip all triangle controls up or down in one step.

The Show pop-up menu lets you choose whether to list all results in a view or only selected results. Since selection plays such an important role in the analysis process, knowing what is currently selected helps you understand what will happen when you create a new analysis or assign or remove variables.

Select results

The Select button at the top of the results browser lets you select and scroll to results in a view.

• Select one or more result titles

• Click Select

Shift-click or click and drag to select several adjacent results. Control-click (Windows) or Command-click (Macintosh) to select nonadjacent results. Selecting a heading is equivalent to selecting all the items under the heading.

Shortcut Double-clicking an item is the same as selecting it and clicking the Select button.

When you click Select in the results browser, the view window scrolls to that result (or the first result, if you selected several) and selects the object or objects, and you can work with them all at once—clone them, change their variables, delete them, or whatever you need to do. Thus, the results browser can speed up your editing.

For example, if you have several dozen results involving a key variable, and you want to make them all green, you could use the results browser ordered by variable, select the heading for that variable, click Select, and then select green for the foreground color in the Draw palette to change them all at once.

Also, in a view with many tables and graphs, it might not be easy to find the one you want. The results browser lets you move to the result you want quickly.

View (Windows only) and Window menu

The View and Window menus (Windows) or Window menu (Macintosh) help you keep track of all the windows you have open and makes it easy to switch between them.

(Both Macintosh and Windows) The Window menu lists all open datasets, views, and any open Formula, Series, Random Numbers, Recode, and Create Criteria dialog boxes in front to back order. The active view or dataset window has a check mark next to it. The Window menu also has standard commands for managing windows.

(Windows only) The View menu lists:

1. Tool Bar

2. Status Bar

3. Show/Hide Browsers

4. Variable Browser

5. Results Browser

6. Draw Palette

7. Hints Window

(Macintosh only) The Window menu also lists:

1. The variable browser and results browser

2. The Hints window

3. The Clipboard

Analyze subsets

Thus far, we've discussed how to analyze all the rows of your dataset at once. We've shown how to use Split By to get separate calculations for each group of a nominal variable, or each subgroup from several nominal variables, and we've shown a variety of other analysis controls in StatView's view windows.

Sometimes, you want even more control over the data used in analyses. For example, rather than analyzing males and females in Lipid Data separately, you might want to analyze just males. StatView's dataset windows offer still more ways to focus analyses by controlling the data that go into them.

1. Sort the dataset according to the values of one or more variables. See "Sort data," p. 116. For example, if you draw a line plot connecting Weight values graphed against Age values, you're likely to get a chaotic mess of criss-crossed lines; however, if you sort the data according to increasing Age values, the lines fall into place and become meaningful.

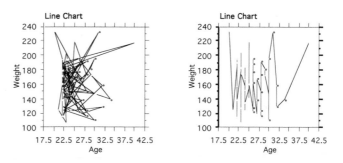

2. Use Include Row and/or Exclude Row to control on a row-by-row basis which rows are used in calculations. See "Include and exclude rows," p. 108. For example, the line chart above has a few outliers with extreme Age values; these commands let you remove those rows from analyses without removing them from your dataset.

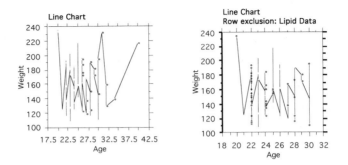

3. Use Criteria to choose by logical expression which rows are used in calculations. See "Create criteria," p. 124. For example, you might *instead* restrict your line chart to cases whose Weight values are under 200 pounds by applying a criterion "Weight ≤ 200." Again, you remove rows from analyses but not from the dataset itself. (You can also *combine* Include/Exclude and Criteria rules.)

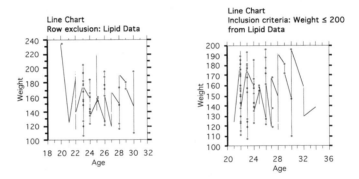

Exercise

The exercise below demonstrates the interaction of the analysis and variable browsers and analysis objects.

Create an analysis, then assign variables

Creating an analysis from scratch is a simple, two step process involving the variable and analysis browsers. To create any analysis, you must select an item from the analysis browser and assign variables to it from the variable browser. You can use the browsers in either order. Try both and use whichever feels more comfortable.

- Open Car Data from the Sample Data folder
- From the Analyze menu, select New View

First, select an analysis from the analysis browser, then assign variables from the variable browser. If you are interested in the degree of correlation among several continuous variables in this dataset, a good place to begin your analysis is with a correlation matrix.

- From the analysis browser, select Correlation/Covariance and click Create Analysis
- Accept the default parameters: click OK

An empty table placeholder (X-box) appears and says that you still need to specify variables.

- In the variable browser, click and drag to select Turning Circle, Displacement, Horsepower, and Gas Tank Size

- Click Add

The analysis calculates and the table updates to show its results.

Correlation Matrix

	Turning Circle	Displacement	Horsepower	Gas Tank Size
Turning Circle	1.000	.747	.482	.618
Displacement	.747	1.000	.764	.719
Horsepower	.482	.764	1.000	.666
Gas Tank Size	.618	.719	.666	1.000

116 observations were used in this computation.

Assign variables, then create an analysis

This time you assign variables first, and then create the analysis. (We add another result to the same view.)

- Make sure that no results are selected (have black selection handles) by clicking in empty space of the view
- In the analysis browser, select Regression

Notice that the variable browser automatically replaces the Add button with Independent and Dependent buttons. You use these buttons to assign variables and specify variable usage simultaneously.

☐ **Variables**
Independent
Dependent
Remove
Split By

- In the variable browser, select Displacement and click Independent
- Select Horsepower and click Dependent

X and Y usage markers in the variable browser now show the roles Displacement and Horsepower will play.

- In the analysis browser, click Create Analysis
- Accept the default parameter settings: click OK

The default regression output appears in the view.

Regression Summary
Horsepower vs. Displacement

Count	116
Num. Missing	0
R	.764
R Squared	.584
Adjusted R Squared	.580
RMS Residual	25.796

ANOVA Table
Horsepower vs. Displacement

	DF	Sum of Squares	Mean Square	F-Value	P-Value
Regression	1	106510.675	106510.675	160.061	<.0001
Residual	114	75859.765	665.437		
Total	115	182370.440			

Regression Coefficients
Horsepower vs. Displacement

	Coefficient	Std. Error	Std. Coeff.	t-Value	P-Value
Intercept	50.444	6.744	50.444	7.480	<.0001
Displacement	.504	.040	.764	12.652	<.0001

Add more results

You generated only the default results for a simple regression. Regression has a triangle next to it in the analysis browser, indicating that several tables and graphs are available as output. In this exercise, you add additional output from the regression analysis to the default results.

- Click the triangle next to Regression

Now you can see all the output available for a regression analysis. There are nine results in the indented list. We also want to see a regression plot for the analysis.

- Make sure at least one of the regression results is still selected (has black handles); if not, click one to select it
- In the analysis browser, double-click Regression Plot

A scattergram of the two variables and the calculated regression line appears.

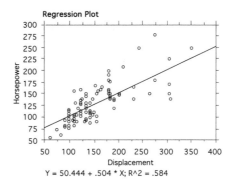

Y = 50.444 + .504 * X; R^2 = .584

Because you had regression results selected, StatView already knew the appropriate analysis parameters and variable assignments you wanted. (If you double-click Regression Plot with no results selected, you have to set analysis parameters again and assign variables again.)

Some analysts like to see every possible result for an analysis all at once—for example, regression and ANOVA tables, plots, interaction plots, residuals, and confidence intervals. Others prefer to look at just a few key results and then decide whether the analysis deserves further examination; they might try several different variable combinations before finding a satisfactory model and only then will they start looking at residual statistics. StatView accommodates either style of work. Start by choosing as many or as few results you want, and then add more results when you want them. By selecting one of the results, you save yourself the trouble of rebuilding the model.

Add variables to existing analyses

Many analyses can incorporate multiple variables in a single analysis. For example, if you select the correlation analysis created above, you can add more variables to the matrix.

- Select the correlation matrix by clicking on it
- In the variable browser, select Weight and click Add

The correlation matrix immediately recalculates:

Correlation Matrix

	Turning Circle	Displacement	Horsepower	Gas Tank Size	Weight
Turning Circle	1.000	.747	.482	.618	.752
Displacement	.747	1.000	.764	.719	.830
Horsepower	.482	.764	1.000	.666	.707
Gas Tank Size	.618	.719	.666	1.000	.847
Weight	.752	.830	.707	.847	1.000

116 observations were used in this computation.

Other analyses compute new results for additional variables. These new results automatically retain the analysis parameters but produce separate results. The simple regression analysis created above is such an analysis.

Select any of the three regression tables or the regression plot you created above. The next variable you assign will use these same analysis parameters.

- In the variable browser, select Weight and click Independent

A completely new regression analysis uses Horsepower as the dependent variable and Weight as the new independent variable. The same four regression results are created (Regression Summary, ANOVA Table, Regression Coefficients and Regression Plot), and the same parameter choices are used. Here we show just the new summary table:

Regression Summary
Horsepower vs. Weight

Count	116
Num. Missing	0
R	.707
R Squared	.499
Adjusted R Squared	.495
RMS Residual	28.299

Selecting an existing result saved you the trouble of reassigning Horsepower as the dependent variable and clicking OK in the Regression dialog box. Any selected analysis forwards information to a new analysis.

Adopt variables for new analyses

The variables in a selected result can be used in a completely different analysis, just as they can be used to create additional output for the same analysis.

- Click to select the correlation matrix previously created
- In the analysis browser, double-click Frequency Distribution
- Accept the default dialog box settings: click OK

The default output for frequency distribution appears in the view. (Your results appear in a single vertical column in the view. We rearrange them to conserve space.)

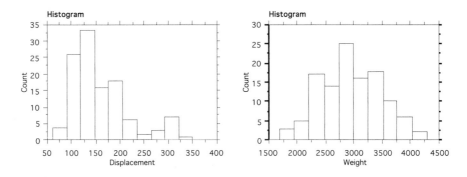

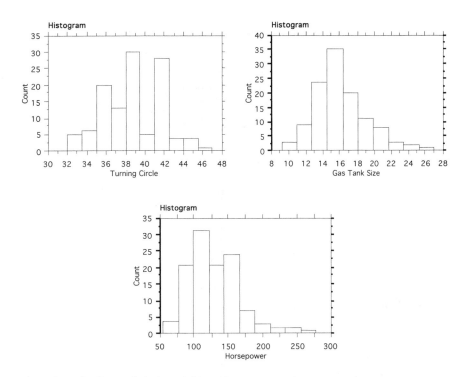

Any selected results forward their variable assignments to the next results you create.

Split analyses by groups

You can break results down by groups of a nominal variable without reorganizing your dataset. (Note that StatView also allows you to set criteria to restrict analyses to a subset of your dataset. See "Create criteria," p. 124.)

To try this, you can split the correlation matrix into separate matrices for each country.

- Click to select the correlation matrix previously created
- In the variable browser, select Country and click Split By

Now you have a separate correlation matrix for each country represented in the dataset:

Correlation Matrix
Split By: Country
Cell: Japan

	Turning Circle	Displacement	Horsepower	Gas Tank Size	Weight
Turning Circle	1.000	.760	.649	.752	.738
Displacement	.760	1.000	.944	.932	.920
Horsepower	.649	.944	1.000	.864	.822
Gas Tank Size	.752	.932	.864	1.000	.908
Weight	.738	.920	.822	.908	1.000

30 observations were used in this computation.

Correlation Matrix
Split By: Country
Cell: Other

	Turning Circle	Displacement	Horsepower	Gas Tank Size	Weight
Turning Circle	1.000	.448	.313	.564	.603
Displacement	.448	1.000	.845	.791	.859
Horsepower	.313	.845	1.000	.768	.748
Gas Tank Size	.564	.791	.768	1.000	.786
Weight	.603	.859	.748	.786	1.000

37 observations were used in this computation.

Correlation Matrix
Split By: Country
Cell: USA

	Turning Circle	Displacement	Horsepower	Gas Tank Size	Weight
Turning Circle	1.000	.679	.450	.581	.765
Displacement	.679	1.000	.801	.658	.793
Horsepower	.450	.801	1.000	.432	.545
Gas Tank Size	.581	.658	.432	1.000	.845
Weight	.765	.793	.545	.845	1.000

49 observations were used in this computation.

This is how easy it is to calculate statistics for different subgroups of your data. It is a flexible and interactive process, and it follows the way you think. Best of all, you do not need to touch your dataset.

Save a view

You can save a view at any time:

- From the File menu, select Save or Save As
- Specify a filename and folder location
- Choose a file format
- Click Save

As a view

When you save a view in the default format (*.SVV for Windows or StatView 4.1+ View for Macintosh), you save all aspects of your work — the analyses, the variables used, anything you have drawn, etc. When you reopen the view using Open from the File menu, you can resume your work right where you left off.

If you save a view whose dataset is untitled (because you have not saved it), StatView cannot find the dataset when you later reopen the view. For that reason, StatView warns that you should save the dataset first.

If you close a dataset whose variables are used in open views, those variables are removed from the results. StatView warns you and gives you a chance to cancel closing the dataset.

As a template

You can use any view you save as a template. See the next chapter, "Templates," p. 161.

If you plan to use the view as a template, consider saving it in the Template folder (Windows) or StatView Templates folder (Macintosh) or a subfolder of that folder. You can then access it from the Analyze menu. A view stored elsewhere can be opened as a template through Open View As from the File menu; see "Assign different variables," p. 158.

To save disk space, you might prefer not to save calculated results with a view you plan to use as a template. See "View preferences," p. 232.

As a text file

You can save views as plain ASCII text files for use with word processors such as Microsoft Word. Text files contain all the text and data from tables but only the titles and notes of graphs.

As a PICT file

(Macintosh only) You can also save views as PICT files for use in drawing or painting applications, as well as some word processing applications. Such files contain a PICT representation of all the information in the view (tables, graphs, all text and drawn objects).

As a WMF or EMF file

(Windows only) You can also save views as WMF or EMF files for use in drawing or painting applications, as well as some word processing applications. Such files contain a metafile representation of all the information in the view (tables, graphs, all text and drawn objects).

Reopen your work

You can reopen any view you save.

- From the File menu, select either Open *or* Open View As (see below)
- Select a view file
- Click Open

Use original variables

To open your work exactly as you left it, select Open from the File menu. Open reopens the view in its own window, with its original variable assignments.

Assign different variables

To open a view with different variables, either from the same dataset or from a new dataset, select Open View As from the File menu.

When you open a view using Open View As, StatView asks whether to use the original dataset or a different dataset, whether to add the view's results to a new view window or the current (topmost) view window, and whether to offer you a chance to Assign Variables differently:

```
═════════════ Opening a View ═════════════

This view should:
  ⊙ Open original dataset(s)
  ○ Be applied to different dataset(s)
Where should work go?
  ⊙ Create new view     ○ Add to top view

  ☐ Always show Assign Variables dialog box

        [ Cancel ]      [  OK  ]
```

Open original dataset   This choice opens the dataset(s) the view uses. Usually StatView can find the original dataset, even if it has been renamed or moved. If not, StatView asks you to find the dataset.

Be applied to different dataset(s)   This choice lets you select a different dataset, so you can use the view as a template for different data.

Create new view   This choice displays the results in a new view window.

Add to top view   This choice places the results at the end of the topmost (current) view window, after all existing tables and graphs. If no views are open, this choice is dimmed.

Always show Assign Variables dialog box   Check (turn on) this option when you want to use the view as a template for different data.

From the original dataset

If you want to use the original dataset but make different variable assignments, check Always show the Assign Variables dialog box (turn the option on). The dialog box shows the original assignments. Drag variables back and forth between the assignment slots and the scrolling list until you have the assignments you want.

```
╔═══════════════════════════════════════════════════════════════╗
║ ▒▒▒▒▒▒▒ Assign Uariables for "Nutrition analysis" ▒▒▒▒▒▒▒     ║
║ Please double click or drag the desired uariables into the proper slots ║
║ in the template.                                              ║
║    Template:                         Uariables:              ║
║    Calorie groups:              ⇧     Data:  │ Candy Bars 2 │ ║
║   Ⓜ│Calorie groups        │          Order: │ Dataset order │║
║    Total fat g:                      Name              ⬖ ⇧   ║
║   ⓒ│▒▒▒▒▒▒▒▒▒▒▒▒▒▒▒▒▒│            Serving/pkg       ⓒ ▓     ║
║              ▲                       Oz/pkg            ⓒ     ║
║    Cholesterol g:                    Calories      M  ⓒ     ║
║   ⓒ│                 │               Total fat g       ⓒ     ║
║    Saturated fat g:                  Saturated fat g   ⓒ     ║
║   ⓒ│                 │               Cholesterol g     ⓒ     ║
║    Sugars g:                         │Sodium mg     │  ⓒ     ║
║   ⓒ│Sugars g        │ ⬇            Carbohudrate g M ⓒ⬇     ║
║                              ( Cancel )      (( OK ))       ║
║                                                          ◳  ║
╚═══════════════════════════════════════════════════════════════╝
```

From different datasets

You can assign variables from different datasets in one of two ways.

The first method is to choose Be applied to different dataset. StatView asks you to open the dataset and then presents the Assign Variables dialog box.

The second method is easier when you want to use variables from several datasets including the original one. Choose Open original dataset, but check Always show Assign Variables dialog box. You can then use the Data pop-up menu in the Assign Variables dialog box to select different datasets.

The Assign Variables dialog box lists all the variables in the dataset, and all the variable slots that need to be filled for this view. You assign variables from the variables list into slots by dragging or double-clicking. See the next chapter, "Templates," p. 161.

Print a view

You can print the contents of a view. Before you print, scroll through the view to see whether any tables, graphs, or drawn objects fall on a page break. Page breaks are shown by red hashed lines. You can avoid splitting results across page breaks by fixing them yourself or by having StatView fix them for you:

• From the Layout menu, select Clean Up Items
• Click Clean Up

Another thing to check is the number and configuration of pages in your document. Use Drawing Size from the Layout menu to set the size and shape of the overall document. This determines how many pages will be printed.

Check Print and copy lines at 1/4 width in the View Preferences dialog box to reduce all line widths to approximately 1/4 of their specified size. See "View preferences," p. 232. This option affects only printed and copied results; there is no discernible difference on the screen.

To print a view:

- From the File menu, select Print

Templates

StatView view documents—collections of completed analyses and annotations—are two documents in one:

1. You can reopen a view and its original dataset(s) to resume analysis where you left off. You can continue working with analysis objects (tables or graphs), which are still linked to their dataset. You can add and remove variables, clone and adopt to build new results, and use drawing and formatting tools to put results together in a complete presentation.

2. You can open a view and apply it as a template to a different dataset. A **template** is a collection of one or more analyses and all their data links, parameter settings, layout, and all other visible characteristics *except* variable assignments. You simply assign new variables to use throughout the template, and StatView computes all the results at once.

Views saved in the Template folder (Windows) or StatView Templates folder (Macintosh) are listed in the Analyze menu for fast, easy use as templates.

How does opening a view differ from applying a template?

Opening a view is the same as opening a document created in any program. In Excel, you reopen a document and resume working on your spreadsheet. In Word, you reopen your document and resume writing and editing. In StatView, you reopen a view and continue working with your analysis results.

Applying a template is more like opening a stationery document in Word or Excel, where the page is blank, but certain things such as your company name and address, margins, headers, and font choices are set up. But StatView goes even further: a template sets up the analyses, formatting, annotations, and everything for any number of analyses and variables. For example, you could do an entire drug study, save the view, and then reopen it with data for a different drug. You specify which new variable is like each old variable, and then StatView redoes the whole analysis with those substitutions.

How can I use templates?

Because a template is simply a view document that is opened a certain way, building a template is simple: you just build a view the usual way, make any formatting changes and annotations you want, and save it. If you want to use it from the Analyze menu, save it in the Template folder (Windows) or StatView Templates folder (Macintosh). To use a view saved in other location as a template, select Open View As from the File menu.

Templates let you do several things:

1. Create any analysis without using the analysis browser or variable browser. StatView has numerous pre-built templates that perform the analyses in the analysis browser and many other special combinations of analyses suited for particular tasks. You select templates from an hierarchical Analyze menu. You can add your own templates to the menu, and you can reorganize the hierarchy of the Analyze menu to suit your needs.

2. Combine different types of analyses into sets you can compute all at once. For example, you might build your own template combining QC charts, histograms, cell plots, and your own special ANOVA model. Then you can use the template to do these analyses with each new dataset.

3. Replay complex sequences of analyses, graphs, annotations, and formatting choices consistently and effortlessly. If you have to produce the same sales report each month, build the report once, save the view, and reuse it as a template with each month's new sales numbers.

4. Harness the expertise of a consultant. You can take a problem to a specialist who can assemble the appropriate analyses in a template that you can use over and over again.

5. Build analyses that others can repeat error-free, without your assistance. All they need to learn is how to open the template and assign the right variables.

Use templates

Templates reduce analyses of any complexity to two simple steps: you select a template, then you assign variables. StatView does the rest.

If a view window is the active (topmost) window, template results appear in the window below (after) any previous results. If some other type of window is topmost or if no view is open, template results automatically appear in a new view window.

- If you want to add results to an existing view, make that view the active window
- From the Analyze menu, select a template
- Drag variables from the browser on the right into the assignment slots on the left
  (If necessary, use the Data pop-up menu to open a dataset or choose among open datasets.)
- Click OK

Assign variables to templates

After you select a template, you must assign variables. Fill each assignment slot in the left side of the Assign Variables dialog box by dragging a variable from the browser on the right.

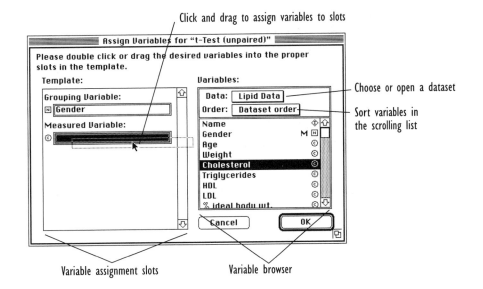

Click and drag to assign variables to slots

Choose or open a dataset

Sort variables in the scrolling list

Variable assignment slots

Variable browser

Variable browser

Use the Data pop-up menu to select among open datasets. The name of the currently active dataset is shown. Click on the menu to choose another open dataset, and choose Other to locate and open a previously saved dataset.

Use the Order pop-up menu to choose how to sort variable names in the scrolling list:

Dataset order	The order in which variables appear in the dataset's columns (left to right).
Alphabetical	Alphabetical order by variable name, with nonalphabetic names first.
Variable class	Grouped in order by continuous, nominal, and informative.
Usage	Variables already mapped to assignment slots appear at the top; remaining variables appear in alphabetical order.

Variables appear in a scrolling list. Icons next to variable names indicate their data class: ⓒ for continuous and Ⓝ for nominal. (Informative (◈) variables are not listed, because you cannot assign informative variables to analyses or templates.)

Compact variables have triangle controls ▷ and ⓒ symbols. Click the triangle to tip it downward ▽ and display the category of the variable, marked nominal Ⓝ.

▷ Effectiveness ⓒ   ▽ Effectiveness ⓒ
                         Time   Ⓝ

An M usage marker appears next to any variable that has been mapped to an assignment slot.

Template list

Labeled slots in the Template list show the various roles variables play in the template. Hints for each slot tell how the variable(s) are used.

Icons to the left of each slot indicate which class the variable(s) must have: ⓒ for continuous, Ⓝ for nominal, and ✳ for compact. Since markers in the variable browser show which class each variable has, it is easy to match variables to slots correctly. You cannot put a nominal variable in a continuous slot, or a continuous variable in a nominal slot. You can drag entire compact variables into compact variable slots, and you can drag the nominal and continuous portions of compact variables into any slots calling for nominal and continuous variables.

Template slots are flexible:

1. You do not need to use every slot; some can remain empty.

2. You can assign as many variables to each slot as you want. Each slot grows to accommodate as many variables as you assign. StatView produces multiple or compound results as needed to analyze all the variables you assign; for details, see "Multiple and compound results," p. 135.

Assign variables to slots

You can assign variables to slots in any of several ways.

1. Click and drag a variable from the list into a slot.

2. Double-click a variable to assign it to the highlighted slot. Then, the next slot is selected and you can double-click to assign variables to it.

3. Control-double-click (Windows) or Command-double-click (Macintosh) to assign several variables to the current (selected) slot.

4. Click and drag to move a variable from one slot to another.

Press the Tab key to move the selection from the currently highlighted slot to the next slot immediately below it. Press Shift-Tab to move the selection to the previous slot.

Remove variables from slots

If you assign a variable to the wrong slot by mistake, you can remove it three ways:

1. Click the variable in the slot and press Delete.

2. Drag the variable from the slot back to the variable list.

3. Double-click the variable in its slot.

Manipulate results

When you finish assigning variables and click OK, results appear in a view. If the active (topmost) window is a view, results appear in that view after existing results. If the top window is not a view, results appear in a new, untitled view.

If the Recalculate box in the view is unchecked (turned off), empty graph and table placeholders (X-boxes) appear rather than completed results. When you are ready to see your results, check the Recalculate box (turn it on). See "Control recalculations," p. 138.

You can manipulate template results the same way as any other results. See the previous chapter, "Analyses," p. 131, for instructions on using analysis and variable browsers and the Edit Display and Edit Analysis buttons. Also see the next two chapters, "Customizing results," p. 179, and "Drawing and layout," p. 203. For instructions on working with each type of analysis and its results, see its chapter in *StatView Reference*.

Exercise

In this exercise, you apply one of StatView's installed templates to generate a basic set of descriptive statistics from these data, then continue by adding results from a regression template.

Please close any datasets or views before starting this exercise.

- From the Analyze menu, select Descriptive Statistics and then Descriptive Statistics (Point to Descriptive Statistics, and then select Descriptive Statistics from the submenu.)

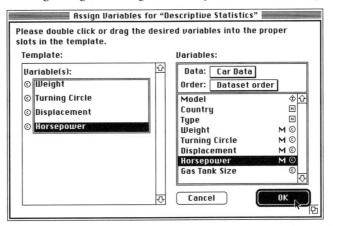

- Open Car Data from the Sample Data folder
- Double-click to assign Weight, Turning Circle, Displacement, and Horsepower

The slot has a ⊚ marker, indicating that you can only assign continuous variables to it. Try double-clicking a nominal variable (☒). An alert tells you that the class of the variable is incorrect for that particular slot.

- Click OK

A new view shows this table of basic descriptive statistics:

Descriptive Statistics

	Mean	Std. Dev.	Std. Error	Count	Minimum	Maximum	# Missing
Weight	2957.629	535.664	49.735	116	1695.000	4285.000	0
Turning Circle	38.586	3.132	.291	116	32.000	47.000	0
Displacement	158.310	60.409	5.609	116	61.000	350.000	0
Horsepower	130.198	39.822	3.697	116	55.000	278.000	0

Now we use a regression template to determine whether a linear relationship exists between gas tank size and the weight of the car. Because a dataset is already open, we won't need to choose a new one.

- From the Analyze menu, select Regression/Regression--Simple
- Drag Gas Tank Size to the Dependent slot
- Drag Weight to the Independent slot
- Click OK

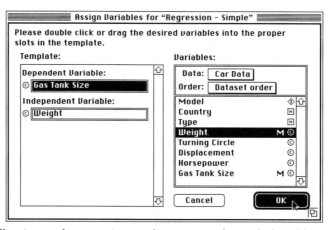

Our view is still active, so the regression results appear underneath the table we already had.

Regression Summary
Gas Tank Size vs. Weight

Count	116
Num. Missing	0
R	.847
R Squared	.717
Adjusted R Squared	.715
RMS Residual	1.643

ANOVA Table
Gas Tank Size vs. Weight

	DF	Sum of Squares	Mean Square	F-Value	P-Value
Regression	1	780.014	780.014	288.914	<.0001
Residual	114	307.779	2.700		
Total	115	1087.793			

Regression Coefficients
Gas Tank Size vs. Weight

	Coefficient	Std. Error	Std. Coeff.	t-Value	P-Value
Intercept	1.858	.860	1.858	2.161	.0328
Weight	.005	2.860E-4	.847	16.997	<.0001

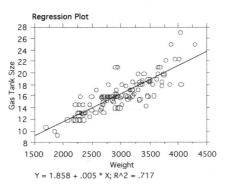

Now we have a Regression Summary, an ANOVA Table, a Regression Coefficients table, and a Regression Plot.

Manage templates

The Analyze menu contains an hierarchical menu of templates. These are prebuilt templates for producing most of StatView's analyses and graphs, organized according to type of analysis.

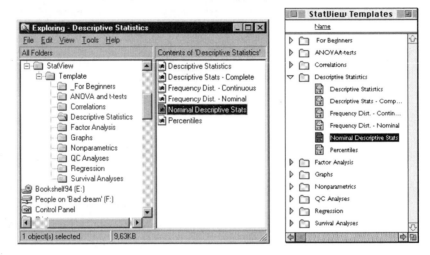

This menu is dynamic—you can rearrange it simply by rearranging the contents of the Template folder (Windows) or StatView Templates folder (Macintosh). This flexibility lets you organize your StatView templates for the way you like to work. The default organization of the menu reflects the way templates are installed in folders within the main folder:

Rearrange templates

You may change the Analyze menu hierarchy simply by rearranging the organization of files and folders inside the Template folder (Windows) or StatView Templates folder (Macintosh).

- Rearrange how templates are stored within the Template folder (Windows) or StatView Templates folder (Macintosh)
  Use the Explorer or File Manager (Windows) or Finder (Macintosh) to create a new folder and file organization. You may nest folders insider each other, up to five folders deep.

- From the Analyze menu, select Rebuild Template List

Group related templates into folders according to categories that make sense to you. You might want to rearrange templates according to the type of data they use, or according to the types of tests they perform, or perhaps according to your current projects. You can add more folders, add more templates, put folders inside folders (as many as five layers deep), and drag files or entire folders to the Recycle bin (Windows) or trash (Macintosh). You can even use aliases (Macintosh only) to point to template files (but not folders) stored elsewhere.

When saving your own views, you might want to use the Create New Folder button (Windows) or the New Folder button (Macintosh) in the Save dialog box to create project folders inside the Template folder (Windows) or StatView Templates folder (Macintosh).

You should not move the template folder itself. This main folder should remain at the top level of the StatView folder. If you move or rename the template folder, StatView asks you to locate it the next time you use a template. StatView then remembers the new location and the new name.

If you change the name or location of the template folder, the only way to restore its default name and location is to discard the StatView Library file. StatView builds a new Library containing the default folder name and location. Note that you lose all preferences you have set, as these are saved in the Library file.

Update the Analyze menu

Any time you add new templates or rearrange templates within the main template folder, you must update the Analyze menu:

- From the Analyze menu, select Rebuild Template List

StatView examines the folder structure inside the template folder and then builds an hierarchical menu. Folders and files are alphabetized.

Build templates

You are not limited to templates provided with StatView. You can also make custom templates of your own. The previous chapter, "Analyses," p. 131, discusses how you can create your own analyses from scratch and save them as templates. The next chapter, "Customizing results," p. 179, shows how to use Edit Display to format table and graph results.

Once you are skilled in these areas of StatView, you are ready to design basic templates. If you want to design templates for reports and presentations, you should also become familiar with the topics in the chapter "Drawing and layout," p. 203.

If you need help with the parameters and variable requirements for a particular analysis, see its chapter in *StatView Reference*.

Template tips

When you create a view to reuse as a template, there are several things to take into consideration. Some characteristics that are helpful in working views get in the way in templates, and vice versa.

Give variables general, meaningful names

You use the Assign Variables dialog box to assign variables from any dataset to the slots in the template. The templates list contains separate slots for each variable used in the view you save as a template. Therefore, when you create your template, consider giving your variables generic names that could apply to any dataset rather than names that have a meaning only in a specific dataset. The picture below shows both:

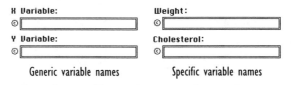

Generic variable names   Specific variable names

Slots take their names from the variables used to create the template, so you may want to rename the variables in your dataset while you're creating a template. You might create a dummy dataset with generic names you can use for template construction. Variables used to build templates needn't contain data.

When the Assign Variables dialog box first appears, it pre-assigns any variables to slots with matching names. So, if you are repeating an analysis on datasets with the same variable names, it is worthwhile to use specific variable names in the template. This saves you the trouble of dragging variables into slots and removes still another opportunity for error.

Do not save results

You can save disk space by not saving results with views you plan to use as templates. In View Preferences, uncheck Save analysis results with view (turn the option off). The option takes effect for the *next* view you create; it does not change a view already created. Remember to turn this option back on after creating templates so that your regular views retain their results. See "View preferences," p. 232.

Turn Recalculate off

You may want to disable calculation when adding results from several templates to one view so you do not have to wait for each set of results to calculate before you can add results from another template. See "Control recalculations," p. 138.

Format information

In a few cases, formatting information saved with a template does not apply to all output:

1. For analyses that generate multiple results (rather than compound results) for additional variables, formatting information applies only to the number of tables or graphs present when the template was created. See "Multiple and compound results," p. 135.

2. For analyses that generate multiple results (rather than compound results) for the groups of Split By variables, formatting information is retained only for the first group of the Split By variable. See "Multiple and compound results," p. 135.

Note that many default formatting instructions can be globally set using View, Table and Graph preferences.

Change templates

The easiest way to change a template is to Open it from the File menu, make your changes, and save it again. To avoid renaming the variable assignment slots, either use the original dataset or create a new dataset with the same generic names.

Exercise

This exercise shows you how to build two simple templates. One generates a customized graph, and the other generates a custom analysis with special parameter settings.

Customize a graph

If you are writing an article for publication, you may want all your scattergrams to have exactly the same format. You can customize a single scattergram, save it in the Template folder (Windows) or StatView Templates folder (Macintosh), and use the template to create all the scattergrams. There is no need to repeat all the formatting steps for each new scattergram.

First, change one of the preference settings so the template you create uses less hard disk space.

- From the Manage menu, select Preferences
- Select View and click Modify
- Uncheck Save analysis results with view
- Click OK
- Click Done

When you use a scattergram template, the Assign Variables dialog box contains slots for the variables assigned to each axis. We want these slots to have generic names, so we'll use variables named X variable and Y variable.

- Open Tree Data from the Sample Data folder
- Rename Trunk Girth to be X Variable
  (Click the variable name cell, type the new name, and press Tab.)
- Rename Weight to be Y Variable
  (Don't forget to press Enter or Return.)
- From the Analyze menu, select New View
- In the analysis browser under Bivariate Plots, select Scattergram and click Create Analysis
- Click OK to accept the default parameters
- In the variable browser, select X Variable and click the X Variable button
- In the variable browser, select Y Variable and click the Y Variable button

The scattergram appears in the view.

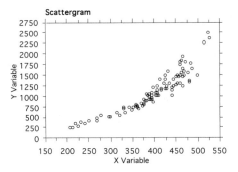

Now we remove the title, customize X and Y axis lengths, change the font and size of the axis values and labels, and change the position of major and minor tick marks.

- Make sure the graph is selected and click Edit Display
- Uncheck Show title (turn the option off)
- Specify a Vertical measurement: 2 inches
- Specify a Horizontal measurement: 2 inches
- Click OK

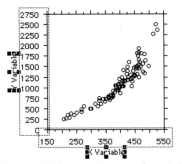

- Shift-click to select the axis labels and scales

- In the Text menu, change Font to Helvetica (or your favorite) and change Size to 12

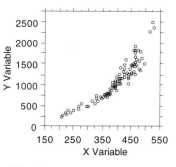

- Shift-click to select the X and Y scales

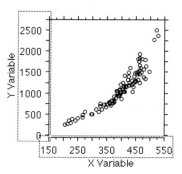

- Click Edit Display
- Click More Choices and use pop-up menus to select major and minor tick marks that straddle axes:

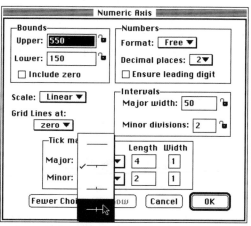

- Click OK and repeat these choices for the second axis
- Click in the empty space of the view to deselect the graph

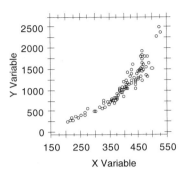

You have finished customizing the graph and are ready to save this view as a template.

- From the File menu, select Save
- Specify a filename: My Scattergram
- Choose some location in the Template folder (Windows) or StatView Templates folder (Macintosh)
- Close both the view and the dataset (do not save changes)

You are now ready to use this template to format a new scattergram. You can use this template with any dataset.

- Open Car Data from the Sample Data folder
- From the Analyze menu, select Rebuild Template List
- From the Analyze menu, select My Scattergram
  (If you chose a subfolder in the Template folder (Windows) or StatView Templates folder (Macintosh), the template appears under that heading in the hierarchical Analyze menu.)
- Drag Turning Circle to the X Variable slot
- Drag Displacement to the Y Variable slot
- Click OK

A new view opens, and a scattergram with the same format appears.

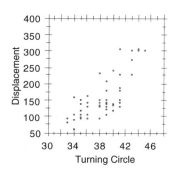

- Close this view and Car Data (do not save changes)

In view preferences, you might want to restore the option Save analysis results with view.

Modify an existing template

A template lets you name and save all the parameters and output of a particular analysis. You can modify parameters and add results to any of the templates that ship with StatView. You can also start from scratch and build your own analysis template with the parameters and results you desire.

We will modify the Regression--Simple template that ships with StatView. That template includes a scattergram with a regression line, and we want a template that also draws 95% confidence bands for the regression line. Also, we want to add a plot of residuals vs. fitted values. Again, we want to use generic variable names.

- From the File menu, select New
- Name the first variable Dependent
  (Click the Input Column cell, type Dependent, and press Enter or Return)
- Name the second variable Independent
- From the Analyze menu, select Regression/Regression--Simple
- Drag Dependent to the Dependent Variable slot and Independent to the Independent Variable slot
- Click OK

The view window fills with a number of empty analyses. Notes beneath the placeholders read, "There were not enough observations to compute this result." That's not surprising; our dataset has no cases. It doesn't matter, though; we can still make our changes and save a new template.

- Make sure at least one of the empty results is still selected
- Click Edit Analysis
- Click More Choices
- Check Slope (turn the option on) for Plot confidence bands
- Click OK

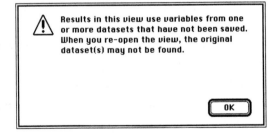

- In the analysis browser under Regression, double-click Residuals vs. Fitted

We've changed the regression plot to include confidence bands, and we've added a plot of residuals vs. fitted values. Now, we can save our view as a new template.

- From the File menu, select Save
- Specify a filename: Regression--Simple, conf
- Choose a location inside the Template folder (Windows) or StatView Templates folder (Macintosh) (perhaps the Regression folder)
- Click Save

StatView warns that you haven't saved your dataset. Since you don't intend to use the empty dataset again, that doesn't matter.

> ⚠ **Results in this view use variables from one or more datasets that have not been saved. When you re-open the view, the original dataset(s) may not be found.**
>
> OK

- Click OK
- Close both the view and the dataset

You are now ready to use this template with any dataset to perform a simple regression.

- From the Analyze menu, select Rebuild Template List
- From the Analyze menu, select Regression/Regression--Simple
- Open Car Data from the Sample Data folder
- Drag Gas Tank Size to the Dependent slot
- Drag Weight to the Independent slot
- Click OK

A new view with simple regression results appears. Note that the regression plot includes confidence bands, and we also have a plot of residuals against fitted values. We've rearranged the results to fit the page.

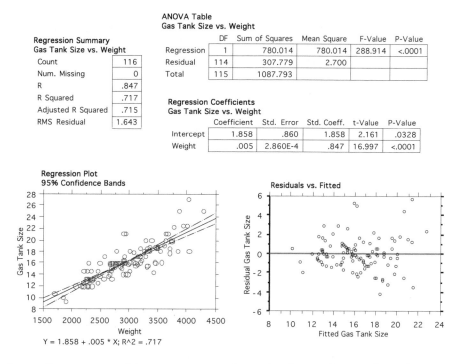

ANOVA Table
Gas Tank Size vs. Weight

	DF	Sum of Squares	Mean Square	F-Value	P-Value
Regression	1	780.014	780.014	288.914	<.0001
Residual	114	307.779	2.700		
Total	115	1087.793			

Regression Summary
Gas Tank Size vs. Weight

Count	116
Num. Missing	0
R	.847
R Squared	.717
Adjusted R Squared	.715
RMS Residual	1.643

Regression Coefficients
Gas Tank Size vs. Weight

	Coefficient	Std. Error	Std. Coeff.	t-Value	P-Value
Intercept	1.858	.860	1.858	2.161	.0328
Weight	.005	2.860E-4	.847	16.997	<.0001

Regression Plot
95% Confidence Bands

$Y = 1.858 + .005 * X; R^2 = .717$

Residuals vs. Fitted

In view preferences, you might want to restore the option Save analysis results with view.

Customizing results

StatView includes all the features of a graphing program, with numerous features enabling you to enhance the clarity and visual impact of your graphs and tables.

1. You can set global preferences that establish defaults for every graph and table you create. Before producing any results for a presentation, you should set preferences to suit your most general needs. For example, if you are preparing a journal article, you should set preferences to match your results to that journal's style guidelines.

2. Edit Display lets you change tables and graphs individually. Many options duplicate those that you can set globally with preferences, so Edit Display provides a way to override your default settings for specific graphs. Other options for controlling features specific to certain result types or data situations are unique to Edit Display, because they are options that can be modified only locally, one result at a time.

3. Draw tools let you change lines, colors, fill patterns, etc. used in graphs and tables.

4. Finally, a complete palette of drawing and text tools lets you modify, annotate, and amplify the information shown in graphs and tables. Layout tools help you arrange results on the pages of a presentation. StatView's drawing and layout tools are discussed in the next chapter, "Drawing and layout," p. 203.

This chapter discusses preferences briefly and then shows how to use Edit Display and Draw tools to customize individual tables and graphs. For graphs, you can change number formats, axis bounds, tick marks, interval widths, labels and symbols, grid lines, fills, colors, patterns, line widths and text formats. You can also transpose the horizontal and vertical axes. For tables, you can change number formats, borders, row heights, fonts, sizes, and styles, lines and thicknesses, colors, and pen patterns. You can also transpose rows and columns.

Preferences

Preferences let you establish global settings for graphs and tables. Your preference settings determine the defaults used for every graph and table you create. By contrast, Edit Display lets you change these and other settings for any single graph or table you select.

Before producing any results for a presentation, you should set preferences to suit your most general needs. You should establish through preferences the usual measurements, fonts, and colors you expect to see. You should decide in advance whether you want square or rectangular graphs, big points or little points, differing colors or fill patterns. You should decide whether you like tables with borders or without, single- or double-spacing, few or many decimal places. If you are planning to publish your results, you should set preferences to match any style rules your publication may have established.

Preferences are discussed in detail in a later chapter, "Tips and shortcuts," p. 221. Here we merely call your attention to the choices available.

See "Graph preferences," p. 228, to learn how to set default height and width, numeric formatting for scales, axis frames (how many edges are drawn around a graph), point size and types (e.g., circles, squares, diamonds, stars, etc.), fill patterns (blank, solid, hatched, checkered, etc.), and colors. Also choose how compound graphs (see "Multiple and compound results," p. 135) should distinguish between variables or groups: by different point types, by different colors, or by different fill patterns.

See "Table preferences," p. 231, to learn how to set numeric formatting, borders, and line-spacing.

See "View preferences," p. 232, to learn how to control for both tables and graphs the default font and the thickness of lines in printed output.

Edit Display dialog boxes

The Edit Display button at the top of the view window lets you customize any graph or table in a view window:

- Click to select the graph or table

- Click Edit Display

Shortcut Double-clicking a result has the same effect as selecting it and clicking Edit Display. Note that both Right-double-clicking and Alt-double-clicking (Windows) or Option-double-clicking (Macintosh) an analysis is the same as selecting it and clicking Edit Analysis. However, a view preference lets you switch these shortcuts. See "View preferences," p. 232.

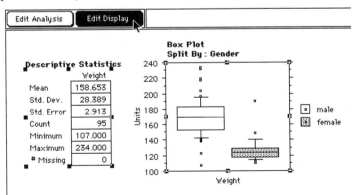

- Choose the options you want

- Click Show to preview your changes

- Click OK to apply your changes

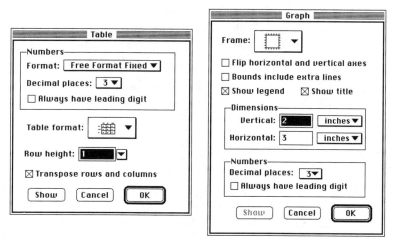

Subsequent sections, "Graphs," p. 183 and "Tables," p. 197, discuss these dialog boxes in detail.

Preview changes

Both formatting dialog boxes have a Show button which lets you preview formatting changes as you make them. After choosing options, click Show to see the effects of the options on the graph or table in the view. The dialog box is still open for you to adjust your choices. Click OK to implement the changes, or click Cancel to abandon all changes, close the dialog box, and return the graph or table to its original state.

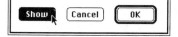

Undo changes

Any formatting changes you make, whether through Edit Display, drawing tools, or layout tools, are reversible. If you make a mistake, choose Undo immediately to return your graph to its previous state. You can only Undo the single most recent action. To undo earlier actions, you must retrace your steps—e.g., return to Edit Display and restore previous settings.

Clipboard commands

You can use standard Edit menu commands with tables and graphs. However, please note that any StatView table or graph copied into the clipboard *becomes a static picture* when pasted back into a view. This picture is *not* a dynamic object. You can no longer use Edit Display or Edit Analysis, change variable assignments, or update results with criteria, inclusion, or Recalculate. You should *not* use clipboard commands to move objects around.

Recalculate controls all the objects in a view at once, so using static pictures is a handy way to maintain a view of data in several states at once. If you want to compare results with criteria or inclusion against those without (for example), Copy and Paste the results as a picture. Next, change the dynamic object (the original results). Finally, compare the two results side by side.

(An alternative is to extract a subset to a different dataset and create results with variables from that smaller dataset alongside results from the full dataset's variables. Note that StatView lets you work in many views and datasets at once.)

Cut and Copy

Cut removes a selected object or component (a table or graph, or a part of one) from the view and places a copy into the clipboard. Copy places a copy of a selected object or component in the clipboard but leaves the original in the view unharmed.

If you mistakenly Cut a graph title or legend, you can restore it with Edit Display's Show title and Show legend options.

Duplicate

Duplicate places a second copy of a selected object or component (a table or graph, or a part of one) in the view, below and to the right of the original. Duplicate is equivalent to using Copy and then Paste.

Clear

Clear removes a selected object or component (a table or graph, or a part of one) from the view but does *not* place a copy in the clipboard. You can select and clear the following components: titles, entire legends (not parts of legends), axis labels, and notes.

If you select and clear a plot (the representation of a variable or group within a graph), axis, whole graph, or whole table, the entire table or graph is cleared.

If you mistakenly Clear a graph title or legend, you can restore it with Edit Display's Show title and Show legend options.

Paste

Paste places the contents of the clipboard in the view, at the point of the most recent mouse click. If the most recent mouse click location is no longer visible, Paste centers the pasted object(s) in the visible portion of the view.

If you resize a pasted picture, you can restore its original size by double-clicking the object.

Graphs

You can edit many aspects of a graph's appearance. Some formatting changes apply to an entire graph, others to particular components of a graph. To make changes to an entire graph, you select the entire graph and click Edit Display. To change a component of a graph, you select just that component and click Edit Display. To make still other changes, you select graphs or components and work with Draw tools.

This diagram identifies many major graph components.

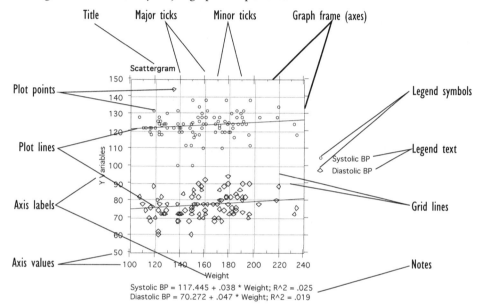

This table explains each component:

Title	The text above a graph that identifies the analysis, variables, and criteria or row inclusion in effect.
Frame	The set of axes that border a graph—a closed rectangle or L-shape
Interior	The area inside a graph but outside the plot
X axis	The horizontal or X-axis (abscissa)
Y axis	The vertical or Y-axis (ordinate)
Axis values	The numbers or words along an axis that label points on the axis
Tick marks	Small hatch marks along an axis that identify intervals of the scale
Axis labels	Text below the X axis and left of the Y axis that indicate what variable or quantity is plotted on that axis
Plot	The points, bars, lines, or boxes that represent a single variable or group in a graph
Grid lines	Vertical and horizontal dotted lines at each major tick interval
Plotted lines	Regression lines, confidence bands, or normal distribution curves superimposed on a graph
Legend	Symbols and text identifying how variables or groups are depicted in the graph

Notes	Text below a graph, such as a regression equation or a message explaining why the graph is empty
Reference lines	Lines indicating means, standard deviations, or other computed values

Select graphs

With a whole graph selected you can:

1. Change thickness, color, and pen pattern for all lines in the graph.
2. Change the color of the whole graph.
3. Add a color or fill to the graph's interior.
4. Use Edit Display to change the graph as a whole.

If the cursor isn't an arrow, first choose the selection tool from the Draw palette.

To select an entire graph, click directly on the frame or interior of a graph. Do not click a bar, point, line, text item, or any other component.

To select several graphs, Shift-click them, or click and drag a marquee around them.

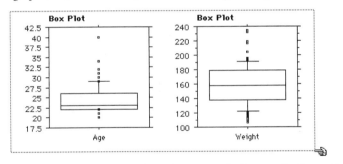

You can also use the Results Browser to select objects; see "Select results," p. 148.

Black handles show that a graph is selected. You can also check the Result Selected note in the upper right corner of the view, or use Show Selection in the Results browser:

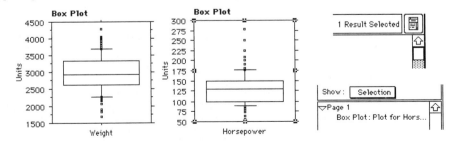

Select components

If the cursor isn't an arrow, first choose the selection tool from the Draw palette.

To select a component, click that component directly. Shift-click to select several components at once.

Black selection handles show when certain types of components are selected, while dotted lines show selection for other types of components.

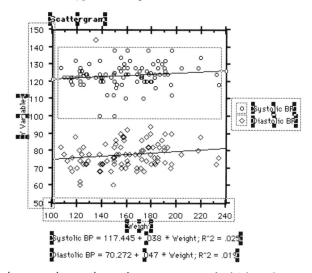

This table shows how to select each graph component and which tool to use to change an aspect of the component.

Component	How to select it	Tool
Font, size, style, alignment, and angle of text items (titles, legend text, axis labels, axis values, notes)	Click the text	Text menu
Color of text items	Click the text	Draw palette
Axis frame type	Click the frame	Edit Display
Line width, pen type, color of graph frame	Click the frame	Draw palette
Color and fill of graph interior	Click blank space inside the graph	Draw palette
Line width, pen type, color	Click the axis numbers	Draw palette
Bounds, intervals, scales, numeric format	Click the axis numbers	Edit Display
Length, width, and position of tick marks	Click the axis numbers	Edit Display
Whether and where grid lines appear	Click the axis numbers	Edit Display
Line width, pen type, fill pattern, point type, point size, color of a plot (box, bar, point, or line)	Click the plot (box, bar, point, or line)	Draw palette
Thickness, pen type, and color of plotted lines	Click the line	Draw palette

| Orientation and frame of legend | Click anywhere in the legend | Edit Display |
| Point type, point size, fill pattern, and color of legend symbols | Click the symbol | Draw palette |

Overlay graphs

You can superimpose a graph on another to create a double layer graph. Select one graph and drag it into position over the other graph. If one plot hides another, adjust the plot's fill attributes and consider using Move to Front and Move to Back commands from the Layout menu. Also consider deleting or making invisible redundant scales, axes, etc.

Resize graphs

To resize any graph, select the whole graph, then click and drag one of its selection handles to a new location. Drag a corner handle to resize a graph's height and width at once; drag a side handle to change height or width alone.

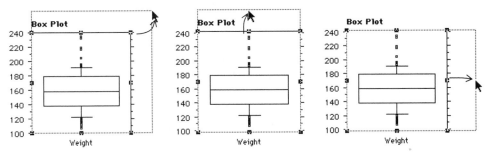

All components of the graph move to stay in the same relative location to the graph.

Move graphs or components

You can move an entire graph and most components of a graph: the title, legend, axis, axis labels, notes. If you move the axis, it is constrained to the respective horizontal or vertical direction. If you move the graph as a whole, all components move together and stay in the same positions relative to each other.

- Click and drag the graph or component

Do not drag selection handles; dragging handles resizes rather than moves the graph or component.

Shortcut You can use cursor arrow keys to move any selected graph or graph component. If the grid is turned on, each keystroke moves the object one grid unit in the direction of the arrow. If the grid is turned off, each keystroke moves the object one screen pixel. In this context, "grid" refers to an underlying grid in the view window itself, not the grid lines that can be used to show tick intervals inside a graph's interior; for more information, see "Turn Grid On/Off," p. 217.

Change text items

You can change the font, size, style, and color of any text item in a graph: graph titles, notes, axis labels, axis values, and legend text. You can also change the alignment and orientation of any text item except in legends. You can change components individually or all at once.

To format or edit a text component, select only that component. To select several text items, Shift-click to select them at the same time. Then, use Text menu items to change the font, size, style, justification (left-alignment, right-alignment, or centering), and rotation. Use the pen color tool in the Draw palette to change the color of text components. Use the text tool in the Draw palette to edit the contents of a text item.

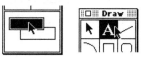

You cannot edit axis scale values with text tools.

If you use the text tool to edit any text, that text no longer updates when the graph updates.

Change overall structures

While StatView displays many different graphs, they share a common overall structure, which can be changed with the Graph dialog box. You can choose a graph frame, transpose two axes, hide or show titles and legends, and set the height and width for any graph. To use the Graph dialog box:

• Select the entire graph (click its frame)

• Click Edit Display

Any changes you make in this dialog box apply only to the selected graph. If you want to change several graphs, select them all at once. Click Edit Display for a series of Graph dialog boxes, one for each graph, in the order in which you selected the graphs.

Frame Choose from three different styles in the pop-up menu.

Flip horizontal and vertical axes Check this option (turn it on) to transpose the horizontal and vertical axes, changing the orientation of the graph.

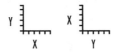

Bounds include extra lines Check this option (turn it on) to ensure that default axis bounds do not exclude calculated lines (such as the three standard deviation lines in univariate charts).

Show legend Check this box to display the graph legend.

Show title Check this box to include titles showing analysis type, variables assigned, and criteria/row inclusion in effect.

Dimensions Specify the horizontal and vertical dimensions in inches, centimeters, picas or points.

Numbers Choose a number of decimal places for numbers in axis scales (see "Decimal places," p. 80). Check Always have leading digit to include a leading zero in fractional values (e.g., 0.25).

Choose box styles

You can choose from among four different box styles for box plots:

- Inside a box plot, click the plot (the actual box-and-whisker)
- Click Edit Display

![Box Plot dialog. Title bar reads "Box Plot". Text: "Select a box plot style:" with four box plot style icons. Buttons: Show, Cancel, OK.]

The default style uses regular boxes and includes outliers as points. The second style uses regular boxes but excludes outliers. The third style uses boxes with notches showing the 95% confidence interval for the median and includes outliers. The fourth choice uses notched boxes but excludes outliers.

Connect or separate lines for univariate line plots

You can choose whether all points in univariate line plot are connected with a single line, or with a separate line for each group. Examples of both are shown below; the default is separate line segments for each group.

- Inside a univariate or cell line chart, click the plot (one of the lines)
- Click Edit Display
- Turn the option on or off

- Click OK

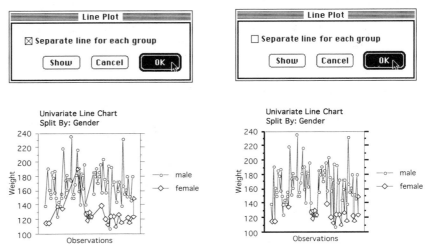

Connect or separate lines for cell line charts

You can choose whether all points in cell line charts are connected with a single line, or with a separate line for each variable. Examples of both are shown below; the default is to connect the variables.

- Inside a cell line chart, click the plot (one of the lines)
- Click Edit Display

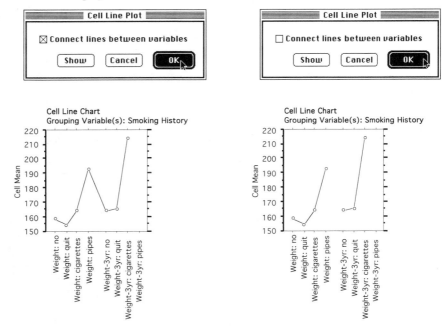

Change axes

StatView uses three different types of axes: a numeric axis for displaying continuous measurements, a cell axis for displaying information on groups or subgroups, and an ordinal axis for displaying the order of a point in a dataset. Axis values appear at major tick intervals along both vertical and horizontal axes.

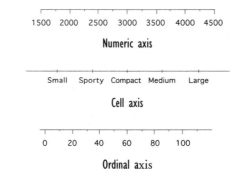

Bivariate plots can have either numeric or cell axes for both the X and Y axes. Univariate plots always have an ordinal X axis and can have either a numeric or cell Y axis. Frequency distributions, percentile plots, and comparison percentiles always have two numeric axes. Cell plots and box plots have a cell X axis and a numeric Y axis. Pie charts have no visible axes.

Each type of axis has its own dialog box. To edit an axis:

• Click axis numbers to select an axis

• Click Edit Display

• Choose options

• Click OK

Axis values can be rotated using commands Rotate Right and Rotate Left from the Text menu. Note that long axis values are legible only when they are perpendicular to the axis.

Numeric axes

StatView offers two dialog boxes for numeric axes: one with fewer choices and one with more choices.

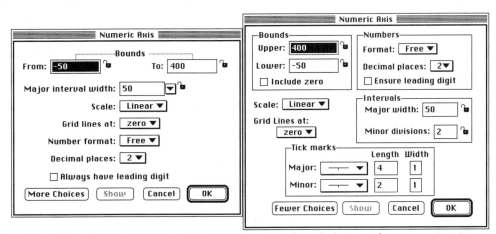

Bounds Specify maximum and minimum values. Check Include Zero if you want StatView to calculate its own bounds but ensure that zero is included in those bounds.

Use the lock controls to choose whether these values should be locked (🔒) so that any recalculations of the graph (for changing data conditions) do not change them, or unlocked (🔓) so that recalculations do change the values as needed. If you specify a value, that value is locked by default. Click a lock to toggle from locked to unlocked, or *vice versa*.

Major and minor intervals Specify how wide the interval between major tick marks should be, and specify how many minor intervals you want between major tick marks. For example, the following axis has major intervals of 500 and 2 minor intervals within each major interval:

1500   2000   2500   3000   3500   4000   4500

When you first create a graph, intervals default to widths appropriate to the bounds. If the axis bounds change, major and minor interval widths automatically update. You change the intervals by typing in the text boxes. The Fewer choices dialog box has a pop-up suggesting "good" major interval widths.

Use the lock controls to choose whether these values should be locked (🔒) so that any recalculations of the graph (for changing data conditions) do not change them, or unlocked (🔓) so that recalculations do change the values as needed. If you specify a value, that value is locked by default. Click a lock to toggle from locked to unlocked, or *vice versa*.

Tick marks Choose the placement for major and minor tick marks from pop-up menus. Specify a length in points for major and minor tick marks. It is common to make major tick marks longer than minor tick marks. Specify the width (thickness) for major and minor tick mark lines in pixels.

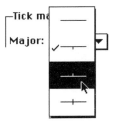

Scale Axis scales are linear by default, or you can choose logarithmic scales of base *e*, 10, or 2.

Grid lines Choose whether to display grid lines at major or minor ticks, at zero, or not show any grid lines. Horizontal and vertical grid lines can help show where values fall.

Numbers Choose numeric format and number of decimal places (see "Format," p. 79 and "Decimal places," p. 80). Check Ensure leading digit to include a leading zero in fractional values (e.g., 0.25). (To change formatting for a date/time axis, change the display format for the date/time variable in the dataset attribute pane.)

Cell axes

Your formatting choices for cell axes are not as extensive as for numeric axes. You can change the style of tick marks, the position of axis values, how many of them are shown, and determine whether or not to show grid lines. There is only one dialog box for cell axes. To make any of these changes, select the axis by clicking on its values and click the Edit Display button. The following dialog box appears:

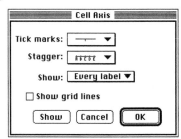

Axes for nominal variables are inherently different from numeric axes since a cell axis does not define a range of values but instead lists the labels of groups or the names of variables. Cell axes use tick marks to identify different groups. The tick marks for a cell axis have no relation to a numeric width.

Small   Sporty   Compact   Medium   Large

Tick marks Choose the placement for tick marks.

Stagger Choose the stagger pattern that makes axis labels most legible.

Show Choose how many labels to show.

Below are some of the possibilities:

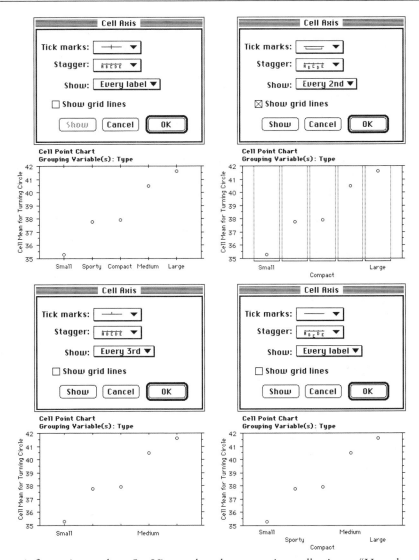

For more information on how StatView orders the groups in a cell axis, see "How does Stat-View use ordering in nominal variables?," p. 238, and "How can I reorder category variables?," p. 238.

Ordinal axes

Ordinal axes are used only for univariate plots. By default, ordinal axes have no tick marks nor scale values. By default, ordinal axes show the order of points in a dataset only by relative position. Check Show ticks and values (turn the option on) if you want to see a numeric scale for row numbers. (Note: to select an ordinal axis, click carefully just below the axis line, away from the Observations label.)

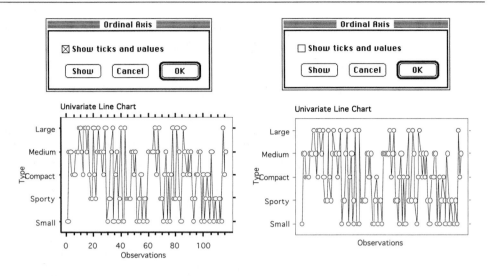

Change legends

Compound graphs—graphs that depict several variables or groups within a single axis frame—have legends that identify how each variable or group is distinguished. (See "Multiple and compound results," p. 135.) A legend serves as a key to the graph, and you can use it to change how lines, points, bars, etc. are drawn in the interior of a graph.

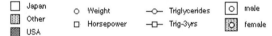

To change the overall format of a legend:

- Click the legend to select it
- Click Edit Display

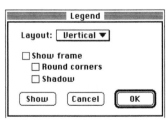

Layout Choose vertical, horizontal, or two-column orientation for the legend. Each are shown below:

• Small					
◇ Sporty					
▣ Compact	• Small	◇ Sporty	▣ Compact	▴ Medium	◆ Large
△ Medium					
◆ Large					

• Small	◇ Sporty
▣ Compact	▴ Medium
◆ Large	

Frame Check options on and off to control whether and how the legend is framed. Possibilities are shown below.

Once you change the layout and frame style of the legend, you may want to move it below or above the graph (particularly with horizontal legends). You can move it by selecting the legend and dragging it to a new location anywhere in the view.

You can change legend text items with the text tool in the Draw palette and commands from the Text menu. If you cut or clear a legend, you can bring it back by selecting the entire graph and clicking Edit Display.

Change plotting symbols

For a scattergram, you can change point style, size, and color. For a bar chart, pie chart or box plot, you can change fill patterns, colors, lines, and pen patterns. For a line chart you can modify lines and points. There are two ways to select the plotting symbols of a graph.

1. Select the interior of the graph
2. Select symbols in the legend
   (You can change all the symbols by selecting the entire legend. For example, you could change every single point to a particular size or color)

Once a plot is selected, use Draw palette tools to make changes.

Point styles and sizes

Points are the plotting symbols in scattergrams, line charts, percentile plots, compare percentile plots and in box plots. To change a point, select it and choose a type and/or size from the Draw palette. Choose the null symbol (ø) for invisible points, which are often desirable for line plots.

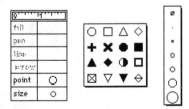

Fill patterns, pen patterns, and line thicknesses

The Draw palette's fill, pen, and line tools are handy for calling attention to items in graphs. You can thicken lines and fill them with patterns, or add patterns to the plotted shapes within a graph. You can also add a fill to the interior of a graph, making the plot itself stand out more.

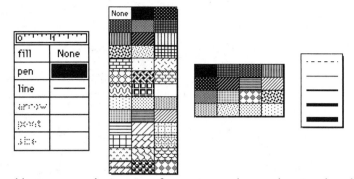

Fill You can add a pattern to the interior of an entire graph, or to bars in a bar chart and histogram, slices of a pie chart, and boxes of a box plot. To add a fill to a graph's interior, select the entire graph and choose a pattern from the fill pop-up menu.

Pen pattern For any line, you can choose from sixteen pen-type choices. All lines default to a solid pattern. Pen patterns have greater visual impact with thicker lines. (PostScript printers interpret some patterns as halftones, so a single pixel screen line may print as a gray line with some patterns.)

Line thickness You can change the thickness for the following lines: a graph frame, tick marks, boxes in a plot, pie chart divisions, bars in a chart, the simple and polynomial regression lines and the normal curve of a histogram. All line widths default to a single point line. (To print hairlines, see "View preferences," p. 232.) Choose the top, dotted line for invisible lines.

Change colors

Pop-up menus at the bottom of the Draw palette let you choose colors for the pen, fill, and background (the empty view area outside graphs). For each component you select, the pen and fill color menus change different aspects of the graph.

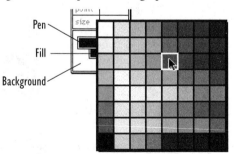

Control-click (Windows) or Command-click (Macintosh) to select both pen and fill colors at once.

The table below describes the components that can be selected and what each pop-up menu controls.

Component	How to select	Pen color changes	Fill color changes
Frame	Click the frame	All lines connected to the frame including axis tick marks	The interior of the graph
Axis	Click an axis value	Axis values, axis line, tick marks, grid lines	
Plot	Click the plot	Points or lines in the plot	The fill of bars, boxes or pies
Regression line or normal curve	Click the line	The line	
Legend symbol	Click the symbol	Points or lines in the plot	The fill of bars, boxes or pies
Legend as a whole	Click the interior of the legend	Points or lines in the plot, legend text	The fill of bars, boxes or pies
Any text item	Click the text	The text	

Tables

You can edit many aspects of a table's appearance. Some formatting changes apply to the entire table, others to a particular component of a table. To make changes to an entire table, you select the entire table and click Edit Display. To make other changes, you select tables or components and work with Draw palette tools.

This diagram identifies major table components:

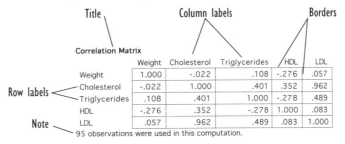

Select tables

With a whole table selected you can:

1. Change thickness, pen pattern, and color of all lines in the table.

2. Change the color of text for the whole table.

3. Change the font, size, style, alignment, and angle for all text components.

4. Use Edit Display to change the graph as a whole.

If the cursor isn't an arrow, first choose the selection tool from the Draw palette.

To select an entire table, click directly on the borders or interior of a table. Do not click a title or note.

To select several tables, Shift-click them, or click and drag a marquee around them.

Descriptive Statistics		Descriptive Statistics	
	Weight		Cholesterol
Mean	158.653	Mean	191.232
Std. Dev.	28.389	Std. Dev.	35.674
Std. Error	2.913	Std. Error	3.660
Count	95	Count	95
Minimum	107.000	Minimum	115.000
Maximum	234.000	Maximum	285.000
# Missing	0	# Missing	0

You can also use the Results Browser to select objects; see "Select results," p. 148.

Black handles show that a table is selected. You can also check the Result Selected note in the upper right corner of the view, or use Show Selection in the Results browser:

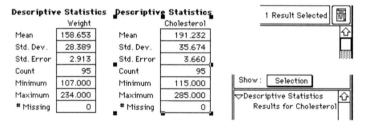

Select components

If the cursor isn't an arrow, first choose the selection tool from the Draw palette.

To select a component, click that component directly. Shift-click to select several components at once.

Black selection handles show when components are selected.

Correlation Matrix					
	Weight	Cholesterol	Triglycerides	HDL	LDL
Weight	1.000	-.022	.108	-.276	.057
Cholesterol	-.022	1.000	.401	.352	.962
Triglycerides	.108	.401	1.000	-.278	.489
HDL	-.276	.352	-.278	1.000	.083
LDL	.057	.962	.489	.083	1.000

95 observations were used in this computation.

This table shows how to select each table component and which tool to use to change an aspect of the component:

Component	How to select it	Tool
Borders, line-spacing, and orientation of entire table	Click a row or column label or anywhere inside the table	Edit Display
Line thickness, pen pattern, and color of entire table	Click a row or column label or anywhere inside the table	Draw palette
Font, size, and style of values inside the table, row labels, and column labels	Click a row or column label or anywhere inside the table	Text menu
Font, size, style, alignment, and angle of title and notes	Click the title or notes	Text menu
Color or text of title	Click the title	Draw palette
Font, size, style, alignment, and angle of note	Click the note	Text menu
Color or text of note	Click the note	Draw palette

Resize tables

You can resize tables several ways:

1. Resize the whole table by dragging selection handles.
2. Change column widths one at a time by dragging column borders.
3. Choose a different font size for the whole table from the Text menu. See "Change text items," p. 200.
4. Change row heights with Edit Display. See "Row height," p. 201.

Resize whole table select the whole table, then click and drag one of its selection handles to a new location. Drag a corner handle to resize a table's height and width at once; drag a side handle to change height or width alone.

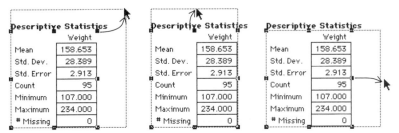

Change column widths To change the width of any column (including the borderless column of row labels), position the cursor over a column border. When the cursor changes to a cross-arrow (✛), click and drag the border to a new location.

Correlation Matrix

	Weight	Cholesterol	Triglycerides	HDL	LDL
Weight	1.000	-.022	.108	-.276	.057
Cholesterol	-.022	1.000	.401	.352	.962
Triglycerides	.108	.401	1.000	-.278	.489
HDL	-.276	.352	-.278	1.000	.083
LDL	.057	.962	.489	.083	1.000

95 observations were used in this computation.

Correlation Matrix

	Weight	Cholesterol	Trigl...	HDL	LDL
Weight	1.000	-.022	.108	-.276	.057
Cholesterol	-.022	1.000	.401	.352	.962
Triglycerides	.108	.401	1.000	-.278	.489
HDL	-.276	.352	-.278	1.000	.083
LDL	.057	.962	.489	.083	1.000

95 observations were used in this computation.

Move tables or components

You can move an entire table, its title, or its note(s). If you move the table as a whole, its title and notes move together and stay in the same positions relative to each other.

- Click and drag the table or component

Do not drag selection handles; dragging handles resizes rather than moves the table or component.

If you want to move only the title or the note, select whichever one you want to move and drag it to a new location. Moving a title or note has no effect on the body of the table.

Shortcut You can use cursor arrow keys to move any selected table or table component. If the grid is turned on, each keystroke moves the object one grid unit in the direction of the arrow. If the grid is turned off, each keystroke moves the object one screen pixel. For more information about the grid, see "Turn Grid On/Off," p. 217.

Change text items

You can change the font, size, style, and color of text inside tables, row and column labels, titles, and notes. You can also change the alignment and orientation of table titles and notes. You can change text components individually or all at once.

To format or edit a text component, select only that component. To select several text items, Shift-click to select them at the same time. To select all text items at once, select the entire table. Then, use Text menu items to change font, size, style, alignment, or angle. Use the pen color tool in the Draw palette to change the color of text components. Use the text tool in the Draw palette to edit the contents of a text item.

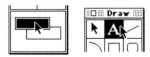

You cannot edit table values or labels with text tools.

If you use the text tool to edit any text, that text no longer updates when the analysis updates.

Change overall structure

While StatView produces many different types of analyses in tables, they share a common overall structure, which can be changed with the Table dialog box. You can change a table's numeric formatting, borders, and row heights, and you can change its orientation.

To use the Table dialog box:

• Select the entire table

• Click Edit Display

Numbers Choose numeric format and number of decimal places (see "Format," p. 79 and "Decimal places," p. 80). Check Always have leading digit to include a leading zero in fractional values (e.g., 0.25).

Table format Choose a set of borders from the pop-up menu, or select Other to design your own.

Select Other to get a Borders dialog box in which you can design your own table format. First choose a line style, then click any border that should use the style.

Row height Specify a line-spacing for the table, e.g., 1 for single-spacing, 2 for double-spacing, etc. The base height for single-spacing varies according to font size.

Transpose rows and columns Check this option (turn it on) exchange rows and columns, thus making a wide table tall or *vice versa*.

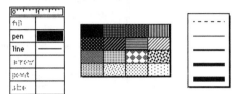

Descriptive Statistics

	Weight
Mean	158.653
Std. Dev.	28.389
Std. Error	2.913
Count	95
Minimum	107.000
Maximum	234.000
# Missing	0

Descriptive Statistics

	Mean	Std. Dev.	Std. Error	Count	Minimum	Maximum	# Missing
Weight	158.653	28.389	2.913	95	107.000	234.000	0

Change line thicknesses and pen patterns

The Draw palette's pen and line tools are handy for calling attention to tables or reducing the visibility of borders in tables. You can thicken lines and change their pen patterns.

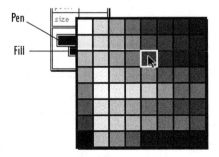

Line Thickness You can change the thickness for border lines. Table borders default to a single point line. (To print hairlines, see "View preferences," p. 232.) Choose the top, dotted line for invisible lines.

Pen pattern You can choose from sixteen pen-type choices. Table borders default to a solid pattern. Pen patterns have greater visual impact with thicker lines. (PostScript printers interpret some patterns as halftones, so a single pixel screen line may print as a gray line.)

Change colors

Pop-up menus at the bottom of the Draw palette let you choose colors for the pen and fill. Use the pen color tool to change the color of text inside a table, and the fill color to change the color of table borders. To change the color of a title or note, select it directly and change the pen color. Control-click (Windows) or Command-click (Macintosh) to select both pen and fill colors at once.

Pen

Fill

Drawing and layout

StatView includes many drawing features to help you customize the results of your analyses. Using StatView as your drawing program has two advantages:

1. You can change data and analyses, updating results automatically, without having to rework presentations.

2. You can save your finished presentation as a template to apply to other datasets.

In this chapter, we discuss Draw tools you can use to add lines, shapes, and text to complete and enhance your results. Then we discuss Layout tools that let you assemble your customized tables and graphs in an attractive, full-color presentation.

The previous chapter ("Customizing results," p. 179) discusses how you can use Edit Display and tools from the Text menu and Draw palette to customize StatView's graphs and tables.

Draw tools

Tools in the Draw palette let you draw shapes and type text in the view. Other Draw palette tools let you customize these shapes and text, as well as tables and graphs. (Using drawing tools to customize graphs and tables is discussed in the previous chapter, "Customizing results," p. 179.)

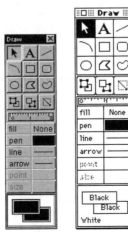

(Windows only) To show the Draw palette, select Draw Palette from the View menu. Drag its title bar to reposition it.

(Macintosh only) The Draw menu is a tear-off palette. Click the menu, then quickly and smoothly drag it to a new location. (If you hesitate or drag too slowly, StatView might mistake your movement for an attempt to select a tool.) Drag its title bar to reposition it. If you prefer, you can use Draw tools from the menu; you do not have to tear off the palette.

You can place the Draw palette anywhere on the screen, so that it is handy but does not obstruct your results.

Select objects

The selection tool ▶ activates the usual arrow cursor, which lets you select and move tables, graphs, shapes, and text.

Add text objects

You can add text anywhere in the view, to label or comment on a result, or to modify a text component of a result.

- From the Draw palette, select the text tool
- Click where you want to enter text

- Type your text; press Enter (Windows) or Return (Macintosh) to start a new line

As you type, the box expands to the right and downward to hold your text.

Drag selection handles Select the selection tool, select a text object, and drag its selection handles to resize a text box. After you resize a text box yourself, its width becomes fixed; any further text you add wraps to additional lines to stay within the established width. (You must reselect the text tool to add more text.)

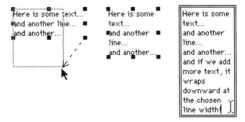

You can also set the width of a text object in advance: rather than clicking once and beginning to type, click and drag a box with the text tool and *then* start typing.

Change text objects Use Text menu commands to format text objects you add with the text tool, or to customize text components of graph and analysis objects (see "Change text items," p. 187 and p. 200).

You can change font, size, style, and justification (left-alignment, right-alignment, or centering) used in text objects. Just select characters with the text tool or a whole text object with the selection tool, and then choose commands from the Text menu.

You can rotate entire text objects left or right (to make text sideways or upside-down). Just select the text object(s) with the selection tool, then select Rotate Left or Rotate Right commands from the Text menu. You can edit rotated text just as you do normal text. While you are editing rotated text, StatView displays the text in normal position. When you are finished editing, the text again appears rotated. You cannot rotate just selected characters.

Use the pen color tool in the Draw palette to change the color of selected characters or objects; see "Change colors," p. 212.

Draw objects

You can draw the following shapes:

Shape	Tool	Keyboard modifiers
text	**A**	
line		Hold the Shift key while drawing to constrain to a 45 or 90 degree angle.
arc		Hold the Shift key while drawing to constrain to an arc from a circle.
rectangle		Hold the Shift key while drawing to constrain to a square.
rounded rectangle		Hold the Shift key while drawing to constrain to a rounded square.
ellipse		Hold the Shift key while drawing to constrain to a circle.
polygon		Hold the Alt key (Windows) or Option key (Macintosh) while drawing to preview a closed polygon.
spline		Hold the Alt key (Windows) or Option key (Macintosh) while drawing to preview a closed spline.

To draw a shape other than a polygon or a free-form curve:

- Select the tool for that shape
- Click and drag until the shape is the desired size

The cursor changes back to the selection tool as soon as you release the mouse. To return to the previous tool, hold the Control key (Windows) or Command key (Macintosh).

A corner/center control lets you draw some shapes beginning either in the shape's center or at its corner. To choose the starting point of a rectangle, rounded rectangle, ellipse, arc or line, click the control to toggle it between the two different states: 🔲 draws and reshapes objects from center to corner, and 🔲 draws and reshapes objects from corner to corner.

You can resize and reshape most shapes by selecting the shape and dragging one of its black selecting handles. Hold the Shift key while you drag to constrain movement vertically, horizontally, or at a 45° diagonal. Check the state of the corner/center control before resizing or reshaping.

Rounded rectangles

After drawing a rounded rectangle, you can use Edit Display to change how corners are rounded.

- Select the drawn shape
- Click Edit Display

You can either round the ends of the rectangle for an oval, or you can round just the corners with an arc of the radius you choose. The unit of measure for the radius is either inches or centimeters, depending on your Custom Rulers settings (see "Custom Rulers," p. 217).

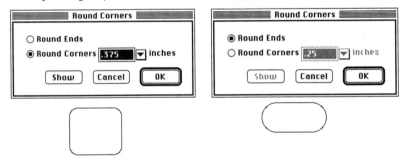

Arcs

After drawing an arc, you can reshape it by dragging its selection handles or using Reshape from the Edit menu.

Drag selection handles Click and drag any of the eight black selection handles to change the shape of an arc.

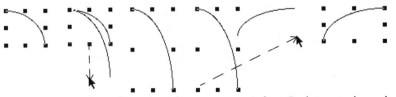

Reshape mode Select Reshape from the Edit menu to switch to Reshape mode, and select it again to exit Reshape mode when you are finished. In Reshape mode, the cursor changes to a reshaping crosshair (✛). Reshape mode lets you change the way an arc is defined. Usually, arcs are determined as the arc quarter section that inscribes the rectangle, so no matter where you drag the corners of the rectangle, the arc you get is just 90 degrees of a circle; see the left figure. By comparison, in Reshape mode the arc is constrained to the same circle, but you can choose a bigger or smaller angle of the circle, as in the right figures.

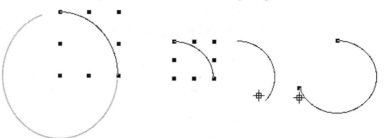

Shortcut (Macintosh only) Hold the Control key to switch temporarily to Reshape mode, and release the key to exit Reshape mode.

Polygons

The polygon tool lets you draw open or closed polygons. A closed polygon is one that has no gaps—it ends where it starts. An open polygon is one with an "empty" edge. Below, the left figure is closed and the right is open.

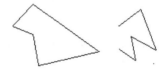

To draw a polygon:

- Select the polygon tool
- Click (and release) at the starting point
- Click where you want the next vertex
- Continue clicking each new vertex
- To finish, either click the starting point (for a closed polygon) or double-click a final point (for an open polygon)

Preview While you're clicking vertices, hold the Alt key (Windows) or Option key (Macintosh) to preview what a closed polygon would look like—in other words, to see what the final shape would look like if you were to finish by clicking the starting point. To force closure, hold the key while double-clicking the final vertex.

Drag selection handles Click and drag any of the eight black selection handles to resize a polygon.

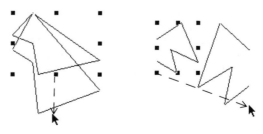

Reshape Select Reshape from the Edit menu to switch to Reshape mode, and select it again to exit Reshape mode when you are finished. In Reshape mode, the cursor changes to a reshaping crosshair (⊕), and you can:

1. Change the shape of a polygon: click and drag any vertex to a new location.

2. Open a closed polygon: Control-Alt-click (Windows) or Command-Option-click (Macintosh) the line segment you want to remove.

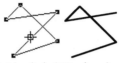

3. Close an open polygon: Control-Alt-click (Windows) or Command-Option-click (Macintosh) either the starting point or the finishing point.

4. Remove a vertex to reduce the number of edges: Alt-click (Windows) or Option-click (Macintosh) the vertex.

5. Add a vertex to any edge: Alt-click (Windows) or Option-click (Macintosh) the edge where you want the vertex

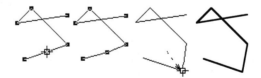

Shortcut (Macintosh only) Hold the Control key to switch temporarily to Reshape mode, and release the key to exit Reshape mode.

Splines

The spline tool lets you draw open or closed free-form curves based on cubic splines, similar to Bezier curves. An open curve is one that doesn't start and end at the same point. Below, the left figure is closed and the right is open.

- Select the spline tool
- Click (and release) at the starting point
- Click where you want the first vertex (the first change of direction)
- Continue clicking each new vertex
- To finish, either click the starting point (for a closed curve) or double-click a final point (for an open curve)

Preview While you're clicking vertices, hold the Alt key (Windows) or Option key (Macintosh) to preview what a closed curve would look like—in other words, to see what the final shape would look like if you were to finish by clicking the starting point. To force closure, hold the key while double-clicking the final vertex.

Drag selection handles Click and drag any of the eight black selection handles to resize a curve.

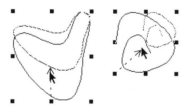

Reshape Select Reshape from the Edit menu to switch to Reshape mode, and select it again to exit Reshape mode when you are finished. In Reshape mode, the cursor changes to a reshaping crosshair ($\oplus$), and you can:

1. Change the shape of a curve: click and drag any single vertex to a new location. Or, select any vertex to see its velocity handles (tangents) and then drag those handles to change the angles of the arcs connecting that vertex to adjacent vertices.

Velocity handles   Vertices

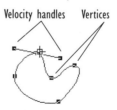

As you drag the end of a velocity handle, you change both the angle of the line and the velocity of the curve at that point; the curve redraws so that the line is still tangent. Usually, the opposite velocity handle remains aligned to the one you are dragging, but you can hold the Alt key (Windows) or Option key (Macintosh) while dragging to leave the opposite handle fixed, thus creating a corner.

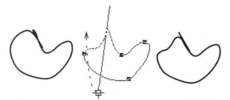

2. Open a closed curve: Control-Alt-click (Windows) or Command-Option-click (Macintosh) the line segment you want to remove.

3. Close an open curve: Control-Alt-click (Windows) or Command-Option-click (Macintosh) either the starting point or the finishing point.

4. Remove a vertex: Alt-click (Windows) or Option-click (Macintosh) the vertex.

5. Add a vertex to any curve: Alt-click (Windows) or Option-click (Macintosh) the edge where you want the vertex.

Shortcut (Macintosh only) Hold the Control key to switch temporarily to Reshape mode, and release the key to exit Reshape mode.

Import objects

You can paste objects from other applications into the view.

- In the other application, copy text or a picture
- In a StatView view window, paste the object

Pasted text can be manipulated the same was as text created by StatView. However, you cannot manipulate a picture except to resize it by dragging its black selection handles. To return a resized picture to its original size, double-click it.

Change fill patterns, pen patterns, and line types

The Draw palette's fill, pen, and line tools let you change the appearance of drawn objects. You can fill shapes with patterns, change lines to arrows, and change the thickness and pen pattern of lines.

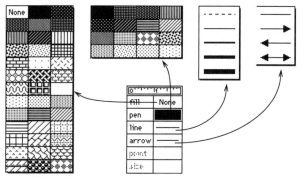

Fill pattern Select any drawn shape (except a line) and choose a fill pattern to add a pattern to its interior. Choose None for a transparent (empty) fill. (None and white fill are not the same.) Closed shapes fill as you would expect; open curves and polygons fill as though a line connected the first and last vertices, and open arcs fill as though lines connected their endpoints to their center points.

Pen pattern Select any drawn shape and choose a pen pattern to change the appearance of its edges. All lines default to a solid pattern. Pen patterns have greater visual impact with thicker lines. (PostScript printers interpret some patterns as halftones, so a single pixel screen line might print as a gray line with some patterns.)

Line thickness Select any drawn shape and choose a line thickness for its edges. All line widths default to a single point line. (To print hairlines, see "View preferences," p. 232.) Choose the top, dotted line for invisible lines.

Arrow Select any drawn line or arc and choose one or two arrowheads. You cannot add arrowheads to the other kinds of shapes.

Change colors

Pop-up menus at the bottom of the Draw palette let you choose colors for the pen, fill, and background (the empty view area outside graphs). You can change the pen color for any object, including text, and you can change the shape color for any object you can fill. You can also change the background of the entire view.

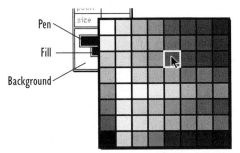

Control-click (Windows) or Command-click (Macintosh) to select both pen and fill colors at once.

Color preferences

You can use Color Preferences to change StatView's color palette. StatView can display any color in each slot of the color palette; the number of colors available depends on your monitor. If you have a monochrome monitor, you can still use colors with a color printer. See "Color Palette preferences (Macintosh only)," p. 226.

Layout tools

Commands in the Layout menu let you manage page layout and arrange, move, lock, group, overlay, and clean up objects. Layout tools apply also to drawn objects grouped to analysis results.

Control page layout

Drawing Size from the Layout menu lets you control how many pages wide and tall your view is. As you produce results, StatView automatically adds new pages to the bottom of the view, and then starts a second column of pages, etc. If you want a view to be wide rather than tall, you must create the additional pages using the Drawing Size dialog box. You can also use Drawing Size to remove blank pages after deleting results.

- From the Layout menu, select Drawing Size
- Click and drag to indicate the page layout you want
- Click OK

Each white rectangle represents one page in your document. Pages are added to or removed from the active view when you click OK. StatView can handle both portrait and landscape printer settings for page orientation.

You cannot set the drawing size smaller than the number of pages needed by any results currently present. A view preference lets you limit drawing size for printing or export to other applications; see "View preferences," p. 232.

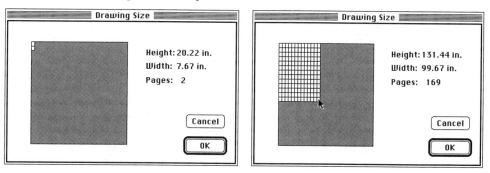

Arrange objects

Clean Up Items from the Layout menu lets you neatly arrange graphs, tables, and drawn objects in the view. This command always works with all results in a view; it is not necessary to select objects before using Clean Up Items

- From the Layout menu, select Clean Up Items

Clean up by Choose whether to keep objects in their current order or to sort them by analysis type.

Distance between items Specify how far apart to space each item. The distance you specify is rounded to the nearest grid unit if the grid is on (see "Exercise," p. 215). The default distance is 0.25 inches.

Ignore page breaks By default, Clean Up Items forces extra space between objects as needed to keep objects from being split over page breaks; avoiding page breaks is preferable for printing, unless you need to tile especially large objects across several pages, e.g., for a poster. However, some people prefer to check this option (turn it on) while working on analyses to save screen space. On the screen, page breaks are depicted with dotted red lines.

Align to left margin By default, Clean Up Items doesn't reposition items horizontally. You can check this option (turn it on) to align all items along a left margin determined by the Horizontal distance setting.

Additional alignment commands appear in the Draw palette; see "Align to Grid," p. 218 and "Align Objects," p. 218.

Move objects

To move objects individually, select the object and drag it to a new location. Be careful not to drag black selection handles; dragging selection handles resizes objects. If you accidentally resize an object, immediately select Undo from the Edit menu.

(Here as in other chapters, **objects** are tables, graphs, table or graph components, drawn shapes, or text items. Most objects can be arranged, moved, and edited with the same basic techniques. For drawing and layout purposes, all objects work the same way *unless* a particular type of change would destroy the nature of the object. For example, you cannot edit numbers in a table (wrong numbers would do you no good), and you cannot move a plot outside its graph frame (a plot would be meaningless outside its axis context).

Lock and unlock objects

You can lock any object to prevent it from being moved or edited accidentally. A locked object cannot be moved, edited, resized, or reshaped. The black selection handles for a locked object are grayed or dimmed. However, you can still select and copy objects, change variable assignments, and change analysis parameters. StatView still recalculates results if their data condition changes.

- Select the object
- From the Layout menu, select Lock

To unlock a locked object so you can again move or edit it:

- Select the object
- From the Layout menu, select unlock

Group objects

You can select two or more objects and group them together so they act as one object. You can group any combination of results, drawn shapes, and text items. If you use Draw tools to make modifications to results, you might want to group them to those results so that they move together and stay intact when you Clean Up or rearrange results. Unless text additions and shapes are grouped with their tables and graphs, they do not move together.

• Select the objects

• From the Layout menu, select Group

To ungroup grouped objects:

• Select the group (or several groups)

• From the Layout menu, select Ungroup

You can also group grouped objects together. Ungrouping compound groups works one "group level" at a time. For example, if you group a pair of objects, then group another pair of objects, and finally group the two grouped pairs, later ungrouping the foursome produces two grouped pairs that could in turn be ungrouped.

When you change variables for grouped results, it affects all the results.

Overlap and overlay objects

Objects in the view are layered in front of previously created objects. (The last object you create or draw is "on top" or "at the front." Each previous object is one layer behind its successor.) If objects do not overlap, this layering is irrelevant. However, if objects overlap, the objects in front obscure objects behind. You can re-layer objects with Draw tools and Layout menu commands.

To move an object, select it and choose the appropriate command or tool. If you select several objects, they move as a group.

Draw palette	Layout menu	Action
	Move to back	Moves the selected object all the way back, behind all other objects
	Move to front	Moves the selected object all the way forward, in front of all other objects
	Move Backward	Sends the object one layer back
	Move Forward	Brings the object one layer forward

Exercise

This exercise shows how to accentuate a table by layering it above a drawn, filled rectangle to create a frame.

• Create any graph or table, e.g., a Descriptive Statistics analysis

• In the Draw palette, select the rectangle tool

- Click and drag to draw a rectangle around the table

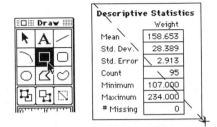

- Make sure the rectangle is still selected (has black selection handles)
- Select a fill pattern from the Draw palette

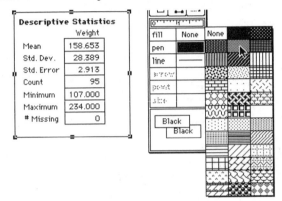

Don't be alarmed! Your filled rectangle *should* now be in front, completely hiding the table behind it.

- Make sure the rectangle is still selected
- Click the Move to back tool in the Draw palette

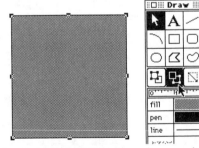

- Select the rectangle tool and draw a smaller rectangle around the table
- Choose a solid white fill for this rectangle
  (Make sure the smaller rectangle is still selected)
- From the Layout menu, select Move Backward
  (Make sure the smaller rectangle is still selected)

Now you have a layer of three objects: a table in front, a white rectangle in the middle, and a gray rectangle at the back.

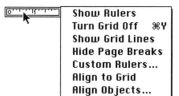

Rulers and grid lines

Ruler and grid commands in the Draw palette help you align objects neatly.

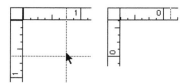

Show/Hide Rulers Choose whether to show horizontal and vertical rulers along the top and left edges of the view. When rulers are visible, hatch marks in the rulers show exactly where your cursor is positioned at that instant, which helps you draw and move objects precisely.

To move the origin (zero) of a ruler, click and drag the zero-position tick mark. To reset the origin back to the edge of the window, click the box in the upper left corner where the rulers intersect.

Turn Grid On/Off Choose whether to have objects snap into alignment with an even grid in the view window. The grid affects objects you create and objects you draw. Grid lines are spaced at each inch or centimeter, depending on your system configuration and Custom Rulers setting, and objects snap into alignment at each tick division along the ruler (not just at the drawn grid lines). The grid is on by default.

If you create or position an item when the grid is off, you can later snap it to the grid by selecting the object(s), turning the grid on, and selecting Align To Grid.

Show/Hide Grid Lines Choose whether to make grid lines visible in the view window. Grid lines are never printed.

Show/Hide Page Breaks Choose whether to make page breaks visible in the view window.

Custom Rulers Select Custom Rulers if you want to change the ruler measurement units, grid spacing, or the colors used for page breaks and grid lines.

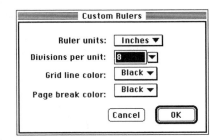

For example, below is the upper left corner of a view window in which rulers and grid lines are shown. Using Custom Rulers, we specified centimeter ruler units and two divisions per centimeter. We turned Align to Grid on, which forces the cursor to align to a ruler tick mark at all times—notice the dotted lines in the rulers showing exactly where the cursor is located.

Align to Grid Align to Grid snaps selected objects into alignment with the grid. (You must turn the grid on to use this command.) Objects align by the rectangle they inscribe—in other words, what aligns to the grid is the smallest rectangle you could draw around every part of the object, including titles, legends, notes, etc., with a tiny margin. You can see this rectangle when you start to drag the object.

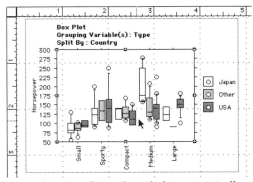

Align Objects Align Objects lets you align selected objects vertically and horizontally.

- Select the objects you want to align
- Select Align Objects from the Draw palette
- Choose whether to align or distribute objects according to their tops, bottoms, rights, lefts, middles, or sizes
- Click Align

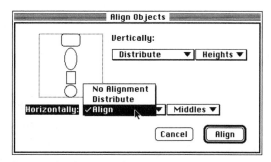

As you make choices, the sample objects in the corner move to demonstrate how your choices will affect the objects. The choices above centered all the objects and distributed them vertically for even graphs.

You can quickly bring together two objects that are far apart in the view by selecting them in the Results Browser and then using Align Objects.

Tips and shortcuts

Tool Bar (Windows only)

The StatView tool bar provides one-step access to many of the most frequently-used StatView commands. To hide or show the tool bar, select Tool Bar from the View menu.

If you forget the function of a tool, pause with the cursor positioned over the tool for a tip.

Help

StatView offers a number of ways to get help online, while you're working.

1. Hints (both Windows and Macintosh)
2. Help (Windows only)
3. Status bar (Windows only)
4. Tool tips (Windows only)
5. Apple Guide (Macintosh only)
6. Balloon Help (Macintosh only)

Each of these systems meets a different need:

Hints give suggestions about what you are doing in StatView—how to use a new window, how to complete an analysis, what to do next, how to resolve an error, etc.

Help has brief discussions of the StatView environment (its windows, commands, and general organization) and gives general advice and step-by-step instructions for common tasks. Windows Help is a hypertext system: you can click any highlighted words or phrases to get brief definitions or to jump to related topics.

Status bar messages, **Tool tips**, and **Balloon Help** teach you the functions of items you see on the screen: menu items, buttons, and so on.

Apple Guide answers questions about how to do things by leading you step-by-step through the process—if necessary, asking you questions along the way, pointing out where you should look, and even doing steps for you.

Hints window

The Hints window is a floating window that contains helpful information about every item on the screen. You can make it visible any time by selecting Hints Window from the View menu (Windows) or Hints from the Window menu (Macintosh). The Hints window appears automatically in some situations, but does not close automatically. You can hide it by clicking its close box. You can resize it and move it anywhere on your screen.

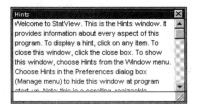 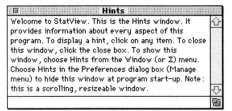

You can also use Hints Preferences to control when the window automatically appears. When you are first learning StatView, it might be helpful to keep the Hints window visible so you get instant feedback on how to use the program.

The Hints window displays two different levels of helpful information. Interface hints (Windows) or Balloon hints (Macintosh) appear in the Hints window when you click on an item of interest in the dataset, a view or a dialog box. Similar information is available through Balloon help (see below). Informational hints offer more detailed information. They explain the following features:

1. definitions of the functions in the Formula, Recode, Series, Random Numbers and Criteria dialog boxes

2. variable usage for template slots in the Assign Variables dialog box

3. dimmed options in analysis dialog boxes when you edit an analysis

4. error messages

Help (Windows only)

Help offers brief discussions of StatView's windows, menus, dialog boxes, and commands. It also gives step-by-step instructions on how to complete common tasks in StatView. StatView's Help is a hypertext system, in which you can navigate freely between topics by clicking underlined words. To start Help, press F1 or select a command from the Help menu.

Status bar (Windows only)

The Windows status bar at the bottom of the main StatView window describes menu items and buttons in the dataset, view, and browser windows. The status bar also informs you of the progress of StatView's calculations.

status bar ——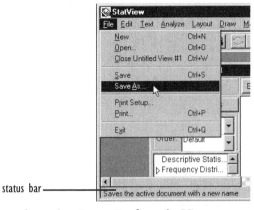

To show or hide the status bar, select Status Bar from the View menu.

Tool tips (Windows only)

To learn the function of a tool on the tool bar, pause with the cursor positioned over a tool.

Apple Guide (Macintosh only)

StatView harnesses the power of Apple Guide active assistance with its own StatView Guide. StatView Guide goes beyond the passive information found in typical online help systems, enabling you to learn while you work. Rather than searching through lengthy help text, you can simply follow StatView Guide's step-by-step instructions and actually complete the task while you learn. StatView Guide gives you the same sort of help you get when an expert sits down with you and not only explains things but shows you what to do: it guides you from start to finish as you create any statistical test, table, or graph in StatView.

Use StatView Guide

To use StatView Guide, launch StatView and select StatView Guide from the Help menu on the right side of your menu bar.

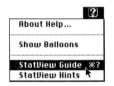

This launches StatView Guide. Click Topics for an overview:

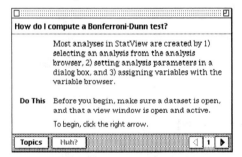

Select a topic and phrase and click OK to begin. StatView Guide leads you step by step through the analysis you want to complete:

For more information about how to use Apple Guide, switch to the Finder and select About Apple Guide from the help menu.

Balloon help (Macintosh only)

Macintosh Balloon help explains almost all program features: the choices in dialog boxes, buttons in the view and dataset windows and all browsers, all the parts of the dataset and views. To use balloons:

• Select Show Balloons from the Help menu on the right end of the menu bar

Menu commands are only described by balloons (and status bar messages in Windows). All other balloon help is duplicated in the Hints window.

Error messages

When an error occurs, StatView generates an error message. The Hints window automatically appears to display the error message, often an explanation of why the requested action cannot be completed. In the Hints Preferences dialog box, you can set an option to have StatView beep when it displays an error message.

Alert messages

An alert message warns you of potentially dangerous situation or advises you of the consequences of an action you requested. Alert messages sometimes appear in a box with a single OK button. You can set a preference to have these appear in the Hints window instead, which automatically opens when there is an alert message to display. The advantage to this setting is that your work is not interrupted by an alert box, yet you still see the alert message.

Preferences

You can set preferences that govern the behavior of many different parts of StatView.

- From the Manage menu, select Preferences
- Select the type of preferences you want to change
- Click Modify

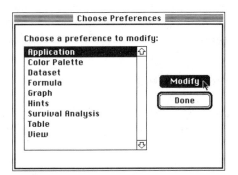

When you are finished setting preferences, click Done.

All preferences are stored in the StatView Library. If you move or delete the Library, all preferences return to their original settings. While this can be a convenient way to undo numerous changes, you should be aware of the other effects of discarding your Library file; see p. 233.

Application preferences

Application preferences affect the overall application.

Windows zoom (Macintosh only) Occupy full screen tells StatView to make its windows as large as your monitor allows. Leave room for Finder icons lets you see your hard disk, the Trash, etc. along the right edge. Your choice takes effect the next time a new window is opened.

Browsers' appearance Choose the font and size you want for the variable, analysis, results, and function browsers. You can type a specific size not in the pop-up menu. Your choice takes effect the next time you open StatView.

Initially hide which browsers? Usually, the analysis and variable browsers are automatically shown; the results browser is only shown when you ask for it. Check any browser you *don't* want to see; uncheck any browser you *do* want to see.

Use System's Temporary Folder Check Use System's Temporary folder if you want temporary files stored inside the temporary folder (Windows) or the System folder's temporary folder (Macintosh). Uncheck the option if you want to store them in the StatView folder. (Temporary files are written to store information from memory-intensive operations.)

Color Palette preferences (Macintosh only)

StatView can display any color in each slot of the color palette; the number of colors available depends on your monitor. If you have a monochrome monitor, you can still use colors with a color printer.

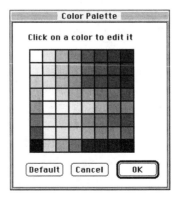

On a color system, you can edit the color palette:

- Click the color slot you want to change
- In the standard color picker, specify a new color
- Click OK

Your changes take effect immediately.

Dataset preferences

Enter key moves When you type a value and press Enter on the numeric keypad, the cursor either moves down to the cell in the next row of the same column, moves right to the same row in the next column, or stays in place, according to your choice. Your choice takes effect immediately. While editing, you can use cursor arrow keys (up, down, left, right) to enter a value and move a different direction.

Font and Size Choose the font and size you want the dataset to use. You can type a specific size. Your choice takes effect for the next new dataset. You can change any individual dataset with the Text menu.

Decimal places Choose how many decimal places you usually want to see for variables with type real. Your choice takes effect for the next new column. You can change individual columns with the Decimal Places pop-up menu in the attribute pane.

Silently accept ambiguous values If you enter an ambiguous date/time value, such as 8/11 (which could mean either August 11 or 8 November), StatView can either warn you, or silently trust that you know what you're doing.

When opening datasets from other platforms StatView stores real numbers and does its computations to the fullest precision of the machine you are using. This precision varies between platforms (see "Type," p. 73). When you import a dataset created on another platform, StatView usually recomputes dynamic formulas so that its values are computed the way they would be computed on your current platform. If you prefer, they can be converted to static formulas that are not recomputed. (See the online documentation for details about file formats that can be opened by your version of StatView.)

Formula preferences

Formula Preferences	Formula Preferences
Default appearance: Font: Arial Size: 8 Cancel OK	Default appearance: Font: Geneva ▼ Size: 9 ▼ Cancel OK

Font and Size Choose the font and size you want the formula window to use. You can type a specific size. Your choice takes effect for the next new formula window. You can change any individual Formula window with the Text menu.

Enlarging the font size beyond 12 or 14 point might render the buttons in the keypad of the Formula dialog box illegible.

If you want to use formulas to work with double-byte text strings, such as with Kanji characters, you must set the Formulas font to an appropriate font, such as Osaka.

Graph preferences

Graph preferences let you change the default display for all graphs, while Edit Display lets you fine-tune each graph individually.

Graph Preferences

Default size
Vertical: 1.5 inches
Horizontal: 2.25 inches

Default numbers
Axis format: Free Format
Axis decimal places: 2
Other decimal places: 3
☐ Always have leading digit

Order in which to choose points, fills, and colors
First ○ □ △ ◇ ＋ ✕ ● ■ ▲ ◆ ◑ ◨ ⊠ ▽ ▼ ◇ Last
First Last
First Last

Default frame:

Default point:
size: ○ ▼

Distinguish cells by: Point/fill and color

Cancel   OK

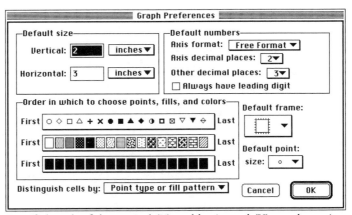

Default size Specify length of the vertical (Y) and horizontal (X) axes by typing values and choosing scale units (inches, centimeters, picas or points). Graphs can be resized individually.

Default numbers Choose the numeric format and number of decimal places to display along axes, titles, notes, and labels. To include a zero before the decimal point (e.g. 0.25 instead of .25), check Always have leading digit.

Default frame Select which graph frame (which combination of axes) you want.

Default point size Choose a size from the points in the Default Point Size pop-up menu.

Order in which to choose points, fills, and colors Choose the order in which you want point types, fills, and colors to be chosen for graphs. Click and hold the item you want to modify, then select a choice from the pop-up menu and release the mouse button. Do not drag across the bar itself. As you change the position of one color, point, or fill in the order, the others adjust; for example, if you choose black for your first variable, the item that is currently black changes to the color that had been first.

Distinguish cells by For compound graphs (see "Multiple and compound results," p. 135) that show more than one group variable, StatView automatically assigns a different point type, color, or fill pattern to each variable so that they can be easily distinguished. Choose which parameter you want to vary between variables. For example, choose color if you want different variables to have the same point type and fill pattern but different colors.

Hints preferences

Display hints window when it contains Check Interface hints (Windows) or Balloon hints (Macintosh) if you want to see hints for buttons, menu commands, and other interface items. Check Informational hints if you want to see general informational hints. Leave both options unchecked if you don't usually want to see any hints at all.

Font and Size Choose the font and size you want the hints window to use. You can type a specific size.

Initially show hints window Check this option if you want StatView to show the Hints window automatically each time it starts. Uncheck it if you prefer not to see hints.

Beep for each error message Check this option if you want StatView to beep when displaying error messages. Uncheck it if you want error messages to appear silently.

Show alert messages in hints window Check this option if you want to see error messages in the hints window rather than in alert boxes.

Survival Analysis preferences

Use "More choices" dialog as default By default, you see the "Fewer choices" versions of the nonparametric and regression model dialog boxes. If you do not routinely need to edit the "More choices" parameters, leave the boxes unchecked. If you prefer to see all the parameters each time, check the boxes. Each dialog box lets you switch freely between more and fewer choices; your choices determine what you see first.

Retain covariate matrix after regression calculations StatView can either save or discard the intermediate covariate matrices it computes. Retaining the matrices consumes RAM; discarding them saves RAM but can slow down the subsequent calculations of additional model results.

Censor variable = 0 means observation is This option specifies how your censor variable is coded. If you choose Uncensored, 0 values in the censor variable are taken to mean that corresponding event times are *uncensored*, and any other (nonzero) values in the censor variable indicate *censored* event times. If you choose Censored, the opposite is true: 0 values indicate *censored* event times, and any nonzero values indicate *uncensored* event times.

Table preferences

Table preferences govern the way table results are displayed by default. In this context, **tables** are results from any statistical analysis that take the form of words and numbers arranged in rows and columns—as opposed to **graphs**, which are results from any analysis that take picture form, such as scattergrams and box plots. ("Tables" include but are not limited to contingency tables.)

You can change the appearance of any individual table by clicking Edit Display.

Default numbers Choose the numeric format and number of decimal places to display in tables. To include a zero before the decimal point (e.g. 0.25 instead of .25), check Always have leading digit.

Table format This option lets you choose how borders are drawn between rows and columns. Choose an appearance type from the pop-up menu.

Row height Specify how many lines of text to use for each row; e.g., choose 1 for single-spacing, 2 for double-spacing, etc.

View preferences

View preferences govern the way view windows behave, print, and save. Your choices take effect with the next new view window.

Font and Size   Choose the font and size you want the view window to use. You can type a specific size.

These settings affect any results you generate with the analysis browser, including table and graph titles, numbers, axis labels, and legends. You can override these settings for any individual table or graph element with the Text menu. Your choice also controls the defaults used for the Draw palette's text tool.

Print and copy lines at 1/4 width   Check this option on to reduce all single line widths to approximately one quarter of their specified size when they are printed with most printers. Otherwise lines are single-pixel lines. Your choice also affects tables, graphs or drawn objects that are copied and pasted into another application. Your choice takes effect immediately and applies to existing as well as subsequently-drawn objects. The option does not affect screen display.

Limit document size   (Windows) Check this option (turn it on) to limit the number of pages in view documents; this prevents out of memory problems when printing by establishing a maximum document size of approximately 54"×54" that should work trouble-free for any 300dpi printer. Uncheck the option (turn it off) if you need to print larger documents.

(Macintosh) If you save your views as PICT files and read them into MacDraw II, you need to constrain the document size so it does not exceed the capabilities of MacDraw II. Clicking Limit document size to MacDraw II limits the total number of pages in a view to the number of pages that MacDraw II can contain. (MacDraw drawing size is 9 pages high by 13 pages across on a LaserWriter, a bit less than 100"×100"; StatView's document size is 23 pages high by 30 pages across, about 227"×227".)

Save analysis results with view   By default, calculations are saved when you save a view so the results do not need to be recalculated when the file is reopened with its original dataset. You can turn this option off to save disk space. If you create a view to use as a template, it makes sense *not* to save results so the template file is smaller.

Templates appear using view text defaults Usually when you use a template, the text of its output is formatted the way it was when you saved the template. This is what you would expect a template to do. You might, however, wish to override these settings and use the default text settings from view preferences. This is useful when you use templates provided with StatView and want their results to match analyses already in the view.

Copy tables and graphs Usually when you copy a table or graph, a WMF (Windows) or PICT (Macintosh) graphic version of that result is copied, so that you can paste the result into any application and have it look the same. Check this option (turn it on) to copy the result both as text and as a graphic object; one advantage to turning this option on is that you can paste analysis results (tables) into datasets for further study.

Double-click on table/graph Usually double-clicking a table a graph in the view is a shortcut to clicking the Edit Display button; Right-double-clicking or Alt-double-clicking (Windows) or Option-double-clicking (Macintosh) is a shortcut to Edit Analysis. You can switch the shortcuts by choosing Edit Analysis for double-click.

StatView Library

StatView stores information in a Library in the StatView folder. The Library contains all preference settings and information the program needs to speed up certain operations (for example, application preferences and category definitions). It also stores the locations of the Templates and Tools folders. If the Library file is discarded or misplaced, StatView creates a new one with default preference settings. You will have to specify preference settings again.

Example Views and Datasets

In your StatView folder is a folder of example views and datasets that demonstrate special ways of working with StatView. To try these examples, open the view files in StatView.

Dataset Templates

Also in your StatView folder is a folder of "dataset templates." These are datasets that use special formula variables and criteria to compute specialized statistics.

Normality Test

StatView gives you a number of useful techniques for evaluating how well continuous data conform to a normal distribution. Some common techniques are:

1. Plot a histogram of the variable with a normal curve (see "Frequency Distribution," p. 13 of *StatView Reference*).
2. Plot a frequency distribution of the variable's Z-scores (see "Frequency Distribution," p. 13

of *StatView Reference*).

3. Calculate the variable's skewness and kurtosis (see "Descriptive Statistics," p. 1 of *StatView Reference*).

Unfortunately, none of the preceding techniques gives an objective criterion upon which to decide whether a distribution is normal. Therefore, StatView provides a pair of dataset and view templates for checking normality.

First, paste into the template a copy of the continuous variable you want to check.

• In the original dataset, select the variable (double-click its name)

• From the Edit menu, select Copy

• Open the Normality Test template from the Dataset Templates folder

	Measurement		Input Column
	Actual	Ideal Normal	
Type :	Real	Real	Real
Source :	User Entered	Dynamic Form...	User Entered
Class :	Continuous	Continuous	Continuous
Format :	Free Format Fi...	Free Format Fi...	Free Format Fixed
Dec. Places :	3	3	3

Normality Test — Compact / Expand / Criteria: No Criteria

• Click the first cell in the Actual column of the Measurement compact variable

• From the Edit menu, select Paste

A formula automatically computes Ideal Normal values from a normal distribution with the same mean and standard deviation as the variable you pasted.

Next, we use the K-S Normality Test template to test the hypothesis that your Actual values and the computed Ideal Normal values come from the same distribution.

• From the Analyze menu, select QC Analyses/K-S Normality Test

The Assign Variables dialog box appears and automatically assigns the variables to the proper slots, since the variables and the slots share the same names

• Click OK

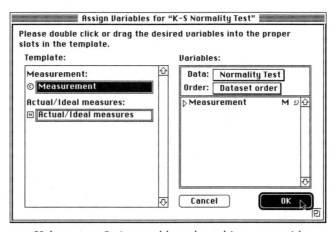

A new view shows a Kolmogorov-Smirnov table and two histograms with normal curves.

If the result of the K-S test is significant (i.e., $p < 0.05$), then the Actual and Ideal variables are probably not from the same distributions. This implies that the Actual variable is not normally distributed, because the Ideal variable is. You should be aware, however, that the K-S test is sensitive to outliers, so you should inspect your data for such cases. The histograms with fitted normal curves let you compare the distributions visually.

Compute Bartlett's Test and Compute Welch's Test

Bartlett's test is a test of homogeneity of variances among groups. A significant p value means that group variances are not equal. Welch's test is a robust one-way ANOVA. Use it instead of one-way ANOVA when Bartlett's test shows that group variances are not equal. Both templates work the same way; we'll demonstrate Bartlett's with the Lipid Data.

- From the File menu, select Open
- Select Lipid Data from the Sample Data folder
- Click Open
- From the File menu, select Open
- Select Compute Bartlett's Test from the Dataset Templates folder
- Click Open

In the left pane, you must provide the counts, means, and standard deviations on separate rows for each group in your model. The easiest way to do this is to copy and paste results from ANOVA means table analysis:

- From the Analyze menu, select New View
- From the analysis browser under ANOVA, select Means Table
- Click Create Analysis
- Click OK to accept the default analysis parameters
- Select a continuous variable (Weight) and click Add
- Select a nominal variable (Gender) and click Add

Means Table for Weight
Effect: Gender

	Count	Mean	Std. Dev.	Std. Err.
male	71	169.282	23.288	2.764
female	24	127.208	16.208	3.308

Then, copy the resulting table as text and paste it into an empty dataset. First, be sure that you have view preferences set to allow copying the table as text:

- From the Manage menu, select Preferences
- Select View and click Modify
- If it is unchecked (turned off), check Copy tables/graphs as both text and metafile Windows) or Copy tables/graphs as both TEXT and PICT (Macintosh) and click OK
- Click Done
- From the Edit menu, select Copy (be sure the means table is still selected)
- From the File menu, select New
- Click in the first empty data cell
- From the Edit menu, select Paste

		Column 1	Column 2	Column 3	Column 4	Column 5
▶	Type:	String	String	String	String	String
▶	Source:	User Entered	User Entered	User Entered	User Entered	User Entered
▶	Class:	Nominal	Nominal	Nominal	Nominal	Nominal
▶	Format:	●	●	●	●	●
▶	Dec. Places:	●	●	●	●	●
1		Means Tabl...				
2		Effect: Gen...				
3			Count	Mean	Std. Dev.	Std. Err.
4		male	71	169.282	23.288	2.764
5		female	24	127.208	16.208	3.308

Now delete the extra cells and change the columns of numbers to have type real:

- Click the variable name cell for Column 5 to select the standard error column
- From the Edit menu, select Delete
- Click and drag over the first three row numbers to select the rows with title text
- From the Edit menu, select Delete
- Select Columns 2, 3, and 4 by dragging over their names
- From the Type pop-up menu for one of the columns, select Real to change all three
- To the warning about loss of data, click Yes

		Column 1	Column 2	Column 3	Column 4
▶	Type:	String	Real	Real	Real
▶	Source:	User Entered	User Entered	User Entered	User Entered
▶	Class:	Nominal	Nominal	Nominal	Nominal
▶	Format:	●	Free Forma...	Free Forma...	Free Forma...
▶	Dec. Places:	●	0	0	0
1		male	71	169	23
2		female	24	127	16

Select the data and paste it into the dataset template:

- Click and drag to select all data cells
- From the Edit menu, select Copy

- From the Window menu, select the Compute Bartlett's/Welch's test window
- Select the empty data cells in the first four columns
- From the Edit menu, select Paste

	Group	Group Counts	Group Means	Std. Dev.	F	p value
1	male	71	169.282	23.288	3.925	.0476
2	female	24	127.208	16.208	3.925	.0476

Finally, read the results from the variables on the right pane of the window.

Make your own dataset templates

Examine the formulas and criteria used in these dataset templates to get ideas for your own dataset templates. Instructions for building dataset templates are given under "Build dataset templates," p. 240.

Common questions

Dataset

How can I record dataset comments?

You can easily annotate datasets by adding one or two string variables to the dataset and typing your comments in those columns. You might record the source of the data and any notes on methodology that you will need to know later. For example, we could document the Candy Bars Data this way:

		NOTES	Brand
▶	Type :	String	Category
▶	Source :	User Entered	User Entered
▶	Class :	Informative	Nominal
▶	Format :	●	●
▶	Dec. Places :	●	●
	1	This dataset, Candy Bars Data,	M&M/Mars
	2	records brand, name, and	Hershey
	3	per-serving nutritional	Hershey
	4	information for 75 popular	M&M/Mars
	5	candy bars. The data were	Charms
	6	gathered by hand at several	M&M/Mars
	7	Berkeley, California convenience	Hershey
	8	stores in July of 1995.	Tobler
	9		Nestle

To prevent yourself from accidentally trying to use the variable(s) as nominal data, be sure to change the class to informative. Also, note that you can copy the cells and paste them into your view document to make the same information accessible in a presentation.

How does StatView use ordering in nominal variables?

StatView automatically sorts the levels of a nominal variable for its graphs and tables—from left to right or bottom to top in graph scales, or from top to bottom in tables. For numeric nominal variables (those with type Real, Integer, Long Integer, Date/Time, or Currency), that means that levels appear from smallest to greatest. For string nominals, that means levels appear in alphabetic order. Category variables are sorted according to the order in which levels are defined. If you define Categories manually using Edit Categories before entering data, that means the order in which they appear in the scrolling list. If you import data or enter data in a variable and then change its type to Category, StatView automatically defines the levels of the Category from the values in the variable, sorted in alphabetical order.

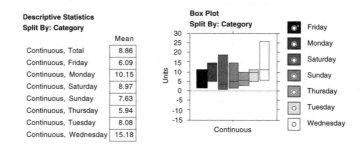

There is one exception to this rule: Pareto Analysis charts and tables show cells in decreasing order of frequency, i.e., groups with the most cases first, least cases last:

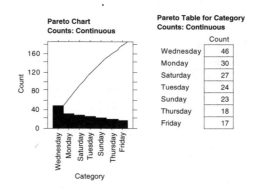

Note: StatView's statistical calculations are not influenced by order in nominal variables—the numerical results are the same no matter how your groups are ordered. In other words, StatView's nominal variables are not ordinal variables.

How can I reorder category variables?

Alphabetical order is not always the best order for informational displays. Generally you should sort information in statistical displays according to the meaning of your data. For example, if you want to demonstrate that groups of patients showed increasing effects from treatments, you might want to sort those groups from least affected to most affected in your plots of the effects. Or, if you are examining sales patterns for each day of the week, you might want to show those days in calendar order.

You might think you could make changes to the order of labels by directly editing your graph or table. However, this is not possible. Instead, you must first create a new column in the Stat-View data set and then redo your analysis with that variable.

- First, determine the order you want; if the list is long or hard to remember, you might want to write it down
- Open your dataset and scroll to the variable you want to reorder
- Insert a column to the right of this column and name it
- Open the attribute pane (if it is closed) by double clicking the control in the upper right corner
- Change the Type of this newly inserted column to Category
- When asked to Choose Category for the column, click New

One at a time, enter the labels for each group, in the order you determined. (Be sure to type each label exactly as it appears in the variable—don't change spelling, spacing, capitalization, etc.)

Edit Category
Category name: Self-defined category
Group label: Saturday
Add · Replace · Delete	Sunday, Monday, Tuesday, Wednesday, Thursday, Friday, **Saturday**	Cancel · Done

- Click Done
- Change the type for the old variable to String, and change its class to Informative
- Select the old column by clicking its name
- From the edit menu, select Copy
- Select the new column by clicking its name
- From the Edit menu, select Paste

Now you have a new copy of your old column. It should look the same; however, in the new column, the levels of the category are ordered according to your definition. Any graphs or tables you produce with this variable will show its levels in that order.

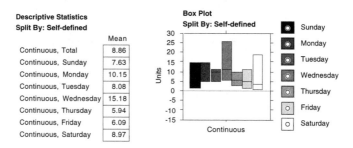

Formulas and criteria

How can I edit formulas?

From the Source pop-up menu, select Dynamic or Static Formula again. This reopens the Formula window so you can edit the formula definition. When you're done making changes, click Compute. Control-click (Windows) or Command-click (Macintosh) Compute to calculate the formula without closing the Formula window.

How can I edit criteria?

From the Manage menu, select Edit/Apply Criteria. Select the criterion you want to change and click Edit. When you're done making changes, click Apply to use the criterion, Save to save changes without applying the criterion, or Select to highlight all rows meeting the criterion. Control-click (Windows) or Command-click (Macintosh) Apply to apply the criterion without closing the Criteria window.

Copy and Paste your favorite formulas

If you find yourself using the same formulas over and over, you might want to Copy them from the Formula window and Paste them into a text document or the Scrapbook (Macintosh). Then you can quickly reuse them in any dataset.

Build dataset templates

If you regularly need to use the same formulas or criteria on different datasets—for instance, for a monthly report—you can build a **dataset template**. Create a dataset with all the variable names, attributes, and formulas you use every week.

	Dates	Gross	Over/short	Tax	Net	Net weekly
1	May 21	$2,274.17	($17.57)	$170.56	$2,086.04	$14,408.60
2	May 22	$2,050.29	$7.89	$153.77	$1,904.41	$14,408.60
3	May 23	$2,255.21	($20.88)	$169.14	$2,065.19	$14,408.60
4	May 24	$2,304.60	($6.04)	$172.85	$2,125.72	$14,408.60
5	May 25	$2,421.45	($3.82)	$181.61	$2,236.02	$14,408.60
6	May 26	$2,273.58	($23.10)	$170.52	$2,079.96	$14,408.60
7	May 27	$2,077.03	($9.99)	$155.78	$1,911.27	$14,408.60

Delete all the rows in the dataset, and save it. (You might want to make this file read only (Windows) or lock this file or make it Stationery using Get Info (Macintosh), so that you don't accidentally save over the template with some month's data.)

		Dates	Gross	Over/short	Tax	Net	Net weekly	Inpu
▶	Type:	Date/Time	Currency	Currency	Currency	Currency	Currency	Real
▶	Source:	User Ente...	Dynamic F...	Dynamic F...	Dynamic F...	Dynamic F...	Dynamic F...	User Ente
▶	Class:	Continuous	Continuous	Continuous	Continuous	Continuous	Continuous	Continuo
▶	Format:	January 1	($1,234,...	($1,234,...	($1,234,...	($1,234,...	($1,234,5...	Free Fori
▶	Dec. Places:	•	2	2	2	2	2	3

Now, each week, import the data into a new dataset and Copy all the cells. Open the template, Paste in the data, and save under a new filename.

When is it faster not to use formulas?

Sometimes it's faster not to use formulas. For example, if you want to recode all the missing values in a dataset with many variables, it might be faster to export or Copy and Paste the data into a word processor, do a global find-and-replace to change all missing values (.) to your new code (say, –999), then import or Paste the data back into StatView.

How can I add confidence intervals or error bars to a plot?

Use a formula to calculate your favorite type of confidence interval or error bar for your Y variable. Then add and subtract those values to the values of your Y variable. Plot all three variables against the X variable, and then edit the display of the plot to use appropriate symbols for the upper and lower confidence or error values.

Suppose you have summary data like these below entered from a published table, and you want to do a cell plot of group means with standard deviation error bars.

	Group	Group mean	Group sd
1	A	2250.227	221.453
2	B	2812.600	360.266
3	C	2815.682	170.847
4	D	3304.833	318.581
5	E	3657.353	293.487

Ordinarily you could use one of the cell plots, but they plot means and error bars computed from raw data. Since you have only the statistics, you must instead compute error values with formulas and then draw a bivariate scattergram.

- Use formulas to compute the upper and lower error bar values:

    "Group mean" + "Group sd"

    "Group mean" – "Group sd"

	Group	Group mean	Group sd	Upper	Lower
1	A	2250.227	221.453	2471.680	2028.774
2	B	2812.600	360.266	3172.866	2452.334
3	C	2815.682	170.847	2986.529	2644.835
4	D	3304.833	318.581	3623.414	2986.252
5	E	3657.353	293.487	3950.840	3363.866

From the Analyze menu, select New View

- From the analysis browser under Bivariate Plots, select Scattergram and click Create Analysis
- Click OK to accept the default plotting parameters
- Assign Group mean, Upper, and Lower to be Y variables; assign Group to be an X variable
- Use Draw tools to change plotting symbols

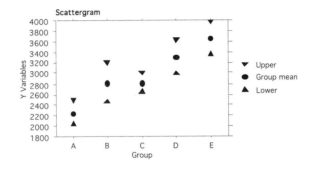

Our plot uses triangle symbols for the error values; you can choose others. You might also want to delete the legend and use the text tool to change the labels.

How can I generate subgroup and labeling variables?

Subgroup data often are recorded in sequence with the same number of measurements per subgroup. Under these circumstances, you could type, copy and paste all of the values for the subgroup variable. But since the values in the measurement variable follow a defined pattern, it is much easier to use a formula to generate the values of the subgroup variable.

Suppose, for instance, there are 8 measurements in each of 15 subgroups, and all measurements from a subgroup are consecutive. This means that the first 8 measurements are from subgroup 1, the next 8 from subgroup 2 and so on. The formula to create these values is:

I+Div(RowNumber–I, 8)

or, more generally:

I+Div(RowNumber–I, X)

where X is the number of measurements per subgroup.

Another pattern in which the measurements could be recorded is that the first measurement from each subgroup is recorded in sequence, then the second measurement from each subgroup, and so on. For the example above with 8 measurements from each of 15 subgroups, this means that the first 15 measurements are from subgroups 1–15, as are next 15 measurements, and so on, for a total of 8 sequences of measurements from subgroups 1–15 (for a total of 120 rows). The formula to create these values of the subgroup variable is:

1+mod(RowNumber–1, 8)

or, more generally,

1+mod(RowNumber-1, X)

where X is the number of measurements per subgroup.

No matter which of these patterns fits your data, once the subgroup numbers are generated, you should make the variable's class nominal; the variable is then ready to be used in any analysis that takes a subgroup variable. If you wish to give the subgroups alphanumeric names (e.g., Sample 1, Sample 2,… etc.), simply create a category in which the ordering of the group labels corresponds with the numeric values of the subgroups. For instance, if the groups are weeks, then make the variable's Type: Category, and create a category whose group labels are: Week 1, Week 2, …, Week 14, Week 15. See "Categories," p. 80, for more information on creating and using categories.

How can I create event times (elapsed time) from start and end times?

You can easily compute event time variables from survival data containing start times and end times.

Suppose you have data on patients suffering from epilepsy. You are interested in whether a particular treatment significantly affects the time that elapses until a patient's next seizure. In this example, each patient has entered the study on a different date. The event time for each patient will be the elapsed time in days from the date of entry into the study until the date of that patient's next seizure (or the date of censoring, which will be the last day of the study).

Your data might look like this:

		Entry Date	End Date	Censor var	Treatment
▶	Type:	Date/Time	Date/Time	String	Category
▶	Source:	User Entered	User Entered	User Entered	Dynamic Form…
▶	Class:	Continuous	Continuous	Nominal	Nominal
▶	Format:	Jan 1, 1904	Jan 1, 1904	●	●
▶	Dec. Places:	●	●	●	●
	12	Oct 3, 1986	Jun 19, 1991	Censored	Dosage 2
	13	Oct 27, 1986	Apr 18, 1991	Uncensored	Dosage 3
	14	Dec 21, 1985	Jun 19, 1991	Censored	Dosage 2
	15	Sep 3, 1988	Nov 29, 1990	Uncensored	Dosage 2
	16	Sep 7, 1985	Mar 21, 1991	Uncensored	Dosage 2
	17	Aug 30, 1988	Dec 20, 1990	Uncensored	Dosage 3
	18	Nov 19, 1985	Jul 22, 1990	Uncensored	Control
	19	Aug 27, 1985	Apr 7, 1989	Uncensored	Dosage 1
	20	Nov 30, 1986	Feb 23, 1989	Uncensored	Dosage 3
	21	Sep 6, 1986	Feb 8, 1990	Uncensored	Dosage 3
	22	Aug 1, 1985	Sep 6, 1989	Uncensored	Control

You can use the DateDifference(?,?,?) to compute event times or elapsed times from these data.

DateDifference("End Date", "Entry Date", 4)

The third argument specifies which time units to use: 1 for years, 2 for months, etc. In this case, we specify 4 for time in days.

QC analysis

How can I draw box plots of subgroup measurements?

Many QC analysts find that box plots give a useful summary of the distribution of sub-grouped data. To generate a box plot quickly, simply select a completed subgroup measurement result (such as an Xbar chart) from the view, then double-click Box Plot in the analysis browser. This adopts variable assignments to produce a single chart with box plots for each subgroup in the same order as those in the QC result.

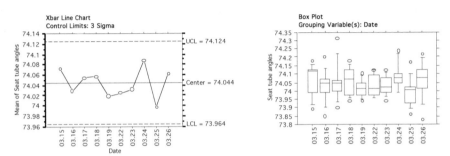

How can I add histograms with normal curves to my capability analyses?

It is often useful to plot a histogram with a normal curve to evaluate whether data are normally distributed. Many QC analysts also like to plot a histogram with a normal curve together with their tables of capability indices. This allows easy visualization of the positions of target values and upper and lower specification limits relative to the actual distribution of the data. Simply select a table of capability indices and adopt its variable assignment for a histogram: in the analysis browser under Frequency Distribution, double-click Histogram. In the Frequency Distribution dialog box, check Show normal comparison (turn it on).

How can I get more information about differences among subgroups?

For subgroup measurement data, analysis of variance can often provide a more fine-grained comparison of differences among subgroups. For instance, an ANOVA with post hoc tests can tell you specifically which subgroups have mean values that differ significantly from the others. Please consult the chapter "ANOVA," p. 73 of *StatView Reference*.

Can I work with compact variables?

Sometimes, data are recorded so that values from each subgroup are in a different variable (column). StatView's flexible data handling allows you to use data in this format simply by compacting all of the subgroups into a single compact variable.

Suppose, for instance, your measurements (or attribute counts) fall into 8 subgroups, each with 10 measurements in separate variables. The data might look something like this:

	Week 1	Week 2	Week 3	Week 4	Week 5	Week 6	Week 7	Week 8
1	55.048	48.300	56.743	58.937	55.866	54.275	54.385	53.744
2	51.515	54.506	56.965	61.027	50.864	53.805	55.197	50.103
3	51.709	45.669	56.985	49.259	53.013	55.602	53.950	55.360
4	48.800	49.805	49.855	51.179	52.535	52.275	48.010	53.131
5	55.172	50.473	51.607	51.251	55.095	46.540	55.286	51.664
6	52.797	50.313	50.343	56.080	48.477	55.612	51.338	51.843
7	51.040	53.337	49.949	48.821	53.253	54.077	52.041	57.768
8	53.540	50.326	49.928	51.285	47.170	44.825	54.445	49.052
9	48.793	51.534	48.223	49.940	49.615	52.718	55.217	54.638
10	51.361	52.544	51.737	54.432	52.335	52.217	50.114	48.526

To compact these variables, select all eight of them, then click the Compact button in the upper left corner of the dataset. When the Compact Variables dialog appears, type in a name for the compacted variable, then click Compact. The compacted variable will look similar to the following:

	Measurements							
	Week 1	Week 2	Week 3	Week 4	Week 5	Week 6	Week 7	Week 8
1	55.048	48.300	56.743	58.937	55.866	54.275	54.385	53.744
2	51.515	54.506	56.965	61.027	50.864	53.805	55.197	50.103
3	51.709	45.669	56.985	49.259	53.013	55.602	53.950	55.360
4	48.800	49.805	49.855	51.179	52.535	52.275	48.010	53.131
5	55.172	50.473	51.607	51.251	55.095	46.540	55.286	51.664
6	52.797	50.313	50.343	56.080	48.477	55.612	51.338	51.843
7	51.040	53.337	49.949	48.821	53.253	54.077	52.041	57.768
8	53.540	50.326	49.928	51.285	47.170	44.825	54.445	49.052
9	48.793	51.534	48.223	49.940	49.615	52.718	55.217	54.638
10	51.361	52.544	51.737	54.432	52.335	52.217	50.114	48.526

When your data are arranged this way, you must add both the continuous and nominal portions of the compacted variable to the chosen analysis, as pictured below.

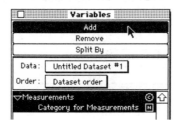

Data arranged this way can be used in any QC analysis that uses subgroup variables, i.e., QC subgroup, *p/np* and *c/u* analyses. You can also use the continuous portion of any compact variable in individual measurement analyses. If you do use a compact variable for the nonconformity and subgroup variables in *p/np* or *c/u* analyses, any Item or Unit Count variables you use should match the number of cases in the continuous portion of the compact. (In the example given above, the continuous portion of the compact variable has $10 \times 8 = 80$ cases.)

Survival analysis

How can I estimate the survival function at other covariate values?

You might wish to evaluate certain regression models for particular covariate values. Suppose, for instance, you would like to evaluate the survival function for the proportional hazards model you computed in the example of the individual who smokes 18 cigarettes per day (on average) and has a type A personality (see "Exercise," p. 191 of *StatView Reference*). From the exercise, the model coefficients table (with results displayed to 9 decimal places) for that model is:

Model Coefficients for Time
Censor Variable: Censor
Model: Proportional Hazards

	DF	Coef	Std. Error	Coef/SE	Chi-Square	P-Value	Exp(Coef)
Cigarettes	1	.013809261	.007746646	1.782611662	3.177704337	.0746	1.013905049
Personality Type: A	1	.624020567	.272504339	2.289947269	5.243858496	.0220	1.866417032

Using the saved values of the baseline survival function, it is a straightforward task to write a formula in StatView that will compute the survival function for specific covariate values of your own choosing.

To save the baseline survival function to a dataset,

- Select one or more of the regression model results in the view, then click the Edit Analysis button. (Note that the following change to the regression models parameters could be made at the time of analysis creation, as well.)

The fewer choices version of the Survival: Regression Models dialog box now appears.

- Click the More Choices button. This brings up the more detailed version of the Survival: Regression Models dialog box.

- To save the baseline values to a dataset, check the Create baseline survival dataset check-box, then click OK.

Because formulas cannot be created in datasets created by analyses, you must copy the Time and Cum. Surv. variables from the Baseline Survival Table dataset and paste them into a new dataset. (For clarity, you might want to change the names of the variables in the new dataset to Event Time and Baseline Cum. Surv., respectively.) In this new dataset, create 2 new columns, one called Coefficients and the other called Covariate values. This new dataset should then appear as below:

	Event Time	Baseline Cum. Surv.	Coefficients	Covariate values
Type:	Real	Real	Real	Real
Source:	User Entered	User Entered	User Entered	User Entered
Class:	Continuous	Continuous	Continuous	Continuous
Format:	Free Format ...	Free Format Fixed	Free Format Fi...	Free Format Fi...
Dec. Places:	3	3	3	3
1	0	1.000	•	•
2	99.000	.999	•	•
3	356.000	.998	•	•
4	364.000	.997	•	•
5	423.000	.996	•	•

From the Model Coefficients Table you know that the coefficient associated with cigarette consumption is 0.013809261 and that associated with type A personalities is 0.624020567. Type these two numbers into the first and second rows of the Coefficients variable. (Because these coefficients are to be used as exponents, errors introduced by rounding will be greatly exaggerated. For this reason, we recommend that you record coefficient values to at least 6 decimal places.)

Now, because you want to compute the survival estimate for a person with a type A personality who consumes 18 cigarettes per day, enter 18 and 1 on the first and second rows of the Covariate values variable. Note that if the person had a type B personality, you would enter 0 in the second row. The dataset should then appear as below:

	Event Time	Baseline Cum. Surv.	Coefficients	Covariate values
Type:	Real	Real	Real	Real
Source:	User Entered	User Entered	User Entered	User Entered
Class:	Continuous	Continuous	Continuous	Continuous
Format:	Free Format ...	Free Format Fixed	Free Format Fi...	Free Format Fi...
Dec. Places:	3	3	3	3
1	0	1.000	.014	18.000
2	99.000	.999	.624	1.000
3	356.000	.998	●	●
4	364.000	.997	●	●
5	423.000	.996	●	●

The final step is to create a formula that uses all of this information to compute the survival estimate. From the appendix "Algorithms," p. 433 of *StatView Reference*, you can see that the equation for evaluating a proportional hazards model at particular covariate values is

$$\hat{S}(T_i;z_i) = [\hat{S}_0(T_i)]^{e^{\hat{\beta}'z_i}}$$

where $\hat{S}_0(T_i)$ is the baseline survival function. So, the StatView formula for evaluating this function is the following:

"Baseline Cum. Surv." ^ e ^ DotProduct(Coefficients, "Covariate values")

Note that DotProduct(?,?) is a Mathematical function.

Now, simply click Compute, and the results are displayed in "Column 5." You can, of course, rename this formula column whatever you like and then save the dataset. If you would also like to plot this computed survival function, assign "Event Time" as an X variable and the formula column as a Y variable to a bivariate chart.

If you frequently need to evaluate proportional hazards models at particular covariate values, you should probably save this dataset for later use as a sort of template. We suggest that you delete all of the rows before saving as a template: that way, the next time you use it, all you will need to do is paste in the new baseline data, then type in the new coefficient and covariate values. You might wish to make the formula column *static*, so that it will not recompute as you are typing in each of the new coefficient and covariate values. Once you are ready to compute the survival function, reopen the formula dialog box, then click Compute.

As you might have guessed, you can also use these same techniques to evaluate any of the parametric models at particular covariate values. For example, from information provided in the appendix "Algorithms," p. 433 of *StatView Reference*, we know that the formula for evaluating an exponential regression model at particular covariate values is

$$\hat{S}(T_i;z_i) \ = \ e^{-T_i e^{-\hat{\mu} - \hat{\beta}'z_i}}$$

where $\hat{\mu}$ is the estimate of the intercept parameter. The StatView formula for evaluating this function would then be:

e^–("Event Time" * e^(–MuHat – DotProduct(Coefficients, "Covariate values")))

where MuHat is the estimated value of the intercept parameter (type the number instead of "MuHat"). You'll notice from this equation that you do not need an estimate of the baseline survival function to evaluate parametric models, but only the event times. Similar equations can be constructed for the other parametric models as well, though the others (Weibull, lognormal and loglogistic) require specification of a scale parameter as well. The complete equations for these other models are in the appendix "Algorithms," p. 433 of *StatView Reference*.

How can I make comparisons among coefficients for linear hypotheses?

Sometimes, you might need to determine if the contribution of a particular group level, or weighted combination of group levels, to a survival regression model differs significantly from that of another group level, or weighted combination of group levels. Suppose, for instance, you have a covariate in a regression model called "Treatment," the levels of which are "Treatment 1," "Treatment 2," and "Control." A simple example of a test of a linear hypothesis would be testing whether the contribution to the model of the "Treatment 1" group is significantly different from that of the "Control" group. A more complex example might test whether an evenly weighted combination of the groups receiving treatments 1 and 2 is significantly different from the "Control" group. If you are familiar with the techniques of analysis of variance (ANOVA), you will recognize that these hypotheses are contrasts. Using the information provided by survival regression models in the Coefficient Covariances Table, you can evaluate such hypotheses.

In their most general form, such contrasts can be computed as follows. If the linear hypotheses for the regression coefficients β (a vector) are expressed in the form $H_0 : H\beta = c$, where H is a matrix (of rank r) of weights for the hypotheses, and c is a vector of constants, then the Wald chi-square statistic (with r degrees of freedom) is given by:

$$\chi^2 \ = \ [H\hat{\beta} - c]'[H\hat{V}(\hat{\beta})H'][H\hat{\beta} - c]$$

For the less general case of testing for the equality of two coefficients β_i and β_j, H is a vector with all elements equal to 0 except $H_i = 1$ and $H_j = -1$ and $c = 0$. The chi-square statistic in this case has 1 degree of freedom and is given by

$$\chi^2 \ = \ \frac{(\beta_i - \beta_j)^2}{V_{11} + V_{22} - 2V_{12}}$$

This equation is applied as follows. Suppose that you compute a regression model that gives results such as these in StatView:

Model Coefficients for Time (days)
Censor Variable: Censor var
Model: Proportional Hazards

	DF	Coef	Std. Error	Coef/SE	Chi-Square	P-Value	Exp(Coef)
Treatment	3	•	•	•	4.549512	.2079	•
Treatment 1	1	-.522397	.409513	-1.275654	1.627294	.2021	.593097
Treatment 2	1	.019237	.347218	.055402	.003069	.9558	1.019423
Treatment 3	1	.298397	.339070	.880045	.774479	.3788	1.347697

Coefficient Covariances for Time (days)
Censor Variable: Censor var
Model: Proportional Hazards

	Treatment: Treatment 1	Treatment: Treatment 2	Treatment: Treatment 3
Treatment: Treatment 1	.167701		
Treatment: Treatment 2	.067560	.120561	
Treatment: Treatment 3	.067107	.066885	.114969

The variable "Treatment" has 4 levels: treatments 1–3, and a control group. The data were entered so that the coefficients displayed are all relative to that for the control group, whose coefficient is 0. (See "Coefficient Initial Values dialog box," p. 182 of *StatView Reference* for details.) Notice that these results are displayed to 6 decimal places; this is recommended to avoid loss of precision in the following calculations.

Suppose that you wish to test the hypothesis that the coefficient for treatment 1 is the same as that for treatment 3. The Wald chi-square statistic would therefore be:

$$\frac{(-0.522397 - 0.298397)^2}{0.167701 + 0.114969 - 2(0.067107)} = 4.538$$

Then, to compute the *p* value associated with this chi-square value, use the following formula in StatView:

1 − ProbChiSquare(4.538,1)

In this example, the *p* value is 0.033. You would therefore conclude that the coefficients from treatments 1 and 3 are significantly different at the 0.05 level.

How can I create step function plots?

In some cases, such as when you would like to plot confidence limits about a Kaplan-Meier survival estimate, you might wish to create your own step function plots. Unfortunately, this plot type is not directly supported in StatView. Using a few simple steps, however, you can create your own step function plots using the bivariate line chart.

These steps can be summarized as follows:

- Copy the variables (including the censor variable) for which you want to create step functions, then paste them into a new dataset.

If you were creating a step plot of the cumulative survival function, you would copy the "Time," "Cum. survival," and "Status" variables from the dataset created by the analysis. If you want to plot confidence limits, copy the upper and lower confidence limit variables as well. (Survival results can be saved to datasets for both nonparametric analyses and regression models; for more information, see the chapters "Survival: Nonparametric," p. 143, and "Survival: Regression," p. 167 of *StatView Reference*.)

- Delete the censored cases from the new dataset.

You could do this in a variety of ways. Probably the easiest way is to define a criterion for the censored cases (e.g., "Censor is 1"), then use that criterion to select only the censored cases, then delete these cases. (Hold the Control key while selecting a criterion from the Criteria pop-up menu.)

- In the new dataset, select and copy all rows of all variables.

- Paste the rows in the input *row* at the bottom of the new dataset.

- Sort the new dataset by "Cum. survival" (descending sort) within "Time" (ascending sort). More generally, the dataset should be sorted by whatever variable will be on the vertical (Y) axis of your step plot, within the variable that will be on the horizontal (X) axis. (Sort by survival within time within group if you want to plot separate survival functions for different groups.)

- Copy the entire "Time" variable in the new dataset.

- Insert an empty row before the first row in the new dataset.

- Paste the contents of the clipboard (copied in step 6) on top of the "Time" variable by clicking on the *name* of the "Time" variable, then choosing Paste from the Edit menu.

- In a view window, plot "Time" as an X variable, and "Cum. survival" and confidence limits variables (if desired) as Y variables on a bivariate line chart.

- Change the point size to ø for the symbols associated with the lines. This removes the symbols from the plot and gives a clean step function, showing only lines.

Troubleshooting

Here we provide tips and troubleshooting information to help you use StatView more efficiently and solve problems you might have with the application. Answers to many questions can be found in the Hints window and these manuals.

General problems

Results appear incorrect

1. Results might seem incorrect if you have too few significant digits displayed in your tables. Change the number of decimal places displayed with the Preferences command in the Manage menu. Choose Table, click Modify, and change the default number of decimal places. To change a single table, select the table and click Edit Display.

2. All statistical routines in StatView have been validated using standard datasets against standard references as well as other commercially available software packages. If you feel that there is an error, please send us information about what you feel is incorrect and why. If you have compared the result to that of another application, please send us the input and

output from that package as well.

Out of memory

If StatView does not have enough memory to perform an operation, it alerts you with a dialog box. If this happens, you need to increase the amount of memory available to StatView.

Unexpected results

StatView's behavior in the view is largely dependent on what results are selected. If StatView creates several tables and graphs when you expect only one, it is probably using variables or analyses from results that are selected in a part of the view not visible in the window. Open the Results browser from the View menu (Windows) or Window menu (Macintosh) to see which results are selected, and look at the Results Selected note in the upper right corner of the window to see the number of results currently selected. See "Determine whether results are selected," p. 133.

Grouped objects can account for unexpected numbers of results appearing. You might intend to add a variable to a single result but effectively assign it to several. If you used the Group command in the Layout menu to group graphs and tables, selecting one of the objects effectively selects them all. The next action you take in the view then applies to all objects in the group. See "Group objects," p. 215.

Random crashes

If the program appears to crash somewhat randomly, try throwing away the StatView Library file; see "StatView Library," p. 233. Take note that doing this restores all default preference settings.

(Windows only) If discarding the Library file does not help, try restarting with the plainest possible configuration. Boot with a generic set of start-up files, and be sure to check whether any recent changes to your hardware or network configuration could be involved.

(Macintosh only) If discarding the Library file does not help, try restarting without loading system extensions. This will reveal whether the difficulty is simply an incompatibility between StatView and an extension or control panel in your system. To restart without extensions, choose Restart from the Special menu, then hold down the Shift key until the start-up screen appears with the message "Extensions off." Also be sure to check whether any recent changes to your hardware or network configuration could be involved.

Problem-solving techniques

If you encounter a problem using StatView or do not understand something about the program, we recommend that you follow these steps:

- If you get an error hint when trying to do something, follow the instructions in the Hints window to solve the problem. In the Formula dialog box, Hints give information about functions that might prove helpful. See "Hints window," p. 222.

- Read this book, using the table of contents or index to locate information.
- See if your question is addressed in this chapter.
- If your question involves setting up an experiment, see if one of the sample datasets provided with the program mirrors your situation. If the problem disappears, you might have a problem in the structure of your dataset. Review the data requirements in the *StatView Reference* chapter for that analysis. Make sure each variable's attribute settings are correct (see "Variable attributes," p. 73). If you imported your data from another application, examine it for possible importing errors.
- Try again with the simplest possible system configuration. On Windows, reboot with plain startup files. On Macintosh, restart and hold the Shift key until you see the message "Extensions off." If the problem disappears, try adding things back one at a time to isolate the problem.
- Try reinstalling StatView. A change in your system or network configuration could have caused a problem, or an application file might have become corrupted.

Importing

It is important to identify the correct separator characters to make the importing process simple and trouble-free. A separator character is a character that occurs between data points and tells StatView where a data point in one column ends and the next begins. Separator characters also define the end of rows in the dataset.

If you are not certain what separator characters are used in a text file you are importing, open the file in a word processing application and choose the setting that enables you to see formatting characters within the document. Formatting characters or **gremlins** are non-textual characters that indicate tabs, spaces, paragraphs and so forth. Each word processing application represents gremlins a little differently, so check the user manual for your application to see how they appear.

If a separator character other than a Tab is used, such as a comma, StatView needs to know. Problems can arise if an improper separator is used in the source file, or if you tell StatView to use a separator character that does not match the one used in the source application.

Spaces as separators

If you choose *spaces* and the text file contains strings with spaces within an individual entry, StatView expects the spaces to indicate separate data points. For example, it would be a mistake to import this text file with spaces as a separator:

```
Employee Age
Kate Bishop 46
David Wong 19
```

In this dataset, spaces appear not only between data points but also inside them. StatView would import this text file as the following three variable dataset:

	Column 1	Column 2	Column 3
1	Employee	Age	●
2	Kate	Bishop	46.000
3	David	Wong	19.000

As you can see, StatView split the employee names in two. To remedy this, you could either separate data points with some other character besides spaces (such as Tabs), or place double quotation marks around distinct data points having spaces within them.

The text file should look like this:

Employee <tab> Age

Kate Bishop <tab> 46

David Wong <tab> 19

or this:

"Employee" "Age"

"Kate Bishop" "46"

"David Wong" "19"

Commas as separators

Another example of an incorrect choice would be to import the following file without specifying commas as a separator:

Name,Age

Yukito,32

Setsuko,35

Armita,30

Choosing Tab, for example, tells StatView to import the file as a one variable dataset:

	Column 1	Input Column
1	Name,Age	
2	Yukito,32	
3	Setsuko,35	
4	Armita,30	

Remedies for common errors

1. If some values in certain rows are shifted to the right, see if the source text file contains groups of the separator character you used (two commas, for instance). If it does, edit out the extra separator characters from the source text file and import the file into StatView again.

2. If some values are shifted to the left in a file imported with space separators, you used a space separator to indicate a missing value. Two or more spaces are condensed into one. If two or more spaces are grouped together, edit those out of the source text file. Type a period with a space on either side into the source file where the missing value belongs and import the file again.

3. If you have an empty data cell (without a missing value symbol), you probably chose the

return character to separate values on a line. Since duplicate returns are not compressed into a single missing value (.), your data will be imported improperly. Check the text file to see if there are any duplicate return characters and remove them.

4. If you want to import a variable of mixed data type (real, integer and string, for instance) or one with errors, choose Make columns with errors have type string in the Import dialog box. This setting turns a variable of mixed data type or a variable with field errors into a variable with a String data type. You can import the dataset and examine the variable to see what caused the errors. Correct the errors and change the variable to the appropriate data type (through the attribute pane).

5. If you have an inordinately large number of missing values in your dataset, check to see if the source text file has formatting characters in it such as dollar signs, percent signs, etc. This is more likely to occur if you import a text file from a spreadsheet application such as Excel.

6. If you are importing a dataset with several nominal variables that share the same group level names, you should import these variables as type String rather than Category. Make sure that the Import non-numeric data as type String option is checked in the import dialog box. This prevents StatView from creating multiple categories with the same group level names.

Printing

If you are having problems related to printing, following these guidelines might remedy the situation.

- Try printing from another application to determine if it is indeed a printing problem or if the problem lies only in the use of StatView.

- Make sure you have your printer and printer drivers correctly installed.

- Some printers require that you install and use special screen fonts; otherwise you might get misaligned print or odd spacing.

- Be sure that enough memory is available for printing.

Formulas and criteria

When I click compute, nothing happens. Why?

- Does the Hints window offer any help? The Hints window tells you when more or fewer arguments are needed, when an argument is the wrong type (such as a variable when a number is expected), and so on.

- Are any variable names or function names misspelled?

- Are you missing any parentheses? You might need to add parentheses to control the order of operations. Extra pairs of parentheses are rarely harmful. StatView highlights unmatched parentheses, so you can fix them. Often error messages about the wrong number of arguments are due to a problem with parentheses.

- Do you have quotation marks around variable names containing spaces? Around text values such as e and π, which are also function names?

Why do I get a column of missing values?

- Are any variable or function names misspelled?
- Does the formula variable have the correct type? New variables have type real by default; you might need to change this to date/time, category, string, or currency before you'll see the results you want.
- Are you missing any parentheses?
- Are any text values misspelled?
- Are all arguments listed in the correct order?
- Do you have quotation marks around variable names containing spaces? Around text values such as e and π, which are also function names?
- Do your variable names contain "reserved words"? Function names, operators, and category level names should not be used in variable names. (Many examples in this reference break this rule so that dataset illustrations are easier to interpret.) For a list of function names, see the table of contents.
- If you can't figure out what might be wrong, Copy just the columns the formula needs, Paste them into a new dataset, and try your formula there. If it works, then the problem has to do with naming conflicts (reserved words, variable name changes, etc.). If you don't have time to figure out where that naming conflict is, Copy the results and Paste them into the full dataset as a user-entered variable.

Why is my recoded variable wrong?

- Does your original variable have any missing values? Look at Missing Cells in the attribute pane. Use the Recode command or use a formula with "if IsMissing(*var*)" if you need to recode missing values to a special group such as "unknown." Consider using IS and ISNOT instead of = and ≠.
- Does your original variable have more values than you thought? Look at Minimum and Maximum in the variable attribute pane. (For nominal variables, which don't have summary statistics, sort on the variable and look for any unexpected values.)
- Did you use "else" to set your last group? If so, any values in the original variable that you forgot end up in that group.
- Did you forget that strings are case-sensitive? "A" and "a" are different values!
- Is your original variable a category variable? If so, be sure to use if…then…else statements rather than arithmetic functions.

See "if ? then ? else ?," p. 341 of *StatView Reference* for some ways to handle these problems.

Why do I get Formula and Criteria windows when I open a dataset?

These open windows indicate definition errors that you need to fix before StatView can compute the variables.

- Did you rename any variables used in formula or criteria definitions? You need to update those formulas or criteria to use the current names.

- Did you edit any category definitions for variables used in formula and criteria definitions? You need to update those formulas or criteria to use the current level names from the new category definition/s.

- Do your variable names contain "reserved words"? Function names, operators, and category level names should not be used in variable names. (Many examples in this reference break this rule so that dataset illustrations are easier to interpret.)

- Was the dataset created in SuperANOVA? Certain functions unique to SuperANOVA cannot be computed in StatView. Edit the definition to use StatView functions and click Compute.

- Was the dataset created in a newer version of StatView? SuperANOVA and older versions of StatView have fewer functions; check to see whether you're using any functions that your program doesn't support. (StatView warns you about any such formulas before saving to older file formats.)

- Was the dataset created on a different type of system? Different platforms do their computations in different levels of precision. Formulas calculated in one version need to be recalculated in another. To suppress recalculations between platforms, choose the Convert dynamic formulas to static option in Dataset Preferences:

```
When opening datasets from other platforms:
✓ Recompute dynamic formulas
   Convert dynamic formulas to static
```

- Was the dataset created with a foreign system? Correct the separator characters used between arguments of a function to match the character used on your system. (To learn the correct character, look at functions listed in the Formula dialog box.)
  The separator character varies according to the international number format in use. For example, a formula with period decimal characters uses commas, but a formula with comma decimal characters uses semi-colons:

RandomNormal(1.5, 3.0)

RandomNormal(1,5; 3,0)

- Try clicking Compute. If it doesn't work, open the Hints window and check for error messages.

Index